Linguistics Series No 1

AN INTRODUCTION TO HISTORICAL LINGUISTICS

Linguistics Series No 1

AN INTRODUCTION TO HISTORICAL LINGUISTICS

Terry Crowley

University of Papua New Guinea Press
University of the South Pacific
1987

USP Library Cataloguing in Publication Data

Crowley, Terry
    An introduction to historical linguistics / Terry Crowley.
    — [Port Moresby] Papua New Guinea : University of Papua
    New Guinea Press ; Suva, Fiji : Institute of Pacific Studies,
    University of the South Pacific, 1987.

        vi, 306 pp. ; 21 cm. — (Linguistics series ; no. 1)
        Bibliography : pp. 298-301.
        ISBN 9980-84-004-8

        1. Historical linguistics 2. Linguistics — Oceania
        I. Title II. Series : Linguistics series (University of
        Papua New Guinea) ; no. 1

    P 140 .C7   410

Published by the University of Papua New Guinea Press
P.O. Box 320, University P.O., N.C.D. Papua New Guinea
and the
Institute of Pacific Studies,
University of the South Pacific
P.O. Box 1168
Suva, Fiji

Typeset by Jacobsons
Text set in 10 on 12 Times
Printed by Fiji Times Ltd., Suva.
Reprinted by Star Printery Ltd., Suva, 1991.

CONTENTS

Acknowledgements   1
Preface   3
Charts of Phonetic Symbols   5
Maps of Languages Referred to in the Text   8

Chapter One – Introduction   11
  1.1 The Nature of Linguistic Relationships   11
  1.2 Attitudes to Language Change   18

Chapter Two – Types of Sound Change   25
  2.1 Lenition   26
  2.2 Sound Addition   32
  2.3 Metathesis   34
  2.4 Fusion   35
  2.5 Unpacking   37
  2.6 Vowel Breaking   38
  2.7 Assimilation   39
  2.8 Dissimilation   47
  2.9 Abnormal Sound Changes   47

Chapter Three – Expressing Sound Changes   57
  3.1 Writing Rules   57
  3.2 Ordering of Changes   64

Chapter Four – Phonetic vs Phonemic Change   71
  4.1 Phonetic Change without Phonemic Change   71
  4.2 Phonetic Change with Phonemic Change   73
  4.3 Phonemic Change without Phonetic Change   79

Chapter Five – The Comparative Method   89
  5.1 Sound Correspondences and Reconstruction 89
  5.2 Reconstruction of Conditioned Sound Changes 103
  5.3 The Reality of Proto-languages   115

Chapter Six – Problems with the Comparative Method   121
  6.1 The Neogrammarians   121
  6.2 Analogy   129
  6.3 Spelling Pronunciation   133
  6.4 Borrowing   134
  6.5 Opposition to the Neogrammarian Hypothesis 135

Chapter Seven — Internal Reconstruction   149

Chapter Eight — Grammatical and Semantic Change   161
  8.1 Grammatical Change   162
  8.2 Semantic Change   179

Chapter Nine — Subgrouping   187
  9.1 Shared Innovation and Shared Retention   188
  9.2 Lexicostatistics and Glottochronology   190

Chapter Ten — Observing Language Change   213
  10.1 The Traditional View   213
  10.2 Indeterminacy   215
  10.3 Variability   220
  10.4 The Spread of Change   226

Chapter Eleven — Causes of Language Change   235
  11.1 Theories of Language Change   235
  11.2 Pidginisation   250

Chapter Twelve — Cultural Reconstruction   263
  12.1 Archaeology   263
  12.2 Oral History   265
  12.3 Comparative Culture ·   268
  12.4 Historical Linguistics   270

Appendix — Data Sets   289
  1. Palauan (Micronesia)   289
  2. Nganyaywana (Northern New South Wales)   289
  3. Mbabaram (North Queensland)   290
  4. Yimas and Karawari (East Sepik)   290
  5. Lakalai (West New Britain)   291
  6. Suena and Zia (Morobe)   291
  7. Korafe, Notu and Binandere (Oro Province)   292
  8. Northern and Southern Paamese (Vanuatu)   292
  9. Motu (Central Province)   292
  10. Sepa, Manam, Kairiru and Sera (Coastal Sepik)   293
  11. Burduna (Western Australia)   294

Language Index   295

Bibliography   298

Index   303

ACKNOWLEDGEMENTS

The present revised form of this textbook owes a lot to my own past students of historical linguistics at the University of Papua New Guinea. It was largely with their help that I was able to locate areas of inadequacy in exemplification and explanation in the previous edition. In particular, I would like to thank Kalesita Tupou and Sam Uhrle for checking and correcting the Tongan and Samoan data in chapter five.

Other people have provided a great deal of input also. Bill Foley of the Australian National University helped a lot with the first edition by providing me with copies of his own comparative linguistics lecture notes and problems — some of his material has found its way into this book. John Lynch read in detail the draft forms of the first and second editions, and made many specific comments to improve examples and explanations. I should also thank Ross Clark of the University of Auckland and Harold Koch of the Australian National University for prescribing the first edition in their courses in historical linguistics — thus giving me the chance to prepare this revised edition.

Vagoli Bouauka of the Geography Department at the University of Papua New Guinea was involved in the preparation and re-drawing of some of the maps and diagrams, for which I express my thanks. I thank Florence Wala, the secretary of the Language Department at the University of Papua New Guinea, for her extreme patience and skill in typing the first edition, as well as the even longer second edition.

Finally, I must also make a formal acknowledgement to Jean Aitchison of the London School of Economics. Her published texts *The Articulate Mammal, Teach Yourself Linguistics* and *Language Change: Progress or Decay?* are, to me, a model of clear and simple expression, and even of ideological soundness. She shows it *can* be done — I just hope I have achieved it.

1

PREFACE

My *Introduction to Historical Linguistics* first appeared in 1981, and was published by the University of Papua New Guinea (UPNG). Along with John Lynch's *Introduction to Phonetics and Phonology, Introduction to Morphological Analysis* and *Readings in the Comparative Linguistics of Melanesia,* these books comprised the beginnings of our *Studying Pacific Languages* series. This series is being written specifically with UPNG students in mind.

Having taught various linguistics courses at this University, we found that the English used by writers of nearly all standard textbooks was far too difficult for English-as-a-second-language speakers. This seemed to be especially true in books dealing with historical linguistics. Also, foreign words abound in textbooks on comparative linguistics, and readers are arrogantly assumed to know what is meant by *Umlaut, Lautverschiebung, spiritus aspirate, un système où tout se tient, sandhi* and so on. Another problem we found was that the examples that are chosen to illustrate points and arguments often involve languages that students have never heard of, or have no familiarity with. (Usually, they involve European languages or American Indian languages.)

We therefore decided to remedy these faults by producing our own series of textbooks. We tried to simplify the language and to explain concepts simply, without simplifying the concepts themselves. We have also tried to draw examples as far as possible from Pacific languages, and from English.

Contrary to my original intentions and expectations, *Introduction to Historical Linguistics* was prescribed for students taking comparative linguistics at the Australian National University and at the University of Auckland. This meant that a textbook that we would have been stuck with for twenty years of teaching at UPNG with our past class sizes in comparative linguistics was actually out of stock after only two years of teaching. This gave me a welcome opportunity to revise the textbook, and to change or add material according to the experiences of myself and of others who have actually used the book as a course text.

The principal changes that I have made are as follows:

(a) Improvements have been made where points have been inadequately (or, in some cases, even inaccurately) explained or exemplified.

3

(b) The original transcription system has been substituted by an IPA-based system for wider appeal.

(c) Footnotes or additional explanations have been added for overseas readers to clarify examples that are familiar only to Papua New Guinean readers.

(d) More problems for solving have been added, and those problems come from a wider range of languages. Specifically, more Australian Aboriginal data has been incorporated. (Anyway, these are clearly Pacific languages also, in the widest sense of the word.)

(e) Some of the maps and diagrams that did not come out well in the first edition have been redrawn in a form that reproduces better.

(f) Some of the material has been presented in a different order. In particular, part of Chapter five has gone to Chapter two, while the rest has gone into a new chapter towards the end, Chapter eleven.

(g) Additional content has been added where it was felt that material was lacking in the first edition. In particular, this edition contains some discussion on the following topics that were not included in the first edition: attitudes to language change, pidginisation and semantic change. There is also a completely new chapter, entitled Observing Language Change, which questions the rigid Saussurean dichotomy between synchronic and diachronic linguistics.

It should be kept in mind that this book *An Introduction to Historical Linguistics* is just that — an introduction. In my course on historical linguistics, I cover practically all of the topics in this textbook in lectures and tutorials. Students should be encouraged to use other textbooks for their wide reading, to look at different topics, or to look at different views of the same topics. At the end of all chapters, I have included a list of supplementary readings, where students can start their wider reading.

Terry Crowley
Pacific Languages Unit
University of the South Pacific
Vila, Vanuatu
1987

PHONETIC SYMBOLS

In this volume, we use an IPA-based transcription system with some modifications commonly used in studies of Pacific languages (including Australian Aboriginal languages). The following tables give the most commonly used symbols. (Symbols in the text that do not appear on the tables are explained as they occur.)

Consonants

	bilabial	labio-dental	dental/alveolar	lamino-dental, dental	retroflex	alveo-palatal	palatal	velar	labio-velar	uvular	glottal
voiced stop	b		d	d̪	ḍ		ɖʲ	g	gʷ	G	
voiceless stop	p		t	t̪	ṭ		ʈʲ	k	kʷ	q	ʔ
voiced fricative	β	v	ð				j	ɣ		ʁ	
voiceless fricative	ɸ	f	θ				ç	x		χ	h
voiced affricate							c				
voiceless affricate							ɟ				
voiced sibilant			z	z̪	ẓ	ʒ					
voiceless sibilant			s	s̪	ṣ	ʃ					
nasal	m		n	n̪	ṇ		ɲ	ŋ	ŋʷ		
lateral			l	l̪	ḷ		ʎ	ĩ			
flap			ř		ṛ						
trill			r̃								
frictionless continuant							ɹ	y	w		

Vowels

	front un-rounded	front rounded	central un-rounded	central rounded	back un-rounded	back rounded
high	i ɪ	ü ʏ	ɨ	ʉ	ɯ	u ʊ
mid	e ɛ	ø œ	ə		ʌ	o ɔ
low	æ a		ɑ			ɐ

5

The following diacritics are also used:

⁓ nasalisation   ₒ voiceless   : vowel length
, syllabic   ´ stress (primary)   ` stress (secondary)

Since the books in the *Studying Pacific Languages* series have been printed in the past with a system of transcription based more on American transcription systems, the following comparisons between the present system and the system used in other publications in the series (and in the first edition of the present volume) are presented:

This edition	First edition
d̡	j
ʄ	c
β	b̦
φ	p̦
δ	d̦
γ	g̦
ç	x̂
ɣ	g̱
ʒ	ž
ʃ	s
ɲ	ñ
ɟ	ĭ
ɾ	r
ʏ	ü
φ	ö
œ	ɔ̈
ʉ	ɨ̵
ɯ	ï
ʌ	ɛ̈

6

Map 1 : Papua New Guinea Languages Referred to in the Text.

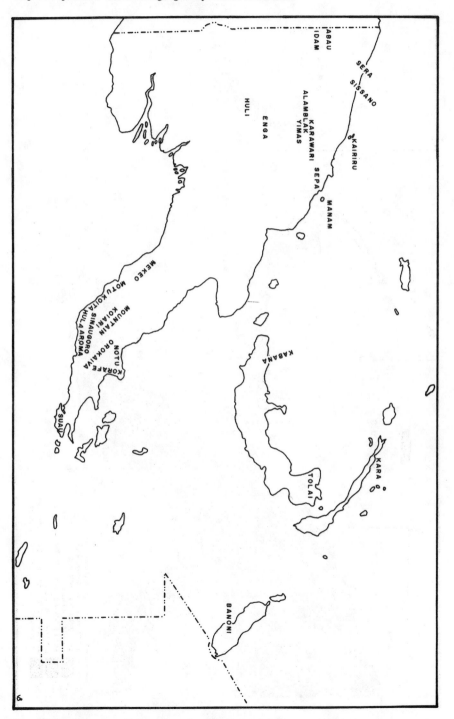

6

Map 2 : Distribution of Tok Pisin and Hiri Motu as Lingua Francas in Papua New Guinea.

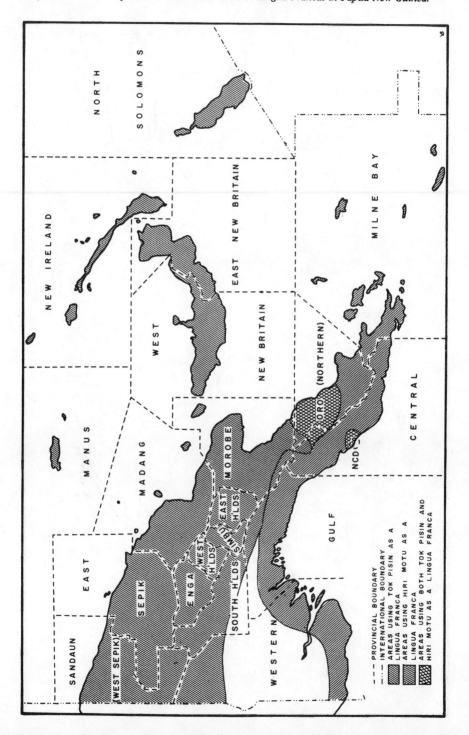

Map 3 : Pacific Languages Referred to in the Text.

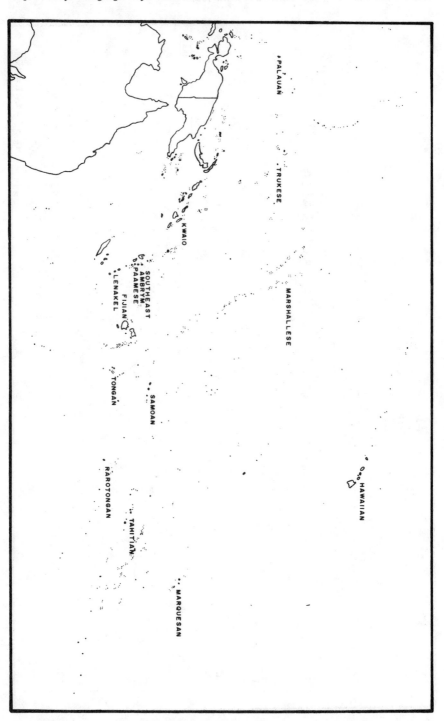

Map 4 : Australian Languages Referred to in the Text.

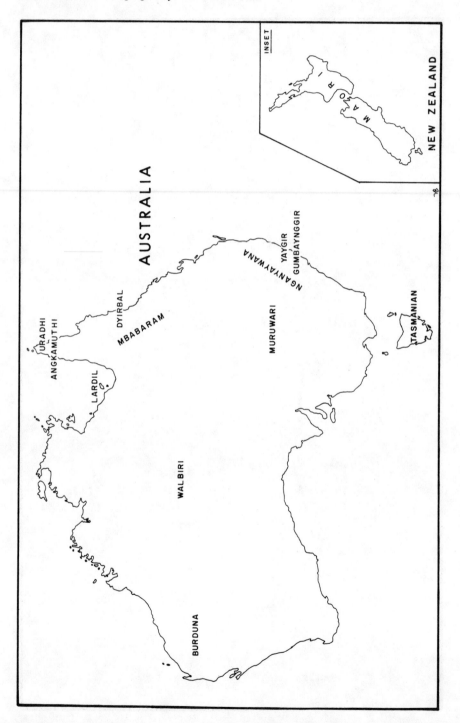

Chapter One

INTRODUCTION

1.1 The Nature of Linguistic Relationships

Many linguists trace the history of modern linguistics back to the publication in 1915 of the book *Course in General Linguistics* by students of the Swiss linguist Ferdinand de Saussure. In this book, the foundation was laid for the scientific study of language. Saussure recognised, as we still do today, that language is made up of a collection of units, all related to each other in very particular ways, on different levels. These different levels are themselves related in various ways. The primary function of language is to express meanings, and to convey these to someone else. To do this, the mental image in a speaker's head has to be transformed into some physical form so that it can be transferred to someone else, who can then decode this physical message, and have the same mental image come into his or her head.

One of the points that Saussure stressed was the fact that we need to make a distinction between studying language from a DIACHRONIC point of view and from a SYNCHRONIC point of view. Up until the time of Saussure, linguistics had basically involved the diachronic study of languages, which meant that scholars were only interested in describing (and explaining) relationships between various aspects of languages *over periods of time*. Linguistics was, until then, a purely historical field of study. Languages at a particular point in time were viewed not so much as systems within themselves, but as 'products of history'. Saussure disputed this interpretation, and said that all languages could (and *should*) be described synchronically, *without reference to history*. When we describe a language synchronically, we describe what are the basic units that go to make up the language (i.e. its phonemes, morphemes and so on), and the relationship between them at that time and that time only. He therefore proposed a rigid boundary line between diachronic and synchronic linguistics that has been part of linguistics since his time (though lately, linguists have come to question such a rigidly stated view). This book is intended to introduce you to the concepts and techniques of diachronic linguistics.

Another important concept that Saussure stressed was the fact that the mental image in a speaker's head and the physical form used to transfer this image is completely arbitrary. This accounts for the fact that a certain kind of domestic animal is called a [sisia] in Motu[1], a [pap] in Tolai[2] a [hunt] in German, a [dɔg] in English and a [ʃiɛ̃] in French. If there were any kind of natural connection between a word and its meaning we would all use the same word.

Saussure would not have denied that some parts of language are strongly iconic, or natural. All languages have onomatopoeaic words like *rokrok* for 'frog' and *meme* for 'goat' in Tok Pisin[3] and *kokoroku* for 'chicken' in Motu. However, words such as these are usually very small in number, and are not an important consideration.

If we compare two different words used by two different groups of people speaking different languages, and we find that they express a similar (or identical) meaning by using similar (or, again, identical) sounds, then we need to ask ourselves this question: why? Maybe it is because there is some natural connection between the meaning and the form being used to express it. On the other hand, maybe it says something about some kind of historical connection.

Let us go on a diversion for a moment, and look at the topic of stories in different cultures of the world. Probably all societies in the world have some kinds of stories that are passed on from generation to generation, telling of the adventures of people and animals a long time ago. Often, these stories are told not just for pure interest and enjoyment, but as a means of preserving the values of the culture of their tellers. The fact that all societies have such stories is not particularly surprising. Even the fact that most societies have stories about animals that speak and behave like humans is not particularly surprising, as all humans of whatever culture are able to see similarities between animals and humans. However, what if we found that two different peoples had a story about a person who died, and who was buried and from whose grave grew a tree that nobody had seen before and that this tree had large green fruit, and that nobody knew what to do with this fruit, but a sign was given by a bird, and the people broke it open and drank the sweet water inside? This story,

---

[1] The language of the Port Moresby area
[2] The language of the Rabaul area
[3] The official name of the English-based pidgin spoken in the New Guinea area.

12

in its basic form is in fact recognised by people from widely separated parts of Melanesia. Surely, if two different peoples share this story about the origin of coconuts in its basic form (though it may differ in detail), then it cannot be accidental. It must indicate something in common about the history of the people.

So, if we came across two (or more) different languages and find they have similar words to express similar meanings, we would come to the same kind of conclusion. Look at the following forms:

	BAHASA INDONESIA	TOLAI	PAAMESE (VANUATU)	FIJIAN
'two'	dua	aurua	elu	rua
'three'	tiga	autul	etel	tolu
'four'	empat	aivat	ehat	va
'five'	lima	ailima	elim	lima
'stone'	batu	vat	ahat	vatu

These similarities must also be due to more than pure chance. Our suggested explanation is that these words have some kind of historical connection.

This connection (and the connection between the stories about the coconut that we looked at earlier) could be of two kinds. Firstly, it could be that three of these four languages simply borrowed these words from the fourth (or that all four borrowed from a fifth language somewhere). Secondly, it could be that these forms all derive from a single set of original forms that has diverged differently in each case. Since these four languages are spoken in widely separated areas, we could guess that the speakers have had little or no opportunity to contact each other until very recent times. Anyway, even if they were in contact, there would seem to be little need to borrow words for things like the basic numbers and the word for 'stone'. They are the sorts of words that people from almost all cultures must know already, so they would hardly need to be borrowed. It might be understandable if the words for 'coffee' or 'iceberg' were similar, as these are certain to be introduced concepts in these areas, which would originally have had no indigenous names. The second explanation would therefore seem to be the most likely, i.e. these forms must be derived from a single original set of forms.

This brings us to the important concepts of LANGUAGE RELATIONSHIP and PROTO-LANGUAGE. These concepts were first recognised in modern scholarship by Sir William Jones, a British judge in colonial India. Jones had studied a wide variety of languages, and in 1786 he delivered a famous speech in which he said:

> The Sanskrit[4] language, whatever be its antiquity, is of a wonderful structure; more perfect than the Greek, more copious than the Latin[5], and more exquisitely refined than either, yet bearing to both of them a stronger affinity, both in the roots of verbs and in the forms of grammar, than could possibly have been produced by accident; so strong indeed, that no philologer[6] could examine all three, without believing them to have *sprung from some common source,* which, perhaps, no longer exists: there is similar reason, though not quite so forcible, for supposing that both the Gothic[7] and Celtic[8], though blended with a very different idiom, had the same origin with the Sanskrit; and the Old Persian[9] might be added to the same family.

This statement added two significant advances to the understanding of language change. Firstly, he spoke of the idea of languages being related. Up until then, people had tried to derive one language from another, often with ridiculous results. For instance, people had tried to show that all modern languages of the world ultimately went back to Hebrew, the language of the Bible. Kings of Europe even went to the extreme of separating newborn babies from their parents to see what language they would speak naturally if they were left alone and not taught. The results varied from Dutch to Hebrew (and none of them are believable). The similarities between Sanskrit, Latin and Greek that Jones was talking about were often explained by saying

---

[4] The language of ancient India, which was until that time little known to Europeans
[5] The ancient language of Italy
[6] An earlier term for historical linguist
[7] The ancient language of northern Europe
[8] The ancient language of western Europe
[9] The ancient language of Iran

that Sanskrit developed *into* Greek, and then Greek developed *into* Latin:

SANSKRIT   →   GREEK   →   LATIN

Jones, however, introduced the idea of the 'parallel' development of languages. The concept he was introducing was therefore the concept of language relationship — the fact that two languages have a common origin means that they belong to a single FAMILY of languages.

Secondly, he spoke of the concept of the proto-language (without actually using the term). When he said that these three languages, and possibly the others he mentioned (and he was later shown to be right), were derived from some other language, he meant that there was some ancestral language from which all three languages were descended by changing in different ways. So, the model of language change and relationship that he proposed to replace the earlier model looks like the model we use today:

PROTO-
LANGUAGE

SANSKRIT   GREEK   LATIN

The concepts of proto-language and language relationship both rest on the assumption that languages change. In fact *all* languages change *all* the time. It is true to say that some languages change more than others, but all languages change nevertheless. But while all languages change, the change need not be in the same direction for all speakers. So, let us imagine a situation like this:

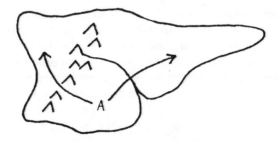

15

There is an area on an island occupied by a group of people speaking a language, called A. Perhaps under pressures from population density, perhaps because of disputes, or perhaps out of pure interest, the people from one area move out across the river and the mountains and settle in other areas. As we have said, all languages change, and language A is no exception. However, the changes that take place in Language A across the mountains and across the river are not necessarily the same as those that take place in the original homeland. Eventually, enough changes have taken place in the three areas so that people can no longer understand each other. So, we now have this kind of situation:

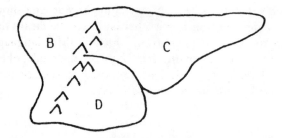

These three languages, B, C and D, still show some similarities, despite their differences. What we say, therefore, is that they are all related languages, all derived from a common ancestor or proto-language. We could therefore draw a family tree diagram for these three languages to look like this:

A
↙ ↓ ↘
B   C   D

This is therefore what we would say about Bahasa Indonesia, Tolai, Paamese and Fijian. They are related languages which are derived from a proto-language, of which we have no written records.

Generally, when a proto-language evolves to produce a number of different daughter languages, we have no written records of the process. In the case of some of the languages of Europe however, we have written records going back some thousands of years, and we can actually observe the changes taking place. Latin was the language of most of Europe at the time of Christ. However, as the centuries passed, Latin gradually changed in its spoken form in different areas so that it was quite different from the older written records. It is important to note that Latin changed in different ways in what is now Portugal, Spain, France, Italy and Rumania. The eventual result of this was that there are different languages in Europe today called Portuguese, Spanish, French, Italian and Rumanian, which are all similar to some extent, because they all go back to a common ancestor. Again, we can draw a family tree that looks like this to describe this situation:

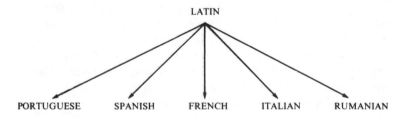

We should ask ourselves this question: did Latin die out? Well, Latin did not die out in the same way that some languages die out. Some languages die out because their speakers die out. The Tasmanian Aborigines, for instance, were badly affected by the diseases introduced by the Europeans and many died. Those who did not die from disease were often shot and poisoned by the Europeans. The last full-blooded Tasmanian died in 1876, and a knowledge of the language died with her. (However, many part-blood Tasmanian Aborigines are still living and proudly identify themselves as Tasmanian Aborigines. Their language, however, is English.) Other languages die out, not because their speakers die out, but because they prefer (for whatever reason) or are forced (by whatever means) to abandon their own language in favour of someone else's. Again, in Australia, we see Aborigines in many areas giving up their own languages in favour of English. The same may happen in Papua New Guinea if people choose to speak Tok Pisin or Hiri Motu[10] instead of their own local languages.

But neither of these situations is true of Latin. A proto-language can in some ways be compared to a baby. A baby changes over time,

---

[10] The Motu-based pidgin that is used as a lingua franca throughout much of the Papuan area

and becomes a teenager, and then an adult, and finally an old person. The baby did not die and then become a teenager. Similarly, Latin did not die and 'become' French. Latin simply gradually changed so that it changed enough that it looked like a different language, i.e. French. The change was gradual, and the change continues. There was no moment when people suddenly realised they were speaking French instead of Latin, in the same way that there is no moment when a baby becomes a teenager. After enough changes had taken place, people compared their own language with the older written forms of Latin, and realised that the changes had taken place. But this is like looking at a photograph of ourselves taken when we were younger. We will certainly look totally different, but the person we can see is definitely not dead!

French has not stopped changing either. The change continues. French may well be the future ancestor language from which a whole family of languages will be derived. So too may English, and Bahasa Indonesia, and Tolai, and Paamese, and Fijian. . . .

1.2 Attitudes to Language Change

Since we are speaking of language change in this book, we should perhaps look at some of the common attitudes that people have towards language change. As we saw in the preceding section, all languages change all of the time. Very often, members of a particular society can actually observe the changes that have taken place. Sometimes, in the case of written languages, people can see the language as it was spoken a number of generations ago, or even a number of centuries ago. In the case of unwritten languages, we obviously cannot observe how the language was spoken that far back in time, but very often, people are able to recognise differences between the way the older people speak and the way younger people speak.

It seems that in almost all societies, the attitudes people have to language change are basically the same. People everywhere tend to say that the older form of a language is in some sense 'better' than the form that is being used today. In Papua New Guinean villages for example, it is not unusual to hear the parents and grandparents of today's generation of children, who have been educated in school, saying that their children do not speak the language 'properly'. In fact, it is even possible to hear university students in this country

18

saying that they cannot speak their *own* language 'as well' as their parents speak it. Very recently on the National Broadcasting Commission, Cecil Abel, a European who was born and brought up in Milne Bay, and grew up speaking both English and Suau, complained that the Suau spoken by young people today was nothing but 'doggerel'. This seems to be a fairly common attitude.

In most cases, if you ask people why they say these things, it turns out that what they mean is that the younger generation doesn't use some of the words that the older generation use, or that the younger generation might use words borrowed from Tok Pisin or English. For instance, in Vanuatu, the younger people on the island of Paama very often say *ka:ren* for 'garden' and *bu:s* for 'bush', while their parents would use the original Paamese words *a:h* 'garden' and *leiai* 'bush', instead of the forms borrowed from Bislama (i.e. Vanuatu Pidgin). Regarding the Suau case that we just mentioned, Cecil Abel went on to say that what he meant by the language these days being 'doggerel' was that some of the expressions used by Suau-speakers of his generation are no longer used by members of the younger generations.

Now, if you go back to the preceding section, you will find that when we were discussing the ideas of Saussure, we said that forms in language are completely arbitrary. That is, there is no natural connection between a word and its meaning. This means that *any* sequence of sounds can express *any* meaning perfectly adequately, as long as the members of the particular speech community *agree* to let those sounds represent that meaning. This means that *ka:ren* and *a:h* are both perfectly adequate ways of expressing the idea of 'garden'; similarly, *bu:s* and *leiai* both express the meaning of 'bush' just as clearly. Neither is 'better', than the other. And no doubt in Suau, the younger generations have their *own* expressions that the older people did not know.

But people still like to insist that the earlier form is always 'better' than the later form, and they still like to say that the newer ways of speaking and writing are 'incorrect'. This applies to speakers of English, just the same as it does to any language. For instance, the following comments once appeared in a letter to the editor in the Post-Courier[11]:

---

[11] The national daily paper published in Port Moresby

19

> The English language is murdered
> daily on the NBC[12] and I regret to
> say particularly in your Post-
> Courier. . . . It is true that English is
> a living and developing language
> and new words and phrases are in-
> troduced from time to time. But the
> essential grammar must be retained.

The writer of this letter was not just complaining about new words
creeping into the language. He was also complaining of the 'loss' of
grammatical standards. In particular, he complained about people
who 'split' their infinitives, by placing adverbs between the word 'to'
and a verb. He objects when people say things like:

> The minister intended *to speedily ex-
> amine* the proposal for the intro-
> duction of vernacular education in
> schools.

and says that only the following sentence is correct:

> The minister intended *speedily to ex-
> amine* the proposal for the intro-
> duction of vernacular education in
> schools.

You can see in the first sentence, it says 'to speedily examine', while
in the second sentence it says 'speedily to examine'. People who
complain like this (and there are many) are ignoring the fact that
probably everybody (even themselves when they are not thinking
about it!) follows the pattern of the first sentence. The writer of the
letter quoted above actually went on to suggest that a good solution
to the problem was for children to be physically punished in school
when they produce 'incorrect' sentences like this!

There was a time when things were different in English, and
people probably *did* speak without split infinitives, but times have
changed. Both of these constructions express the idea completely
adequately. The choice of a particular construction is purely
arbitrary — neither is in any sense 'better' than the other.

As we mentioned earlier, attitudes like these are probably
common to all cultures. Not only this, but these kinds of attitudes

---

[12] The National Broadcasting Corporation

also have a long history. Samuel Johnson was the first person to attempt to write a complete dictionary of the English language. His work appeared about two hundred years ago, and he said that its aim was to:

> refine our language to grammatical
> purity, and to clear it from colloquial
> barbarisms. . . .

However, the choice between what is 'barbaric' and what is 'pure' is completely arbitrary. He always chose to include the 'pure' written forms of the upper classes, and labelled the spoken forms of the lower classes as 'barbaric'.

It has not just been ordinary people who hold these ideas. Even among people who were involved in the study of language change last century, it was a common belief that languages of today were degenerating, and that today's languages were not as 'pure' in structure as they used to be. For instance, one famous scholar, Max Müller, claimed that in the written history of all of the languages of Europe, he could only observe a 'gradual process of decay'. The proto-language from which Latin, Greek and Sanskrit were derived (i.e. the languages that Sir William Jones first mentioned as being related in 1786) was seen as being the most 'pure' form of language that was possible.

The common fault in all of these lines of thinking is that such people all regard language change as unnatural, and wish it would never happen. But all human societies are always changing, and language is just another aspect of human society. Language change is *natural* and *inevitable.* Even if your language uses more English words than it did in your parents' time, it is still your language. In fact, if this were how we measured how 'real' a language is, then English would only be half-English, because about half of the words in an English dictionary originally come from other languages!

READING GUIDE QUESTIONS
1. What statements did Ferdinand de Saussure make that influenced the course of linguistic science from his time on?
2. What is the significance of the discussion of stories told by people of different cultures in this chapter?
3. What possible explanations can we offer if we find that two languages express similar meanings by phonetically similar forms?

4. What do we mean when we say that two or more languages are genetically related?
5. What is a proto-language?
6. What was the significance of the statement by Sir William Jones in 1786 about the relationship between Sanskrit, Latin and Ancient Greek?
7. Does a proto-language die out and then get replaced by its daughter languages? What, for example, is the nature of the connection between Latin and Rumanian?
8. How are people's attitudes to language change and ideas of standard and non-standard forms in language related?

DISCUSSION GUIDE QUESTIONS AND EXERCISES

1. What do you think is the importance to linguists of the fact that Sanskrit, Latin and Greek were written languages?
2. Saussure and the modern linguists who followed him made a great deal of the arbitrary nature of language. How arbitrary *is* language? Consider the following questions:
   (a) What are some words for 'mother' and 'father' in the languages of you and your classmates, or any other languages you know. If these are similar, what reason can you give for this?
   (b) What are the words for 'blow' in your languages or any other languages you know? How similar are these words? Why?
   (c) Examine the pairs of words below in a number of different languages. One word of the pair for each language means 'big' and one means 'small'. Circle the word in each language that you *guess* means 'big'.

Paamese (Vanuatu)	mari:te	titi:te
Russian	malenkiy	bolʃoy
Fijian	levu	lailai
Bahasa Indonesia	kətʃil	besar
Tagalog (Philippines)	maliit	malaki
Kwaio (Solomons)	sika	baʔi
Gumbaynggir (Australia)	barway	dunuy
Samoan	lapoʔa	laitiiti
Dyirbal (Australia)	midi	bulgan
Lenakel (Vanuatu)	ipwir	esuaas

Compare the results across the class. What is going on? Can you explain the results?

What do you think is the importance of such facts to the historical study of languages?

3. The word 'tooth' in English has a long history in English writing, and it goes back to the same source as the German word 'Zahn' [tsa:n] and the Dutch word 'tand' [tant] indicating that these three languages are closely related. Latin also has a root for 'tooth' of the form [dent-] which is more dissimilar to the English form than the German and Dutch forms, suggesting that the languages are less closely related. Later on in English writing, we start finding words in English like 'dental', 'dentist', 'trident' (the fork with three 'teeth' usually held by the devil in pictures) and 'denture' (false teeth). What do you think this indicates about the relationship between Latin and English?

4. Take the Lord's Prayer you know from English. Point out the expressions and constructions that would not normally be used in ordinary speech today. Why do you think people prefer to pray in an old-fashioned form of English that is hard to understand?

5. In Sir William Jones's statement in 1786, he said that the various Indo-European languages he was discussing must have 'sprung from some common source, which perhaps no longer exists'. What did he mean by the comment that the language perhaps no longer exists? Is he saying the language became extinct? Could you think of a clearer way of expressing what he means?

6. For what sorts of reasons may a society give up its language and replace it with somebody else's? Can you think of any examples from your own experience where such a thing has happened, or might happen in the future?

7. Comment on Sir William Jones' statement that Sanskrit, which resembles the proto-language from which Latin and Greek were derived, 'is of a wonderful structure, more perfect than the Greek, more copious than the Latin, and more exquisitely refined than either'.

8. French newspapers contain many English words, like 'football', 'weekend', 'camping' and so on. There are many speakers of French who want to keep the language 'pure', and to prevent the development of 'Frenglish'. There is even a government council, called the French Academy, whose job it is to keep such

words from appearing in the dictionary, and to find good French words for all of these things. What comment would you make to members of this council?

FURTHER READING
1. Arlotto, Anthony, 1972. *Introduction to Historical Linguistics* (Chapter One 'The Scope of Comparative and Historical Linguistics'), Boston: Houghton Mifflin, pp. 1-10.
2. Pei, Mario. *The Story of Language* (Chapter Four 'The Evolution of Language), pp. 35-36.
3. Aitchison, Jean. *Language Change: Progress or Decay?* (Chapter One 'The Ever-whirling Wheel'), pp. 15-31.

Chapter Two

TYPES OF SOUND CHANGE

While it may not be particularly surprising to learn that all languages change over time, as we pointed out in the previous chapter, it may be surprising to learn that languages tend to change in remarkably similar ways. For instance, if we look at the history of the sound [p] in the Palauan language of Micronesia, we find that it has undergone a change to [w] in the modern language. So, ignoring all the sounds except for the underlined sounds, look at the following examples of this change:

PALAUAN

*paqi¹	→	wa?	'leg'
*paqit	→	wa?əδ	'bitter'
*qatəp	→	?aδow	'roof'

Now, if we look at the history of the sound [p] in a completely separate language, which has no known historical connection with Palauan, we may find that exactly the same change has taken place. Let us look at a language called Uradhi, which is an Australian Aboriginal language, spoken on Cape York Peninsula, in north Queensland:

URADHI

*pinta	→	winta	'arm'
*pilu	→	wilu	'hip'
*paṭa	→	waṭa	'bite'

We could easily find other examples in languages of the world of the sound [p] changing to [w]. But we would also find repeated examples of [p] changing to other sounds, for instance [f], or [b] or

---

In the study of the history of languages, the symbol * is used to mark a form that has never actually been heard or written, but which is inferred or reconstructed in a proto-language on the basis of evidence that is available. We will be looking at how we arrive at such reconstructions in Chapter five.

[v]. However, it would be very difficult to find an example of a language in which [p] had changed to [z] or [l] or [æ].

This fact leads uš to try to define likely sound changes and to distinguish these from unlikely sound changes. Having defined which sound changes are likely to occur and which are not, we can then try to classify the various kinds of actually recorded sound changes. To do this, we need to look for as wide a range of possible sound changes in the world's languages and look for generalisations. This is the purpose of this chapter: to try to set out some of the most commonly occurring types of sound changes, and to give examples of each.

2.1 Lenition

The first kind of sound change that we will talk about is that which is called LENITION, or sometimes WEAKENING. The concept of lenition is actually not very well defined, and linguists who use the term often seem to rely more on intuition or guesswork than on detailed understanding of what lenition is. Linguists speak of some sounds as being relatively 'stronger' or 'weaker' than others. Many people would intuitively judge the sounds on the left in the table below to be 'stronger' than those on the right:

STRONGER	WEAKER
b	p
p	f
f	h
x	h
b	w
v	w
a	ə
d	l
s	r
k	ʔ

The generalisations that we can make regarding these correspondences are that voiced sounds can be considered 'stronger' than voiceless sounds. Similarly, stops rank higher than continuants in strength, consonants are higher than semi-vowels, oral sounds are higher in rank than glottal sounds, and front and back vowels rank higher than central vowels.

When phonetic change takes place, it is very often in the direction of strong to weak. That is to say, we would be more likely to find a change of [k] to [ʔ] for example, rather than the other way around, with [ʔ] becoming [k]. Changes of the reverse order are possible of course, though less likely. So, for instance, [naif] in English 'strengthens' the final consonant to become [naip] in Tok Pisin.

Using this intuition as a rough guide to the concept of weakness, we can give actual examples of phonetic lenition or weakening in different languages. The change of [b] and [p] to [f] in the Kara language of New Ireland is one good example of lenition:

		KARA	
*bulan	→	fulan	'moon'
*tapine	→	tefin	'woman'
*punti	→	fut	'banana'
*topu	→	tuf	'sugarcane'

Similarly, the change from [p] to [w] in the Palauan and Uradhi examples given in the introduction to this chapter are examples of lenition. In the Yaygir language of northern New South Wales in Australia, stops are often lenited or weakened to semi-vowels at the beginning of a word, as shown by the following examples:

	YAYGIR	
*ɖa:laɲ	ya:laɲ	'mouth'
*bu:luɲ	yu:luɲ	'belly'
*gaɲa:mbil	yaɲa:mbil	'tongue'

There is one particular kind of lenition that goes under the name of RHOTACISM. The term rhotic is often used to cover all types of 'r' sounds (trills, flaps, glides and so on), as distinct from all types of 'l' sounds. Laterals and rhotics together make up the phonetic class of liquids. The change known as rhotacism refers to the lenition of [s] or [z] to a rhotic between vowels. This kind of change is found in Latin:

		LATIN	
*ami:ko:sum	→	ami:ko:rum	'of the friend'
*genesis	→	generis	'of the type'
*hono:sis	→	hono:ris	'of the honour'

27

There is even evidence in the spelling of modern English that rhotacism has taken place in the history of the language. The plural form of the verb [wɔz] 'was' is [wə:] 'were' (though in many dialects it is [wəɹ]). Assuming that the spelling more closely reflects an earlier pronunciation than the modern pronunciation, we can suggest that the final 'e' of 'were' represents an earlier plural suffix, and that the root was similar to the singular form. So, the plural was probably something like [wase] or [wese] and there was later lenition of the [s] to [ɹ] to give [waɹe] or [weɹe]. It is from this form that the modern form [weɹ] in some dialects is derived: from this form we derived our own pronunciation of [wə:].

A very common kind of sound change that takes place in languages is that one or more sounds tend to be lost or dropped out. This can be viewed as an extreme case of lenition: the weakest a sound can actually be is to not exist at all.

An example from modern English of a sound being lost altogether would be the varying pronunciation of a word like 'history'. While some people will pronounce this as [hɪstəri], other people might simply say [hɪstri], dropping out the schwa vowel [ə] or some people might even say [ɪstri] dropping out the initial [h] as well. Another example from Tok Pisin would be the word we write as 'long' in the sentence:

Em	*Kam*	*long*	*Waigani*
S/he	come	from	Waigani

'S/he is coming from Waigani.'

Many people will actually pronounce this simply as:

Em	kam	lo'	Waigani

It is very common in languages of the world for sounds at the beginnings and ends of words to be lost. In many languages of the Pacific for example, final consonants are very regularly dropped, as shown by the following Fijian forms:

		FIJIAN	
*ɲiur	→	nɪu	'coconut'
*taŋis	→	taŋi	'cry'
*ikan	→	ika	'fish'
*bulan	→	vula	'moon'
*tansik	→	taδi	'sea'
*layar	→	laδa	'sail'
*laŋit	→	laŋi	'wind'

28

Initial consonants are also very frequently dropped. The following examples come from the Angkamuthi language of Cape York Peninsula:

ANGKAMUTHI

*mayi	→	ayi	'food'
*nani	→	ani	'ground'
*ŋampu	→	ampu	'tooth'
*nukal	→	uka:	'foot'
*ɣantu	→	antu	'canoe'
*wapun	→	apun	'head'

There are some kinds of sound loss that are covered by particular terms. These special terms will be discussed below.

(a) Cluster Reduction

When consonants come together in a word without any vowels between them, we speak of consonant 'clusters'. Very often, such clusters get reduced by deleting one (or more) of the consonants. This is one kind of change that has taken place word finally in the history of Tok Pisin with words derived from English.

ENGLISH		TOK PISIN	
kould	→	kol	'cold'
ka:dz	→	kas/kat	'cards'
gʌvəmənt	→	gavman	'government'
dɪstrɪkt	→	distrik	'district'
poust	→	pos	'post'

Even in the history of English itself, cluster reduction has been a common change. Note that the pronunciation of 'government' shows that the [nm] cluster has been reduced to simply [m].

(b) Apocope

APOCOPE, pronounced [əpɔ́kəpi], is simply a name you will come across in textbooks for the loss of word final vowels. This is a very common change in languages, and examples are easy to find. For example, look at the following changes that have taken place in the history of the language of southeast Ambrym in Vanuatu:

		SOUTHEAST AMBRYM	
*utu	→	ut	'lice'
*aŋo	→	aŋ	'fly'
*asue	→	asu	'rat'
*tohu	→	toh	'sugarcane'
*hisi	→	his	'banana'
*use	→	us	'rain'

(c) Syncope

This term, pronounced [síŋkəpi], refers to a very similar process to apocope. Rather than referring to the loss of final vowels, SYNCOPE refers to the loss of vowels in the middle of words. It is syncope which often produces consonant clusters in languages that did not formerly have them. For instance, the common pronunciation of the word 'policeman' as [pli:smən] instead of [pəli:sm ən] is an example of syncope; so too is the pronunciation of 'history' without the schwa that we looked at earlier. In some languages, syncope is a very regular change, as in Lenakel, spoken on the island of Tanna in Vanuatu:

		LENAKEL	
*namataɲa	→	nɔ̃mrɔ̃n	'his eye'
*nalimaɲa	→	nelmɔ̃n	'his hand'
*masa	→	mha	'low tide'

(d) Haplology

Haplology is a kind of sound change that tends to be fairly sporadic and rare in its application. This term refers to the loss of an entire syllable when that syllable is found next to an identical, or at least very similar syllable. This is the process that is involved when we pronounce 'library' as [laibri] instead of [laibrəri]. The word 'England' [ɪŋglənd] was originally 'Angalaland', meaning the land of the Angles (a group of people who settled in Britain and brought with them the English language). The two 'la' syllables were reduced to one by this process of haplology, and we now have only one 'l' in 'England' as a result.

(e) Compression

This is also a kind of change that takes place with only a few words in a language and tends not to be very general. Compression is the process of dropping off one or more syllables from the end or middle of a word. E.g.

administration	→	admin
university	→	uni
Konedobu[2]	→	Kone
Popondetta[2]	→	Pop
Tokarara[2]	→	Tok

A particular kind of compression is the use of 'word mixes' and initials. Examples of phonological reduction by using only the initials include the following:

Preliminary Year[3]	→	PY
Like Good One[4]	→	LGO
Television	→	TV
National Broadcast- ing Corporation	→	NBC

By 'word mixes' we mean forms like the following, in which part of the word is added to a part of another word to make a new word:

Administrative College	→	Adcol

---

[2] Names of towns in Papua New Guinea (PNG), and suburbs of Port Moresby.

[3] The year of matriculation studies offered at the university of Papua New Guinea before a student can go on to degree studies if she or he has not completed six years of high school.

[4] A common rejoinder in PNG English to a sexually suggestive comment when the addressee is not interested (as if to say 'You think you are good enough for me?')

Electricity Commission	→	Elcom
University of Technology	→	Unitech

This kind of change seems to be particularly common in government departments, and in relation to administration generally. In fact, in Indonesia, there has developed a special register of the language commonly used in the newspapers where there are many word mixes of these kinds. Some people in Indonesia actually sometimes find it difficult to read some parts of the newspapers because so many new word mixes and abbreviations are used.

2.2 Sound Addition

While lenition, and particularly the total loss of sounds, is a very common kind of sound change, we also find that sometimes sounds actually get added rather than dropped. On the whole, however, sound addition is rather rare. In modern English, we can see evidence of this kind of change taking place when we hear people saying [sʌmpθɪŋ] instead of the more commonly heard [sʌmθɪŋ] for 'something'. We also have examples such as [noup] 'nope' and [yɛp] 'yep' instead of [nou] 'no' and [ye:] 'yeah' in which the final [p] seems to add emphasis by sharply cutting off the flow of air, symbolising the fact that the speaker's intention is absolutely final.

Sound addition very commonly takes place at the end of words with final consonants, where many languages add a vowel. Many languages tend to aim towards a syllable structure of consonant plus vowel, without consonant clusters and without word final consonants, and the addition of final vowels reflects this tendency. So for instance, when in Motu vowels are added at the ends of words borrowed from English, we have a good example of this process.

MOTU	
gavamani	'government'
maketi	'market'
botolo	'bottle'
traka	'truck'

Some kinds of sound addition are known by specific names in the literature of comparative linguistics. These terms, with examples of the process they refer to are presented below.

(a) Excrescence or anaptyxis

These two terms refer to the same process. EXCRESCENCE (or ANAPTYXIS) refers to the process by which a consonant is added between two other consonants in a word. Although this change operates against the general tendency in languages to produce consonant plus vowel syllable structures in that it creates even longer consonant clusters, it is nevertheless a fairly common kind of change. The insertion of [p] in the middle of the [mθ] cluster in 'something' that we just looked at is an example of excrescence. Excrescence has also taken place in other words in the history of English, and the added consonant is now represented in the spelling system   e.g

ENGLISH

*æmtig	→	ɛmpti	'empty'
*θümle	→	θɪmbl	'thimble' (metal cover placed over finger while sewing to protect it from being pricked)

The excrescent stop that is inserted has the same point of articulation (or is HOMORGANIC with) the preceding nasal in all of these examples. The stop is added to close off the velum (which is open during the production of the nasal) before going on to produce the following non-nasal sound (i.e. stop or liquid).

(b) Epenthesis

The term EPENTHESIS [əpɛnθəsəs] is used to describe the change by which a vowel is added in the middle of a word to break up two consonants in a cluster. This change therefore produces syllables of the structure consonant plus vowel, again illustrating the common tendency for languages to avoid consonant clusters and final consonants. Many speakers of English insert an epenthetic [ɛpənθɛ́tɪk] schwa [ə] between the final consonants of the word [fɪlm] 'film', to produce [fɪləm]. Epenthesis is also a change that has taken place fairly frequently in the history of Tok Pisin. Compare the English and Tok Pisin forms below and note the occurrence of epenthetic vowels in Tok Pisin:

33

ENGLISH		TOK PISIN	
blæk	→	bilak	'black'
blu	→	bulu	'blue'
nɛkst	→	nekis	'next'
sɪks	→	sikis	'six'
skɪn	→	sikin	'skin'
pleis	→	peles	'village'
fɪlm	→	pilum	'film'

(c) Prothesis

PROTHESIS is another term used to refer to a particular type of sound addition, when a sound is added to the beginning of a word. In Motu, for example, when a word began with an [a], a prothetic [l] was added before it, as shown by the following examples:

		MOTU	
*api	→	lahi	'fire'
*asan	→	lada	'gills of fish'
*au	→	lau	'I'

2.3 Metathesis

The change known as METATHESIS [mətǽθəsəs] is a fairly uncommon kind of change. It does not involve the actual loss or addition of sounds or change the appearance of a particular sound; rather, it is simply a change in the order of sounds as they occur. If we mispronounce 'relevant' as 'revelant', this is an example of metathesis.

Metathesis has taken place in the history of some English words and the changed form has become accepted as standard. The English word [bə:d] 'bird' was originally pronounced [brɪd]. This then became [bɪrd] by metathesis, and this is the form we still represent in our spelling system. Of course, the sounds [ɪr] have undergone further changes to become [ə:], though in dialects of English such as American English, the original [r] is still clearly pronounced.

Generally, metathesis is a fairly rare sort of change, and tends to occur in only one or two words in a language. There are cases of fairly regular metathesis however. In the Ilokano language of the Philippines for example, there has been fairly consistent switching of word final [s] and initial [t], as shown by the following comparisons with Tagalog, the national language of the Philippines, which reflects the original situation:

TAGALOG	ILOKANO	
taŋis	sa:ŋit	'cry'
tubus	subbot	'redeem'
tigis	si:git	'decant'
tamis	samqit	'sweet'

2.4 Fusion

Phonetic FUSION is a fairly frequent kind of sound change, in which two originally separate sounds become a single sound, and the resulting single sound carries some of the phonetic features of *both* of the original sounds.

Before we go on to give examples of fusion, we will need to clarify what is meant by the term 'phonetic feature'. All sounds can be viewed as being made up of a number of particular phonetic features, which determine different aspects of the nature of sound. The sound [n] for instance, contains the following features:

1. voiced
2. alveolar
3. nasal
4. continuant
5. consonant

while the sound [æ] contains the following features:

1. voiced
2. low
3. front
4. continuant
5. vowel

Therefore, if we change two sounds to become one as in the process of fusion, we take some of the features of one sound and some of the features of the other sound and produce a new sound different from both, yet also sharing some features with both the original sounds.

35

2.4 Fusion

Let us take an example of a change that is recognised as involving fusion and see how this actually works. The following data comes from French:

		FRENCH	
*œn	→	œ̃	'a'
*bɔn	→	bɔ̃	'good'
*vɛn	→	vɛ̃	'wine'
*blan	→	blã	'white'

(The symbol ˜ over the vowel indicates that the vowel is nasalised, with the air coming out through the nasal passage as well as through the mouth.)
The generalisation that we can make is that:

$$\text{VOWEL} \quad + \quad \text{NASAL} \quad \rightarrow \quad \text{NASALISED VOWEL}$$

Expressing this in terms of features we can say that the 'vowel' feature of the first sound has been kept, while the 'nasal' feature of the second sound has been kept, and a single new sound combining these two features has been created:

1. nasal
2. vowel

A second example of fusion can be quoted from the Attic dialect of Greek. Examine the data below:

		ATTIC GREEK	
*gwous	→	bous	'cow'
*gwatis	→	basis	'going'
*gwasileus	→	basileus	'official'
*leikwɔ:	→	leipɔ:	'I leave'
*yɛ:kwar	→	hɛ:par	'liver'

In the original forms, we had a [g] or a [k] with the features:

1. velar
2. stop

36

and a [w] with the features:

1.   bilabial
2.   semi-vowel

In the fused form in the Attic dialect, we find that we have taken the stop feature of the first sound and the bilabial feature of the second sound to produce either a simple [b] or [p] from an original [gw] or [kw]. Note that the voicing features of the original stop are not changed, so a [gw] produces a [b] and a [kw] produces a [p].

A particular type of phonological fusion is referred to as COMPENSATORY LENGTHENING. This sound change is illustrated by the following forms from Old Irish:

		OLD IRISH	
*magl	→	ma:l	'prince'
*kenetl	→	kene:l	'gender'
*etn	→	e:n	'bird'
*datl	→	da:l	'assembly'

What has happened is that a consonant has been lost, and 'in compensation' for this loss, a vowel has been lengthened. If we introduce the idea of 'phoneme space' or something of this nature, we can treat this as an example of fusion. If each phoneme carried among its collection of features a feature of phoneme space (i.e. the actual space it occupies in a word), then we could say that all features *except* this feature of phoneme space were lost, and that this one feature only was fused with the features of the preceding sound. This new sound ·therefore contained two features of 'phoneme space', which is reflected in the change from a short vowel (one space) to a long vowel (two spaces).

2.5 Unpacking

UNPACKING is a phonetic process that is just the opposite of phonetic fusion. From an original single sound, we find that a sequence of two sounds may develop, each with some of the features of the original sound. In Bislama (Vanuatu Pidgin) for example, the English words [bæg] 'bag' and [slæk] 'slack' appear as [baik] and [slaik].

The sound [æ] has become [ai], and this can be viewed as phonetic unpacking of the features. The vowel [æ] contains the features:

1.   front
2.   low

(among others). The feature low is found in the Bislama vowel [a], while the feature front is found in the vowel [i].

Bislama offers us a second example of unpacking, which is interesting because it shows just how unpacking can be viewed as the opposite of fusion. We saw earlier how nasal vowels evolved in French as the result of phonetic fusion. When words containing nasal vowels in French are borrowed into Bislama, we find that the following change takes place:

FRENCH		BISLAMA	
kamiɔ̃	→	kamioŋ	'truck'
aksidã	→	aksidoŋ	'accident'
televizyɔ̃	→	televisioŋ	'television'
kaʁtɔ̃	→	katoŋ	'box'

Here, the original nasal and vowel features of the final vowel in French are distributed over two sounds, the oral vowels, and the velar nasal [ŋ]. We therefore have a change that can be expressed as:

NASAL VOWEL   →   VOWEL   +   NASAL CONSONANT

2.6 Vowel Breaking

There is another kind of phonetic change that is similar to unpacking in that two vowels evolve out of a single vowel. This process is called vowel breaking. Vowel breaking differs from unpacking however, in that it is not possible to find any transfer of features from an original single vowel to either of the two subsequent vowels. Rather, one vowel simply stays unchanged and some other vowel is added before or after it as a kind of 'off-glide' or 'on-glide'. One of the distinctive characteristics of American English is its 'broken vowels'. What is pronounced by speakers of most dialects as [bæd] 'bad' is often pronounced by Americans as [bæəd] or even as [bæid].

Vowel breaking is fairly common in languages of the world. A good example of a language apart from American English that has fairly regular vowel breaking is the Kairiru language spoken on an island near Wewak:

		KAIRIRU	
*pale	→	pial	'house'
*manu	→	mian	'bird'
*namu	→	niam	'mosquito'
*ndanu	→	rian	'water'
*lako	→	liak	'go'
*pati	→	viat	'four'
*tolu	→	tuol	'three'

(Note also that in this language, there is consistent apocope, or loss of final vowels.)

2.7 Assimilation

Many sound changes can be viewed as being due to the influence of one sound upon another. When one sound makes another sound change so that the two sounds end up being more similar to each other in some way, we call this assimilation. Since assimilation is by far the most common kind of sound change, we will present a fairly detailed discussion of the various sub-types of assimilation, along with numerous examples.

But before we do that, we need to define this concept of phonetic 'similarity'. In fact, we already have at our disposal a means of doing this, if we go back to the concept of phonetic features that we introduced earlier. We can say that two sounds are phonetically more similar to each other after a sound change has taken place if those two sounds have more phonetic features in common than they did before the change. If a sound change results in an increase in the number of shared phonetic features, then we can say that assimilation has taken place.

Let us take, as an example, a word that contains a consonant cluster of the form [np] in some languages. The two sounds in this cluster have the following features each:

39

$$
\begin{array}{ll}
\quad [n] & \quad [p] \\
1.\ \text{voiced} & 1.\ \text{voiceless} \\
2.\ \text{alveolar} & 2.\ \text{bilabial} \\
3.\ \text{nasal} & 3.\ \text{stop}
\end{array}
$$

We could assimilate one or two (or all) of the features of one sound in the direction of the other. For instance, the [n] could lose its nasal feature and replace it with the stop feature of the [p]. This change would be:

$$np \quad \rightarrow \quad dp$$

If, instead of assimilating the nasal feature, the feature of alveolar were to be assimilated to the bilabial feature, we would have:

$$np \quad \rightarrow \quad mp$$

and finally, if the voiced feature changed to voiceless, we would have:

$$np \quad \rightarrow \quad \underset{\circ}{n}p$$

(with the symbol [n̥] representing a voiceless alveolar nasal). These changes all involve the assimilation of only one feature. It is of course possible to assimilate two features at a time, as in the following:

$$np \quad \rightarrow \quad bp \text{ (keeping only the voiced feature)}$$

$$np \quad \rightarrow \quad tp \text{ (keeping only the alveolar feature)}$$

$$np \quad \rightarrow \quad \underset{\circ}{m}p \text{ (keeping only the nasal feature)}$$

All of these changes are examples of PARTIAL ASSIMILATION, because the changed sound always retains at least *one* of the original features by which it is distinguished from the unchanged sound. If *all* of the features are changed to match those of another sound, and the two sounds end up being identical, then we speak of COMPLETE or TOTAL ASSIMILATION. In the case of the cluster [np], an example of total assimilation would be the change:

$$np \quad \rightarrow \quad pp$$

There is yet another dimension that we should discuss regarding this question of assimilation. All of the examples we have just looked at are what are called REGRESSIVE ASSIMILATION. This means that the 'force' of the change operates 'backwards' in the word, i.e. from right to left. It is the features of the [p] in all of the examples above that influence the features of the preceding [n], and this is why we call this regressive asssimilation. This kind of assimilation can be represented in the following way:

$$A \quad \leftarrow \quad B$$

where the arrow represents the direction of the influence.

There is of course, a second possibility in which the direction of the change is reversed, and it is the preceding sound that exerts its influence over a sound that follows it. This kind of situation could be represented by an arrow pointing forward in the word:

$$A \quad \rightarrow \quad B$$

Such a situation, in which the features of a following sound are changed to match those of a preceding sound, is called PROGRESSIVE ASSIMILATION. Of the two types of assimilation, it is regressive assimilation that is by far the most commonly encountered in the world's languages.

If we take the same cluster [np] and this time treat the [n] as the 'influencing' sound rather than the [p] as before, we find that the following changes can all be regarded as partial progressive assimilation:

$$
\begin{aligned}
&np \quad \rightarrow \quad \text{nb (with assimilation of voicing)} \\
&np \quad \rightarrow \quad \text{nt (with assimilation of place of articulation)} \\
&np \quad \rightarrow \quad \text{nm̩ (with assimilation of manner of articulation)} \\
&np \quad \rightarrow \quad \text{nn̥ (keeping only the voiceless feature)} \\
&np \quad \rightarrow \quad \text{nm (keeping only the bilabial feature)} \\
&np \quad \rightarrow \quad \text{nd (keeping only the stop feature)}
\end{aligned}
$$

Progressive assimilation can be total, as well as partial. So, we have the final possibility:

np   →   nn

With two sounds that have only three differing features each, we can see that there are fourteen possible changes that can all be classed as assimilation. This concept therefore covers a wide range of sound changes, and as was said at the beginning of this section most sound changes that take place in languages of the world actually involve assimilation in one way or another.

Rather than try to talk about assimilation in the abstract as we have been doing, we should try to give concrete examples to show how it can work. To begin with, let us look at the pronunciation of the word *klostu* 'nearby' in the Tok Pisin of many older, non-formally educated speakers of the language. Such people may actually pronounce this as [korottu]. Ignoring for the moment the insertion of an epenthetic [o] and shift of [l] to [r], the change that is of particular interest to us is the change of [st] to [tt]. The [s] has totally assimilated in its features to the following [t]. This is therefore a case of total regressive assimilation.

As we have already seen, progressive assimilation is much less commonly encountered and good examples are harder to find. However, in the history of Icelandic, we can give an example of very regular total progressive assimilation.

ICELANDIC

*findan	→	finna	'find'
*gulθ	→	gull	'gold'
*halθ	→	hall	'inclined'
*munθ	→	munn	'mouth'
*unθan	→	unna	'love'

Examples of partial assimilation are more common than examples of complete assimilation. Partial assimilation can involve a wide range of possibilities, as the features that are assimilated may involve place of articulation (including the high, low, front and back features of vowels, as well as the features referring to the place of articulation of consonants), manner of articulation (whether stop, fricative, nasal, lateral and so on) and voicing (whether voiced or voiceless). Assimilation may also involve any combination of these various features.

42

Assimilation of place of articulation is a very common change. We can see the results of this change in modern English with the varying forms of the negative prefix [in-] 'in-'. This is normally pronounced as follows:

ındəvızəbl	'indivisible'
ımbæləns	'imbalance'
ıŋkənsıdərət	'inconsiderate'

The variants are therefore:

ım-	before labials
ıŋ-	before velars
ın-	elsewhere

The [n] has assimilated in place of articulation to the following consonant, i.e. the alveolar feature has been replaced with the feature for place of articulation of the following sound.

The change known as PALATALISATION is also an assimilatory change. By this change, a non-palatal sound (i.e. dentals, alveolars, velars and so on) become palatal sounds, usually before front vowels such as [i] or [e], or before the semi-vowel [y]. Sounds that we can class as palatal include: [ʈ], [ɖ], [s], [z], [ʃ], [ʒ] and some others which are less common. This can be called assimilation because the palatal (i.e. "front") feature of the vowel is transferred to the preceding consonant. One good example of palatalisation that we can give is the change from [t] to [s] in some words in Motu. Look at the following forms:

		MOTO	
*tama	→	tama	'father'
*tanis	→	tai	'cry'
*tumpu	→	tubu	'grandparent'
*topu	→	tohu	'sugarcane'
*tolu	→	toi	'three'
*tina	→	sina	'mother'
*qate	→	ase	'liver'
*mate	→	mase	'die'

Here, we clearly have [t] changing to [s] when it is followed by either of the front vowels [i] or [e]. The [t] of Motu is actually dental rather than alveolar, and the [s] is definitely articulated further back towards the palate. We can therefore say that there has been regressive assimilation of the consonant to the place of articulation of the following vowel. The tongue therefore has less distance to move from an [s] to an [i] or [e].

In the history of English too, we also have examples of palatalisation. The velar stops [k] and [g] became palatalised to [t] and [y] respectively when there was a following front vowel, as shown by the following examples:

		ENGLISH	
*kinn	→	tʃiːz	'cheese'
*kɛːsi	→	tʃaːf	'chaff' (chopped dried grass for feeding horses)
*geldan	→	yiːld	'yield'
*gearn	→	yaːn	'yarn' (thread for sewing)

(Note that the change of [g] to [y] probably involved palatalisation of [g] to [dz], and then lenition of [dz] to [y].)

Phonetic changes in the manner of articulation of a sound to bring two sounds into greater phonetic similarity are also common. Examine the following changes between vowels in the Banoni language of the North Solomons:

		BANONI	
*pekas	→	beɣasa	*pekpek*/'faeces'
*wakar	→	baɣara	'root'
*pakan	→	vaɣana	*'abusin kaikai*/'add meat to staple'
*tipi	→	tsivi	*singsing*/'traditional dance'
*makas	→	maɣasa	'dry coconut'

The intervocalic voiceless stops have become voiced fricatives. This can be viewed as involving the assimilation of two of the features of the voiceless stops to the features of the vowels. The stops have become voiced to match the feature of voicing for the vowels. Not only this however, but the change from stop to fricative is also assimilatory. Vowels, as well as nasals, fricatives and laterals, all carry the feature 'continuant', which means that these sounds can be continued or 'held'. These sounds contrast with those that carry the feature 'noncontinuant', which cannot be held. Such sounds include stops, affricates and semi-vowels. Now, in changing from a stop to a continuant between two other continuant sounds, we have a clear case of assimilation in the manner of articulation, as well as in voicing.

Another very common type of change that can also perhaps be viewed as assimilation of voicing is the change called FINAL DEVOICING. Sounds at the end of a word, especially stops and fricatives (but sometimes also other sounds, even vowels) often change from being voiced to voiceless. In German, the devoicing of final stops has been very regular, e.g:

		GERMAN	
*ba:d	→	ba:t	'bath'
*ta:g	→	ta:k	'day'
*hund	→	hunt	'dog'
*land	→	lant	'land'
*ga:b	→	ga:p	'gave;

We can say that in a case like this, the voiced feature of the original sound is changed to voiceless to match the voicelessness of the following silence at the end of the word.

There is a further aspect to assimilation that we have not yet touched on, and that is the fact that there is a contrast between what we call IMMEDIATE ASSIMILATION and ASSIMILATION AT A DISTANCE. In all of the examples we have looked at so far of assimilation, it has always been a case of one sound being influenced by the sound either *immediately* preceding or following it. These are therefore, all examples of immediate assimilation.

In the case of assimilation at a distance however, a sound can be influenced by another sound not immediately to the left or right of that sound, but perhaps in another syllable altogether. In the Huli language of the Southern Highlands, the Tok Pisin word *piksa* is often pronounced by older people speaking Huli as (kikiɗa] rather than as [pikida] as we would expect. What has happened is that the [p] of the first syllable has assimilated (at a distance) in place of articulation to the [k] of the second syllable.

Sometimes assimilation at a distance like this is a very regular feature of a language, and some type of assimilation may even apply over a whole word. When this happens, we call this HARMONY. Many languages have what we call vowel harmony, which means, basically, the assimilation of one (or more) vowel features of one vowel to other vowels in the word, sometimes even to all other vowels in the word. In Bislama (Vanuatu Pidgin), we find a good example of vowel harmony involving the original transitive suffix [-im] on verbs.

In Bislama, this suffix has three variants, as illustrated below:

BISLAMA	
kuk-um	'cook'
put-um	'put'
sut-um	'shoot'
mit-im	'meet'
kil-im	'hit'
rit-im	'read'
har-em	'feel'
mek-em	'make'
so-em	'show'

Following a syllable with a high back vowel, the [i] becomes [u] and therefore there is assimilation at a distance of the feature 'front' in one syllable to the feature 'back' in another. Following a syllable with a mid or low vowel, the [i] becomes [e] and therefore we can say that there is again assimilation at a distance of the feature 'high' to the feature 'mid' under the influence of the vowel of the preceding syllable.

Sometimes, we can have harmony involving features other than just vowel features. In the Enggano language, spoken on an island off southern Sumatra in Indonesia, there has been a change of nasal harmony, by which all voiced stops became nasals, and all vowels became nasalised following *any* nasal sound in the earlier stage of the language. If a word contained any nasal, then *all* following vowels became nasalised and all voiced stops became the corresponding nasals. So:

	ENGGANO		
*honabu	→	honãmũ	'your wife'
*ehɛ̃kua	→	ehɛ̃kũã	'seat'
*eũʔadaʔa	→	eũʔãnãʔã	'food'

There is one kind of vowel harmony that goes under the name of UMLAUT. This normally refers to the fronting of a back vowel or

46

raising of a low vowel in Germanic languages under the influence of a front vowel in the following syllable. Very often, the following high front vowel was then dropped (by apocope) or reduced to schwa, and the new front vowel became the only way of marking the difference between some words. The irregular plurals of words like 'foot/feet' in English are the result of such harmony. The original singular form was [fo:t] and the original was [fo:ti]. The [o:] was fronted to the front rounded vowel [ϕ:] under the influence of the following [i], so the plural came to be [fϕ:ti]. The final vowel was later dropped and the front rounded vowel became unrounded to [e:] giving [fe:t]. The alternation was therefore between [fo:t/fe:t] which was the origin of the modern English pronunciations of 'foot/feet'.

2.8 Dissimilation

Having explained at length the concept of assimilation, it should be a relatively simple matter to grasp the concept of dissimilation. Dissimilation is precisely the opposite process to assimilation. Instead of making two sounds more like each other, dissimilation means that one sound changes to become *less* like some other sound. Dissimilation, therefore, reduces the number of shared phonetic features between two sounds.

The process of dissimilation is involved in so-called 'tongue-twisters'. Try to say very quickly:

'Peter Piper picked a peck of pickled peppers.'

and the frequent occurrence of [p] and [k] is likely to cause you to mix up the two sounds, or put in another sound in their place, perhaps [t].

One very famous example of dissimilation will be mentioned here because it is frequently encountered in textbooks of historical linguistics, where it is often referred to as Grassmann's Law. This sound change, first recognised in 1862 by the German scholar Hermann Grassmann, took place in both the ancient Sanskrit language of India and the ancient Greek language. In both of these languages, there was a phonemic contrast between aspirated and unaspirated stops. However, when there were two syllables following each other and both contained aspirated stops, then the first of these lost its aspiration and became unaspirated. So, in Sanskrit, the earlier form [bho:dha] 'bid' became [bo:dha] and in Greek, the form [phewtho] with the same meaning became [pewtho]. This is clearly a case of dissimilation at a distance.

An example of immediate dissimilation can be found in Afrikaans, one of the national languages of South Africa. Observe the following changes:

AFRIKAANS

*sxo:n	→	sko:n	'clean'
*sxouder	→	skouǝr	'shoulder'
*sxœlt	→	skœlt	'debt'

In the original forms, there was a sequence of two sounds, both carrying the feature fricative. In Afrikaans, the fricative [x] dissimilated from the fricative [s] to become a stop [k].

2.9 Abnormal Sound Changes

In this chapter, we have looked at a wide range of types of sound changes that we can observe in languages of the world. However, there are numerous examples of sound changes in language that would appear, at first glance to be 'abnormal', in the sense that they do not fit any of the categories we have described. For instance, take the French word for 'hundred', which is [să]. This ultimately goes back to a form that can be reconstructed as [km̩tom], with the symbol [m̩] representing a syllabic nasal (i.e. a nasal that can be stressed in the same way as a vowel). How can the changes in:

$$km̩tom \quad → \quad să$$

be described in terms of the types of changes we have been looking at in this chapter?

The answer to this comes in the fact that while the changes between the two extremes might appear to be abnormal, we can usually reconstruct various intermediate steps that are quite reasonable. Let us imagine that this change in fact took place through the following steps:

kmtom	kemtom	(unpacking of features of syllabic and consonant to two separate h sounds)
kemtom	→ kentom	(regressive assimilation of [m] to [t] in place of articulation)

48

kentom	→	kent	(loss of final unstressed syllable)
kent	→	tent	(palatalisation of [k] to [t] before front vowel)
tent	→	sent	(lenition of stop to fricative)
sent	→	sen	(loss of final consonant)
sen	→	sĕ	(fusion of features of vowel and nasal to produce nasal vowel)
sĕ	→	să	(lowering of vowel)

(Note that while all of these changes actually took place in the history of this word, they did not necessarily take place in the order given. This is not particularly important for the purposes of the present discussion however.)

Sometimes, we find that perhaps an individual sound has changed in a rather unusual way. Although we should keep in mind the types of sound changes described in this chapter as being somehow more likely to occur than others, students of languages will always come up against apparently 'odd' changes. For instance, in the language of Truk in Micronesia, there has been a regular change of [t] to [w], and in Mekeo, spoken around Bereina in the Central Province of PNG, there has been a change of both [d] and [l] to the velar nasal [ŋ]. This latter change is illustrated by the following forms:

		MEKEO	
*dua	→	nua	'two'
*dau	→	nanau	'leaf'

How might we account for such changes? Again, we can suggest a series of more reasonable intermediate changes which have left no trace. The Trukese change of [t] to [w] may have passed through the following stages for example:

$$t \quad → \quad \theta \quad → \quad f \quad → \quad v \quad → \quad w$$

Similarly, the Mekeo change of [d] and [l] to [ŋ] may have gone through the following steps:

$$d \quad → \quad l \quad → \quad n \quad → \quad n \quad →$$

Given a sufficient period of time, it is probably possible for any sound to change into any other sound by a series of changes such as those we have described. It is for this reason that the study of the history of languages has not really been able to go back further than about 10,000 years at the present stage. The changes are simply too great. The changes we have just looked at for instance in the case of French go back only about 5,000 years, while the Mekeo and Trukese changes are only about 3,000 years old.

READING GUIDE QUESTIONS
  1. What is lenition?
  2. What is rhotacism?
  3. What is cluster reduction?
  4. What is the difference between apocope and syncope?
  5. What is haplology?
  6. What is compression?
  7. What is the difference between excrescence and epenthesis?
  8. What is prothesis?
  9. What is metathesis?
 10. What is phonetic fusion?
 11. What is meant by compensatory lengthening?
 12. What is the difference between phonetic unpacking and vowel breaking?
 13. What is the difference between assimilation and dissimilation?
 14. What is the difference between partial and complete assimilation?
 15. What is the difference between immediate assimilation and assimilation at a distance?
 16. What is palatalisation and how can we view this as assimilation?
 17. What is final devoicing, and in what way can this be viewed as assimilation?
 18. What is vowel or consonant harmony?
 19. What is meant by the term umlaut?
 20. What is Grassmann's Law?

EXERCISES
  1. Some of the kinds of phonetic changes described in this chapter could actually be regarded as belonging to more than one of the named categories of changes. For instance, final devoicing was described in section 2.7 as a kind of assimilation, while devoicing was described in section 2.1 as lenition or weakening. Can you find other kinds of sound change that could also be said to belong

50

to other classes of sound change? In fact, could you suggest any major reorganisation of the classification of sound changes presented in this chapter?

2. What do you think the spelling of the following words indicates about the phonetic history of English?

1.	thumb	5.	stone
2.	sing	6.	mate
3.	night	7.	tune
4.	rough	8.	Christmas

What kinds of changes do you think have taken place in the pronunciation of these words?

3. Many English place names have spellings that do not reflect their actual pronunciations, for example:

1.	Cirencester	sistə
2.	Salisbury	s ɔlzbri
3.	Barnoldswick	baːlik
4.	Leicester	lɛtə
5.	Chiswick	tʃizik
6.	Cholmondely	tʃʌmli
7.	Gloucester	glɒstə

What kinds of changes do you think have taken place?

4. Speakers of English for whom English is their mother tongue pronounce the following words as shown:

'social'	souʃəl
'taxation'	tækseiʃən
'decision'	desiʒə n

A frequently heard pronunciation for these words by Papua New Guineans speaking English is:

ʃouʃəl
tækʃeiʃən
dəʃiʒən

What kind of change is this?

5. The following changes have taken place in the Banoni language of the North Solomons:

			BANONI	
1.	*mpaɣa	→	bara	'fence'
2.	*mpunso	→	busa'fill'	
3.	*mpua	→	buɣava	'buai/betel nut'

The change in the initial consonants can be described as fusion. Why?

6. The following changes have taken place in Rumanian. Should we

51

describe these changes as phonetic unpacking or as vowel breaking?

		RUMANIAN	
1. *pɔti	→	pwate	'he is able'
2. *pɔřta	→	pwařtə	'door'
3. *nɔkti	→	nwapte	'night'
4. *floři	→	flwařə	'flower'
5. *ořa	→	wařə	'hour'
6. *eska	→	yaskə	'bait'
7. *ɛřba	→	yařbə	'grass'

7. The following changes took place in Old English. Should we describe these changes as phonetic unpacking or as vowel breaking?

		OLD ENGLISH	
1. *kald	→	keald	'cold'
2. *erδa	→	eorδa	'earth'
3. *lirnyan	→	liornyan	'learn'
4. *melkan	→	meolkan	'milk'

8. In the following data from the northern dialect of Paamese, spoken in Vanuatu, try to say what kind of assimilation has taken place.

		NORTHERN PAAMESE	
1. *kail	→	keil	'they'
2. *aim	→	eim	'house'
3. *haih	→	heih	'pandanus'
4. *auh	→	ouh	'yam'
5. *sautin	→	soutin	'distant'
6. *haulu	→	houlu	'many'

9. In the following data from Toba Batak (Sumatra), try to say what kind of assimilation has taken place.

		TOBA BATAK	
1. *hentak	→	ottak	'knock'
2. *kimpal	→	hippal	'lump of earth'
3. *ʒintak	→	sittak	'draw one's sword'
4. *ʈiŋkəp	→	sikkop	'enough'
5. *pintu	→	pittu	'door'

10. In the following Italian data, try to say what kind of assimilation has taken place.

		ITALIAN	
1. *noktem	→	notte	'night'
2. *faktum	→	fatto	'done'
3. *ruptum	→	rotto	'broken'
4. *septem	→	sette	'seven'
5. *aptum	→	atto	'apt, fit for'
6. *somnus	→	sonno	'sleep'

11. In the following Banoni forms (North Solomons), try to say what sorts of assimilation have taken place.

		BANONI	
1. *manuk	→	manuɣu	'bird'
2. *kulit	→	ɣuritsi	'skin sugarcane'
3. *njalan	→	sanana	'road'
4. *taŋis	→	taŋisi	'cry'
5. *pekas	→	beɣasa	*pekpek*/faeces'
6. *poɣok	→	boroɣo	'pig'

12. Old English has a causative suffix of the form -y, and an infinitive suffix of the form -an, both of which have been lost in the modern language, and their functions have come to be expressed in other ways. Examine the pair of words below in Old English:

drink-an   'to drink'
drink-y-an   'to cause (someone/something) to drink'

How do you think we developed the modern words 'drink' and 'drench' from the first and second Old English forms respectively? What kind of change is involved?

13. In the Marshallese language of Micronesia, the following changes have taken place.

		MARSHALLESE	
1. *mataɲa	→	medan	'his eye'
2. *damaɲa	→	dem^wan	'his forehead'
3. *masakit	→	metak	'pain'
4. *masala	→	metal	'smooth'
5. *nasakaɣu	→	tekay	'reef'
6. *madama	→	meram	'light'

How would you characterise the changes that have affected the vowels?

14. Examine the English and Tok Pisin pairs of words given below. The Tok Pisin forms are all derived from the English forms by some kind of phonetic changes. Try to classify these changes according to the types of sound changes discussed in this chapter. (Not all changes will fit into any particular category. Do not get bogged down with minor or unclassifiable changes. Just deal with the obvious.)

	ENGLISH	TOK PISIN	
1.	æks	akis	'axe'
2.	æutsaid	ausait	'outside'
3.	dæun bilou	tamblo	'down'
4.	ka:dz	kas	'cards'
5.	ɛmpti	emti	'empty'
6.	gʌd dei	gude	'good day'
7.	hɛlp him	alivim	'help'
8.	kæpsaiz	kafsait	'tip over'
9.	mʌŋki	mangi	'boy'
10.	to:tʃlæmp	sutlam	'torch'
11.	stænd bai	sambai	'be prepared'
12.	siŋglet	singlis	't-shirt'
13.	spiə	supia	'spear'
14.	prəpɛlə	porpela	'propellor'
15.	gæmən	giaman	'tell lies'
16.	so:	sua	'sore'

(You may find some of the pronunciations given here for Tok Pisin non-standard. Just discuss the forms as they are given and not how *you* would pronounce them.)

15. From the data in Yimas and Karawari, spoken in the East Sepik Province (Data Set 4), what kinds of changes would you say had taken place in each of these two languages?

16. Examine the forms in Nganyaywana, originally spoken in northern New South Wales (but now extinct) (Data Set 2). The original forms are given on the left. Try to classify the various types of change that have taken place.

17. Refer to the forms in Data Set 3 from Mbabaram (formerly spoken near Cairns in northern Queensland). Try to describe the types of changes that have taken place.

18. In Data Set 1, a series of sound changes in the Palauan language

of Micronesia is presented. Try to classify these changes according to the types of sound change discussed in this chapter.

19. Examine the original forms below in some made up language data. On the right are given three forms. Two of these represent 'reasonable' phonetic changes; the third represents an unlikely development. Your task is to spot the unlikely development in each case and say why.

1.	*papan	paban	pafan	palan
2.	*bua	vua	bea	buo
3.	*kento	klento	tʃento	kentu
4.	*flugmen	fulmen	rulgmen	flugmen
5.	*kni	ni	kini	knis
6.	*okto	oto	oko	olto
7.	*midi	mili	miri	miti
8.	*fati	feti	foti	futi
9.	*bitl	bidl	bitil	bitx
10.	*manu	mwanu	wanu	fanu

20. Examine the original forms below in some made up language data. On the right are two forms, one of which represents the more likely development of the two from the original form. Spot which one this is in each case and say why.

1.	*bugal	buɣal	bungal
2.	*bámbam	bámbəm	bə́mbam
3.	*banargan	banagan	banarlgan
4.	*guma:n	guma:	guma:nt
5.	*ginbal	giŋbal	gimbal
6.	*lumar	lumal	lumap
7.	*ruiai	ruioi	ruiei
8.	*tisga	tisg	tazga
9.	*yiřali	yiřagi	yiřli
10.	*yanbu	yanbe	yanbe
11.	*wilbi	welbi	walbi
12.	*sparu	skwaru	saparu
13.	*komte	konte	komme
14.	*tago	tako	taɣo
15.	*tʃiři	siři	kiři
16.	*saump	somp	saumb

21. Let us assume that in some language, the following sound changes took place. These changes all appear to be quite abnormal in that there is no simple change of features from one stage to the other. Could you suggest a succession of reasonable intermediate steps to account for these changes?

1. b	→	h
2. e	→	l
3. k	→	řˇ
4. k	→	s
5. p	→	w
6. l	→	i
7. k	→	h
8. γ	→	ʔ
9. s	→	ʔ
10. s	→	r
11. t	→	f
12. b	→	l

22. Can we argue that there is some kind of 'conspiracy' in languages to produce CV syllable structures? What kinds of sound changes produce this kind of syllable structure? What kinds of sound changes *destroy* this kind of syllable structure?

FURTHER READING
1. Bloomfield, Leonard. *Language* (Chapter One 'Types of Phonetic Change'), pp. 369-391.

Chapter Three

EXPRESSING SOUND CHANGES

3.1 Writing Rules

When reading the literature of the history of sound changes in languages, you are almost certain to come across various formal rules written by linguists to express these changes. You will therefore need to know how to write and interpret such rules, so this short section of this chapter aims to provide you with this skill.

When a sound undergoes a particular change wherever that sound occurs in a language, we refer to this as UNCONDITIONED SOUND CHANGE. Comparatively few sound changes are actually completely unconditioned, as generally there are at least some environments (however restricted) in which the change does not occur, or in which perhaps some other change takes place. One example of a completely unconditioned sound change that we can give comes from Motu, where there has been unconditioned loss of earlier [ŋ] as shown by the following forms:

		MOTU	
*asaŋ	→	lada	'gills of fish'
*taŋi	→	tai	'cry'
*laŋi	→	lai	'wind'
*taliŋa	→	taia	'ear'

Similarly, in Hawaiian, we can find examples of an unconditioned change of [t] to [k], and another of [ŋ] to [n], as shown by the forms presented below:

		HAWAIIAN	
*tapu	→	kapu	'forbidden'
*taŋi	→	kani	'cry'
*taŋata	→	kanaka[1]	'man'
*ŋutu	→	nuku	'mouth'
*tolu	→	kolu	'three'

---

[1]Note, as a matter of interest, that the Tok Pisin word *kanaka* 'uneducated village person' is related to the Hawaiian word meaning 'man'.

Unconditioned sound changes such as these are the simplest historical changes to express in terms of formal rules. The earlier form is given on the left, and the later form on the right, with the two being linked by an arrow. So, the Hawaiian changes just described can be expressed simply as:

$$t \rightarrow k$$
$$\eta \rightarrow n$$

The Motu change involving the loss of the velar nasal can be expressed as:

$$\eta \rightarrow \emptyset$$

(where the symbol ∅ represents the absence of any sound).

A great many sound changes actually only take place in certain phonetic environments, rather than in all environments in which the sound occurs. Such changes are referred to as CONDITIONED SOUND CHANGES, or sometimes also as COMBINATORY SOUND CHANGES. Most of the sound changes we looked at in the previous chapter are actually conditioned sound changes. A sound change can be conditioned by a great range of different types of environments. Factors to consider include the position of the sound in a word (whether it is initial, final or medial), the nature of the preceding and following sounds, the position of stress, whether or not the syllable is open, and so on. In fact, conditioned sound changes can involve the same kind of range of conditioning factors that we find when we are looking for complementary distribution with allophones of phonemes.

If a change takes place only in a specific phonetic environment, this environment is written following a single slash (/). The location of the changing sound with respect to the conditioning environment is indicated by a line (____). If a change takes place before some other sound, then the line is placed before the sound that conditions the change; if a change takes place after some other sound, then the

line follows the conditioning sound. Some examples of rules expressing conditioned changes that we have looked at, with their
expressions in words, are given below:

	front	
t →s / _____ V		[t] becomes [s] before front vowels (Motu)
x → k /s_____		[x] becomes [k] after [s] (Afrikaans)
p → v / V_____ V		[p] becomes [v] between vowels (Banoni)

(Note that the symbol *V* is the standard symbol to express any
unspecified vowel. Similarly, any unspecified consonant is expressed
by the symbol *C*).

To express the fact that a change takes place word finally or word
initially, we use the symbol # to represent the beginning or end of
a word, as follows:

p → w / # _____   initial [p] becomes [w]
                            (Uradhi)

voiced   → voiceless   final voiced consonants
C   C   / _____#become voiceless
                            (German)

V → ø / _____ #   word final vowels are
                            deleted (Southeast
                            Ambrym)

Elements that are optional (i.e. whose presence or absence does
not affect the application of the rule) are placed in round brackets.
Thus:

V → Ṽ / Ṽ (C) _____   a vowel is nasalised after
                            a nasal vowel, whether or
                            not it is immediately pre-
                            ceded by a consonant
                            (Enggano)

When there are two different sounds involved in a change, this can
be represented by placing the sounds one above the other in curly
brackets. The Enggano nasal harmony rule described in 2.7.

earlier can actually be described more fully in the following way:

$$\left\{\begin{array}{c} V \\ \text{voiced} \\ \text{stop} \end{array}\right\} \rightarrow \left\{\begin{array}{c} \tilde{V} \\ \text{nasal} \end{array}\right\} / \left\{\begin{array}{c} \tilde{V} \\ \text{nasal} \end{array}\right\} (C) \underline{\hspace{2cm}}$$

> a vowel or a voiced stop becomes a nasal vowel or a nasal consonant respectively when there is a preceding nasal vowel or nasal consonant

Also, the Motu palatalisation rule that we looked at earlier can be alternatively expressed as:

$$t \rightarrow s / \underline{\hspace{1cm}} \left\{\begin{array}{c} i \\ e \end{array}\right\}$$
  [t] becomes [s] before [i] or [e]

(Note that although this is an alternative formulation for the change in Motu, it is considered to be a less "elegant" statement because it misses the generalisation that the conditioning environment is the class of front vowels. Rules should always be as general as possible, without being *too* general. They are meant to be interpreted literally, so should not produce changes that did not actually take place.)

EXERCISES

1. If the following changes took place in the made up examples below, which forms are correctly described by the rules that are given, and which forms are incorrectly described? How would you change the rules so that they are completely correct according to the evidence provided?

(a) 1. *bata → wətə
    2. *bite → witi   (i)   b   →   w / #____
    3. *bebu → webu
    4. *ȶabe → ȶəbe   (ii) e   →   i / front vowel____
    5. *abae → bəe
    6. *nebuwe → nebuwe
    7. *ȶeab → ȶiəb   (iii) a   →   ə / ____C

60

8.   *aleb   →   lep
9.   *ut̯ebi →   ut̯ibi
10. *ŋálib →   ŋəlip

(b) 1.   *θapiu   →   θapi
     2.   *situ   →   ʃit   (i) $\left\{\begin{matrix} s \\ \theta \end{matrix}\right\}$ →   ʃ / ____a
     3.   *θiŋapa →   ʃiŋap
     4.   *taśi   →   ta ʃ   (ii) V   →   ø / ____#
     5.   *taθeřu →   taθeř
     6.   *motsu   →   mots   (iii) t   →   ø / $\left\{\begin{matrix} V\_\_V \\ \#\_\_ \end{matrix}\right\}$
     7.   *tuθito →   tuʃit
     8.   *ditso   →   dits
     9.   *aθi   →   aʃ
     10. *maθe   →   maθ

2.   Take the following imaginary original forms and apply the set
     of sound changes below. What should the descendant forms
     look like?

     1.   *epi   (i)   ŋ   →   ø   /____#
     2.   *loku   (ii)   ø   →   a   /C__C
     3.   *aruŋ
     4.   *iŋus   (iii) s   →   ø
     5.   *klosul   (iv)   mid   →   high
     6.   *tiken   V   V   / #____
     7.   *ogfasoŋ

                     (v)   l   →   r
                     (vi)   voiceless → voiceless
                            stop   fricative   /V____V

3.   Take the following imaginary original forms and apply the set
     of sound changes below. What should the descendant forms
     look like?

     1.   *patu
     2.   *kaləp   (i)   p → $\left\{\begin{matrix} f\ /\_\_\_\_\# \\ \theta\ /\#\_\_\_\_ \\ b\ /V\_\_\_\_V \end{matrix}\right\}$
     3.   *aba
     4.   *puri
     5.   *akhep   (ii) t → ʔ
     6.   *ferip

61

7. *sipe

8. *apa

9. entaklo

10. *kleatu

(iii) $k \rightarrow \left\{ \begin{matrix} x \, / \underline{\hspace{1cm}} h \\ \gamma \, / \underline{\hspace{1cm}} 1 \end{matrix} \right\}$

(iv) a $\rightarrow$ e   / e (C) (C) _____

(v) $\left\{ \begin{matrix} i \\ u \end{matrix} \right\} \rightarrow$ ə

4. Examine the Banoni (North Solomons) data below and write a rule that accounts for the developments of the original [t].

BANONI

1.	*tina	→	tsina	'mother'
2.	*tama	→	tama	'father'
3.	*puti	→	putsi	'pull out'
4.	*koti	→	kotsi	'cut'
5.	*mata	→	mata	'eye'
6.	*matua	→	matsua	'rise'
7.	*taki	→	tai	'go'
8.	*topu	→	tou	'sugarcane'
9.	*tipi	→	tsivi	'singsing/traditional dance'
10.	*pinta	→	pita	'fall on someone (of tree)'
11.	*kutu	→	gutsu	'lice'
12.	*mate	→	mate	'die'

5. Express the following rules in words:

(a) b → f / _____ s

(b) s → r / V_____V

(c) ḏ → y / $\left\{ \begin{matrix} \# \underline{\hspace{1cm}} \\ V \underline{\hspace{0.5cm}} V \end{matrix} \right\}$

(d) C → ø / _____ #

(e) V → ø / #C_____ C

(f) ø → i / b _____ 1

(g) m → p / _____ p

6. Express the following changes formally:
    (a) intervocalic [s] undergoes rhotacism while [s] before consonants is deleted
    (b) word initial consonants become [y]
    (c) [h] between vowels changes to glottal stop
    (d) the second member of a consonant cluster is deleted
    (e) apocope
    (f) an epenthetic [o] is added between the two members of a word final consonant cluster
    (g) word final high vowels are deleted while interconsonantal high vowels become schwa
    (h) a prothetic [h] is added before mid vowels

7. Examine the Lakalai (West New Britain) data in Data Set 5 and write rules for all of the changes that have taken place. Which changes are conditioned and which are unconditioned? Express conditioning environments in your rules.

8. Examine the Yimas and Karawari (East Sepik) data in Data Set 4. Try to formulate explicit and general rules for the changes that have taken place in each of the two languages. Given the following original forms, what would you expect the modern Yimas and Karawari forms to be?

    1. *simari   'sun'
    2. *simasim   'sago'
    3. *naŋgun   'mosquito'

9. Examine the Mbabaram data in Data Set 3. Try to formulate explicit and general rules for the changes that have taken place.

10. Examine the Nganyaywana data in Data Set 2. Try to formulate explicit and general rules for the changes that have taken place.

11. Examine the Burduna (Western Australia) data in Data Set 11. Write rules that account for the changes that have taken place between the proto-language and modern Burduna.

3.2 Ordering of Changes

When a language undergoes a whole series of sound changes, it is often possible to reconstruct not only the changes themselves, but also the actual order in which the changes took place. Let us examine the following data from Hawaiian:

HAWAIIAN

*taŋi	→	kani	'cry'
*kaso	→	ʔaho	'thatch'
*takele	→	kaʔele	'back of canoe'
*aka	→	aʔa	'root'
*pito	→	piko	'navel'
*paki	→	paʔi	'slap'
*tapu	→	kapu	'forbidden'
*taŋata	→	kanaka	'man'
*isu	→	ihu	'nose'
*siʔa	→	hiʔa	'firemaking'

This set of data reveals that the following unconditioned changes have taken place;

t	→	k
k	→	ʔ
ŋ	→	n
s	→	h

Of these four changes, we can say something about the order in which they applied. Let us first of all check the first two sound changes and see if we can decide whether [t] shifted to [k] first, or whether [k] shifted to [ʔ] first. Let us assume that the [t] first shifted to [k], and that the shift of [k] to [ʔ] took place after this. If we accept this sequence of events, then changes like the following would take place:

*takele	→	kakele	'back of canoe'
*pito	→	piko	'navel'
*tapu	→	kapu	'forbidden'

If the shift of [k] to [ʔ] *then* took place, these words would also change to become:

ʔaʔele
piʔo
ʔapu

These are in fact not the forms that we find. At the time that [k] shifted to [ʔ], there must still have been a distinction between [k] and [t] otherwise all original [k] and [t] would end up as [ʔ]. If we assume that the two changes applied in the opposite order, then we get the correct results:

PROTO-LANGUAGE	STAGE I k → ʔ	STAGE II t → k	MODERN HAWAIIAN	
*takele	→ taʔele	→ kaʔele	kaʔele	'back of canoe'
*aka	→ aʔa	→ -	aʔa	'root'
*pito	-	→ piko	piko	'navel'
*paki	→ paʔi	-	paʔi	'slap'
*tapu	-	→ kapu	kapu	'forbidden'

We can represent this by placing one rule over another and linking the two in the following way:

$$\begin{pmatrix} k & \to & ʔ \\ t & \to & k \end{pmatrix}$$

But what about the other changes that have taken place? Can we say anything about whether these changes took place before or after (or between) the two changes we have just looked at? In fact, we can only come to conclusions about the ordering of changes when the changed sound or the sounds involved in the conditioning for a change actually *overlap* in some way. In the rule:

$$t \quad \to \quad k$$

the [k] is also involved in the rule:

$$k \quad \to \quad ʔ$$

65

so we *can* come to some conclusions about the ordering of the changes expressed by the rules. However, in the rules:

$$\begin{array}{ccc} \eta & \rightarrow & n \\ s & \rightarrow & h \end{array}$$

none of the sounds overlap, i.e. none of the symbols are involved in the statement of any of the other changes. Therefore we *cannot* come to any conclusion about the ordering. It does not matter in what order we apply the rules — the end results will not be altered in any way. In listing the changes, we indicate the fact that there is no evidence that the change is ordered either before or after any other change by not linking them as we did above. So, we could represent the ordering of these four changes as:

$$\left(\begin{array}{ccc} k & \rightarrow & \textipa{P} \\ t & \rightarrow & k \end{array}\right.$$

$$\begin{array}{ccc} \eta & \rightarrow & n \\ s & \rightarrow & h \end{array}$$

(Since the linking line is what indicates rule ordering, this can just as easily be expressed as:

$$\left(\begin{array}{ccc} k & \rightarrow & \textipa{P} \\ s & \rightarrow & h \\ t & \rightarrow & k \end{array}\right.$$

$$\begin{array}{ccc} \eta & \rightarrow & n \end{array}$$

with no difference.)

Let us now look at a more complicated example, in which conditioned sound changes are involved. The data comes from Banoni, spoken in the North Solomons.

	BANONI		
*koti	→	kotsi	'cut'
*tina	→	tsina	'mother'
*puti	→	putsi	'pull out'
*mata	→	mata	'eye'

*mate	→ mate	'die'
*matua	→ matsua	'rise'
*makas	→ maɣasa	'dry coconut'
*pakan	→ vaɣana	*abusim kaikai*/add meat to'
*kulit	→ ɣuritsi	'skin sugarcane'

The sound changes we will consider are the following:

$$t \rightarrow ts\ /\ \underline{\quad} \overset{\text{high}}{V}$$

$$\emptyset \rightarrow V_x\ /\ V_x\ C\ \underline{\quad}\#$$

The first rule changes [t] to [ts] before the high vowels [i] or [u]. The second change involves the addition of a harmonising vowel after a consonant at the end of a word. The question we should ask ourselves is: can these changes be ordered with respect to each other? If two changes involve some common sound either in the changing sounds or the conditions under which the changes take place, then we must test to see which applied first. Since these two rules both involve vowels, we must test them for ordering.

So, which of these two changes took place first? If we assume that the first change took place first, we could correctly predict the change of [t] to [ts] in all cases but one, and that is the form [kulit] 'skin sugarcane'. This form has no following high vowel, so it does not meet the conditions for the [t] → [ts] change to take place. If we then applied the vowel addition rule after the [t] → [ts] change, we would get [ɣuriti] for this word (if we apply the other incidental consonant changes as well). The fact that the actual form is [ɣuritsi] rather than [ɣuriti] means that there must have already been a high vowel after the [t] when the rule affecting the [t] applied. This shows that, in fact, the rule given second above must actually have applied before the other rule. So:

$$\left(\begin{array}{l} \text{VOWEL HARMONY} \\ \text{[t]→[ts] BEFORE HIGH VOWELS} \end{array} \right.$$

EXERCISES

1.   From an examination of the changes in Yimas (East Sepik) presented in Data Set 4, in what order do you think that the changes must have taken place? Why?

2.   Examine the Motu forms in Data Set 9. Write rules for the changes that have taken place, and state the order in which they must have applied where this is possible. Give reasons.

3.   In Data Set 1, examine the original forms containing [l] and [y] and [n]. What changes did these sounds undergo in Palauan? In what order did these changes take place? Why?

4.   Examine the Mbabaram forms in Data Set 3. Two changes took place:
    (i)   initial syllables were dropped
    (ii)   the final vowels were changed under certain conditions, which can be specified from the data that is available

Can we say which change took place first? Why?

5.   Examine the Nganyaywana data in Data Set 2. The following changes have taken place:
    (i)   all initial consonants were dropped
    (ii)   [a] was added after a final consonant
    (iii)   long vowels were shortened
    (iv)   short vowels in initial syllables were dropped
    (v)   a [y] was added after a consonant following [i] and a [w] after a consonant following [u].

In what order did these changes take place? Can we say something about the ordering of *all* of these changes or just *some* of them? Why?

6.   Look at the following made-up data:

1.	*belod	→	belod
2.	*piθi	→	pisi
3.	*peθu	→	peθu
4.	*riθid	→	risid
5.	*aleθ	→	ales

6.	*peror	→	perod
7.	*θatur	→	θaθud
8.	*biti	→	biθi
9.	*kitip	→	kiθip
10.	*pata	→	paθa
11.	*wati	→	waθi
12.	*doku	→	toku
13.	*diba	→	tiba
14.	*padu	→	patu
15.	*fide	→	fite
16.	*kad	→	kad

These changes can be accounted for by the following rules:

1. t   → $θ$ / V_____V

2. d   →   t / $\left\{ \begin{array}{l} \# \_\_\_\_ \\ V\_\_\_\_V \end{array} \right\}$

3. $θ$ →   s / $\left\{ \begin{array}{l} i \_\_\_ i \\ \_\_\_\# \end{array} \right\}$

4. r   →   d / _____#

In what order did these changes take place?

7.   Look at the following made up data:

1.	*kantar	→	kãtar
2.	*milaŋ	→	minã
3.	*lilomi	→	ninõmi
4.	*lar	→	nar
5.	*fensu	→	fẽsu
6.	*nap	→	nap
7.	*meken	→	mekẽ
8.	*pekol	→	pekon
9.	*firur	→	firur
10.	*femur	→	fẽmur
11.	*santo	→	sãto
12.	*pimfulo	→	pĩfuno
13.	*resu	→	lesu
14.	*rem	→	lẽ

Write the rules that will account for the changes that have taken place, and state the order in which these changes must have taken place.

8. Refer back to the Burduna data in Data Set 11. Of the changes that have taken place, which can be ordered with respect to the others, and why do we need to order the changes in the way we do?

Chapter Four

PHONETIC VS. PHONEMIC CHANGE

When a linguist describes the synchronic sound system of a language, she or he must be aware of the fact that there is a difference between a phonetic description of the language and a phonemic description of the language. A phonetic description of a language simply describes the physical facts of the sounds of the language. A phonemic description of a language however, describes not the physical facts, but the way these sounds are related to each other *for the speakers of that particular language.* It is possible for two languages to have the same physical sounds, yet to have very different phonemic systems. The phonemic description therefore tells us what are the basic sound units for a particular language that enable its speakers to differentiate meanings.

Just as it is possible to describe a language synchronically both phonetically and phonemically, it is possible to make a distinction between a diachronic phonetic study and a diachronic phonemic study of a language. It is possible, therefore, for some sound changes to take place without altering the phonemic structure of a language, though many sound changes *do* alter the phonemic structure of a language. However, it is also possible for a phonemic change to take place in a language without there necessarily being a phonetic change.

4.1 Phonetic Change without Phonemic Change

Many phonetic changes take place in languages without in any way altering the number of phonemes or the relations between them. Such change is therefore purely ALLOPHONIC or SUBPHONEMIC. All that happens is that a phoneme develops a new allophone (or changes its phonetic form slightly), or the distribution of existing allophones of a phoneme is changed.

One example of sub-phonemic change in the history of English involves the phoneme /r/. This phoneme has always been spelt 'r', suggesting that speakers of English have not perceived any change in this sound. However, we do know that earlier, the phoneme /r/ was actually pronounced phonetically as a flap or a trill, as [ř] or [r̃], much more like the Tok Pisin sound than the modern English [ɹ], which is a glide or a frictionless continuant. However, although this sound has changed phonetically, it has not caused any reanalysis of the phonological system to take place. The same words that used to be distinguished in meaning from other words by [ř] or [r̃] are now distinguished instead by [ɹ]. This change can be represented as:

$$/r/:[ř] \sim [r̃] \quad \rightarrow \quad /r/:[ɹ]$$

Another example from the history of English is the phoneme /t/. We now pronounce this as an alveolar stop [t]. Earlier, however, we know that it was pronounced as a dental stop [t̪]. The change from [t̪] to [t] has again not caused any new meaning contrasts to develop − the same words are still distinguished, only by a slightly different phonetic form. Again, this purely allophonic change can be represented as:

$$/t/:[t̪] \quad \rightarrow \quad /t/:[t]$$

The final example we will give of sub-phonemic change comes from Motu. The previous two examples from English involve a change in the phonetic form of the phoneme wherever it occurs i.e. they are examples of unconditioned allophonic change. In the example which follows, we will look at an example of a conditioned sub-phonemic change, or one which simply creates a new allophone in a particular phonetic environment, but which does not change the sound in other environments.

You should remember from chapter two that we quoted Motu as an example of a language that has palatalised [t] to [s] before front vowels, while leaving [t] unchanged in other environments. This change is the only source of the sound [s] in Motu, as no other sound changes have produced an [s] and there was no [s] sound at all in the proto-language. This means that the palatalisation of [t] to [s] did not in any way affect the phonemic structure of the language. All instances of the sound [s] in Motu are in complementary distribution with [t]. The sound [s] only ever occurs before front vowels, while [t] occurs elsewhere. The [s] that developed was simply a new allophone of /t/[1]. The change can therefore be stated as:

$$/t/:[t] \quad \rightarrow \quad /t/: \begin{cases} \text{[s] before front vowels} \\ \text{[t] elsewhere} \end{cases}$$

These three examples have all been examples of sub-phonemic or allophonic change, or changes that only influence the pronunciation of a sound, but not its behaviour in the phonemic system in the language.

4.2 Phonetic Change with Phonemic Change

We saw from the preceding section that a phonetic change need not necessarily lead to a change in the phonemic system of a language. Very often however, phonetic change *does* lead to some kind of phonemic change; we can in fact generally say that phonetic change is a 'tool' of phonemic change. That is, most instances of phonemic change are the result of a phonetic change in that particular sound.

We can actually subcategorise phonemic changes into three different types: phonemic loss, phonemic addition and rephonemicisation.

(a) Phonemic Loss

The term phonemic loss is really self-explanatory. Phoneme loss takes place when a phoneme is lost altogether between different stages of a language. All cases of unconditioned sound loss at the phonetic level necessarily imply complete phonemic loss. An example of such a loss is the loss of the velar nasal in Motu, which we looked at in the previous chapter.

Phoneme loss is often a conditioned sound change, occurring in only some environments. While the loss of the velar nasal in Motu

---

[1] Note that although the Motu spelling system distinguishes 's' from 't', this is only because the missionaries who devised the spelling system were not familiar with the principle of the phoneme and simply assumed that because [s] and [t] needed to be distinguished in English, they should also be distinguished in Motu. Although Motu developed an [s] sound, it did not develop an /s/ phoneme.

is an unconditioned sound change, we frequently find that only some occurrences of a phoneme are lost. This situation is often referred to in the literature as PARTIAL LOSS, in contrast to COMPLETE LOSS. For an example of partial loss in Fijian, refer to the earlier discussion of the loss of final consonants. This change can be expressed as:

$$C \rightarrow \emptyset / \underline{\hspace{1cm}} \#$$

In the example that immediately follows Fijian in chapter two, the Angkamuthi language, we see that there has been partial loss of consonants again, this time in word initial position, following the rule:

$$C \rightarrow \emptyset / \# \underline{\hspace{1cm}}$$

(b) Phonemic Addition

This term is also quite self-explanatory. Phoneme addition takes place when a phoneme is added to a word in a position in which that phoneme did not originally occur. For example, in Motu a prothetic /l/ was added before the vowel /a/, creating a new set of words distinguished by this sound, as we saw in chapter two.

Note, however, that simple phonetic addition does not necessarily lead to phonemic addition. It is possible for a sound to be added without actually affecting the phonemic form of a word. In the Mpakwithi language of north Queensland, for example, words beginning with fricatives and /r/ have added an optional prothetic schwa, e.g.:

/βaði/:[βaði ~ əβaði] 'intestines'
/ðay/:[ðay ~ əðay] 'mother'
/ra/:[ra ~ əra] 'stomach'

There is no separate schwa phoneme in this language. The sound [ə] occurs only in forms such as those just given, and it is completely predictable in its occurrence. Since it is completely predictable, it has no phonemic status. It can, in a sense, be considered to be a word-initial allophone of /ø/:

$$/ø/ : [ø] \sim [ə] \ / \ \#\rule{1.5cm}{0.4pt} \left\{ \begin{array}{c} \text{fricative} \\ r \end{array} \right\}$$

While the phonetic change:

$$ø \ \rightarrow \ ə \ / \ \#\rule{1.5cm}{0.4pt} \left\{ \begin{array}{c} \text{fricative} \\ r \end{array} \right\}$$

(i.e. schwa is added before fricatives and /r/ at the beginning of a word) has taken place, the actual *phonemic* form of such words has not changed. This has therefore been an example of phonetic addition *without* phonemic addition.

(c) Rephonemicisation

The most common kind of phonemic change to result from phonetic change is REPHONEMICISATION. What this involves is the creation of a new pattern of oppositions in a language by simply changing around some of the existing phonemes, or by changing some of the existing phonemes into completely new phonemes. Whereas phoneme addition means adding a new phoneme in a word where there was no phoneme originally, and phoneme loss means deleting a phoneme from a word where there originally was one, when we have rephonemicisation, we simply change around the actual phonemes that are already there in the word. We can recognise a number of different types of rephonemicisation, these being SHIFT, MERGER and SPLIT. We will discuss each of these below.

The first kind of rephonemicisation that we will consider goes under the name of SHIFT. When we say that phonemic shift takes place, what we mean is that two words that were distinguished in the proto-language by a particular sound, are still distinguished in the daughter language, but the distinction between the two words is marked by a different sound. That is to say, a minimal pair in the proto-language will still be different in the daughter language, but the difference will be marked by different sounds. For instance, in the Banoni language of the North Solomons Province, we saw in section 2.7 that voiceless stops between vowels became voiced fricatives (along with a number of other changes). It is quite possible to imagine a minimal pair in the proto-language in which meanings

75

are distinguished by the presence or absence of a voiceless stop. In the modern language however, the same difference in meaning will be marked instead by the presence or absence of a voiced fricative in the same position.

A thoughtful reader should have noticed that this description of phonemic shift does not seem to be very different from what we said earlier about purely phonetic change. When allophonic change takes place, there is also a change in the actual sounds that are used to distinguish meanings. The important difference is that with phonemic shift, the original sound and the new sound must actually belong to different phonemes. In Banoni today, there are pairs to show that voiceless stops and voiced fricatives are phonemically distinct, e.g.:

kasii   'my brother'   γasi   'open'

This therefore shows that when the voiceless stops changed to voiced fricatives, there was an actual shifting around of the phonemes of the language, and not just a shifting around of the allophones within a phoneme.

The second kind of rephonemicisation that we will look at is phonemic MERGER. This is the process by which two separate phonemes end up as a single phoneme. Words that used to be distinguished by some difference in sound cease to be distinguished, and what were originally minimal pairs become HOMOPHONES or HOMONYMS, or words with the same form but different meanings. For instance, the Motu word /lada/ is a homophone and has two meanings: 'gills of fish' and 'name'. In the proto-language from which Motu was derived, there were originally two different words, distinguished by having different phonemes:

*ansan   'name'

*asaŋ   'gills of fish'

There has been a phonemic merger of /ns/ and /s/ as /d/ (as well as a loss of final consonants and the addition of_a prothetic /l/), producing the modern homophone.

We can also find numerous examples of phonemic merger between English and Tok Pisin. For instance, in some cases, the original

76

vowels [ɔ], [a:] and [æ] have all merged as [a]. So, a three-way set of minimal pairs in English such as:

hot	'hot'
ha:t	'heart'
hæt	'hat'

is not distinguished by many speakers in Tok Pisin. The result of this merger is the homophone:

hat	'hot, heart, hat'

Phonemic merger can be represented as:

$$\left. \begin{matrix} A \\ B \end{matrix} \right\} \rightarrow C$$

(though, you should realise that merger can actually involve more than just two sounds). When phomemes merge in this way, there are two possible forms for the phoneme here symbolised as C. Firstly, C could be identical to one of the existing phonemes; or secondly, it could be different from either of the original phonemes (i.e. a completely new phoneme). An example of phonemic merger where the resulting phoneme is phonetically the same as one of the original phonemes is Uradhi, an Australian language of Cape York Peninsula:

URADHI

*paṯa	→	waṯa	'bite'
*pinta	→	winta	'arm'
*wapun	→	wapun	'head'

The original /p/ and /w/ have merged as /w/:

$$\left. \begin{matrix} p \\ w \end{matrix} \right\} \rightarrow w$$

4.2 Phonetic Change with Phonemic Change

An example of the second possibility is Fijian:

FIJIAN

*tuba	→	tuva	'fish poison'
*batu	→	vatu	'stone'
*ubi	→	uvi	'yam'
*pitu	→	vitu	'seven'
*peɲu	→	vonu	'turtle'

The original phonemic distinction between /b/ and /p/ is lost, and the merged phoneme is different from either of the original phonemes, i.e. /v/:

$$\left\{ \begin{matrix} b \\ p \end{matrix} \right\} \rightarrow v$$

We have been talking about merger, but we have not pointed out that there is a distinction to be made between PARTIAL and COMPLETE MERGER. Complete merger means that the sound change that produces the merger is unconditioned, i.e. the change affects that particular sound in all environments it occurs in. Partial merger on the other hand, means that the sound change is a conditioned sound change, i.e. the particular phonemes merge only in certain environments and are kept distinct in others. The example we gave above of Uradhi as an example of the merger of /p/ and /w/ as /w/ is actually an example of partial rather than complete merger. There is evidence for this in the following forms:

URADHI

*wapun	→	wapun	'head'
*wuypu	→	wuypu	'old man'
*pupu	→	wupu	'buttocks'

The merger only takes place word initially; the distinction between /p/ and /w/ is maintained in other positions of the word. We therefore need to re-express this merger rule as a conditioned change:

$$\left\{ \begin{array}{c} p \\ w \end{array} \right\} \quad \rightarrow \quad w \ / \ \# \underline{\hspace{1.5cm}}$$

Phonemic SPLIT is the category of rephonemicisation we now come to. This kind of change has precisely the opposite effect to that of phonemic merger, in that words which originally contained the same phoneme end up having different phonemes. Phonemic split can arise when a single sound changes in different ways in different phonological environments. We can represent this kind of change in the following way:

$$A \quad \rightarrow \quad \left\{ \begin{array}{c} B \ / \ X \\ C \ / \ Y \end{array} \right.$$

However, if there is a conditioned sound change of this type, and the *only* source for the new sound is this change, then we cannot speak of phonemic split. What we will find is that we simply have a case of subphonemic change, as we have only produced a new allophone for an existing phoneme, in a specific environment. This is exactly what has happened in Motu, where the original [t] has changed to [s] in some environments and remained as [t] in others. This cannot be considered to be a phonemic split because no new phonemes are involved. But, if two or more sound changes were to operate at once to produce the same sound as is produced by some other conditioned sound change, then we can speak of phonemic split. For instance, if in Motu, some *other* sound (or sounds) at the same time also shifted to [s] (in some or all of their environments), then there could be no complementary distribution between [t] and [s] as there is now, and we would have to recognise /s/ as a separate phoneme.

4.3 Phonemic Change without Phonetic Change

In this section, we will look at examples in which the *phonemic* status of a sound changes without any actual *phonetic* change taking place.

4.3 Phonemic Change without Phonetic Change

(a) Loss of Conditioning Environment

Originally in English, there was no velar nasal phoneme /ŋ],
though it did occur as an allophone of the phoneme /n/ before velar
sounds. This can be represented as:

$$/n/: \begin{cases} [ŋ] \text{ before velars} \\ [n] \text{ elsewhere} \end{cases}$$

A world like 'singer', which we now write phonemically as /siŋə/, was
originally phonemically /siŋgə/, but phonetically the medial nasal
had the same pronunciation as it has today, i.e. [ŋ]. This is therefore
an example of a phonemic change (i.e. /n/ → /ŋ/) that does not
involve any phonetic change (i.e. [ŋ] → [ŋ]). How did this come
about?

The separate status of the phoneme /ŋ/ came about as the result
of *another* change that caused the loss of the sound that conditioned
the choice between the alveolar and velar allophones of /n/. Look
at the following earlier forms and the changes that they underwent.
The forms are given first phonemically; the second form in square
brackets gives the actual pronunciation in phonetic transcription.

*/sɪn/:	[sɪn]	→	/sɪn/: [sɪn]	'sin'
*/sing/:	[sɪŋg]	→	/sɪŋ/: [sɪŋ]	'sing'
*/læmb/:	[læmb]	→	/læm/: [læm]	'lamb'

Word finally after nasals in English, the voiced stops [b] and [g] were
dropped by a rule of the form:

$$\begin{Bmatrix} b \\ g \end{Bmatrix} \rightarrow \emptyset \, / \text{ nasal} \underline{\qquad} \#$$

This explains the presence of the so-called 'silent b' in words like
'climb', 'lamb', 'thumb' and so on. Now, you will remember that it
was the presence of a velar phoneme earlier in English that conditioned the choice of a velar allophone of the phoneme /n/ rather
than an alveolar allophone. So, phonemic /sɪng/ was phonetically
[sɪŋg]. However, once the final /g/ was lost, the [ŋ] now came to be
in contrastive distribution with the [n], whereas before the two were
in complementary distribution. As evidence of this, we find the
minimal pair /sɪŋ/ 'sing' and /sɪn/'sin'. Here, we can see that

80

although the velar nasal did not change *phonetically* in English, its *phonemic* status has changed because its original conditioning environment has been lost.

Another well known example of this kind of change is the development of umlaut in Germanic languages. This term is introduced in chapter two in the discussion of assimilation at a distance. Umlaut is the changing of a vowel of a root to become either more front or more high in certain morphological categories. So, we have in English irregular plurals such as:

foot	feet
tooth	teeth

We saw earlier that the original plural suffix was /-i/ and that the original forms of the roots were /foːt/ and /toːθ/ respectively. There then took place a purely allophonic change, by which all back rounded vowels became front rounded vowels when the following syllable contained a front vowel. So, although there was no phonemic change in the plural, there was a change in the phonetic form of the plural of these two words under the influence of the following plural suffix. Thus:

/foːtiː/: [foːti] → /foːtiː/: [føːti]	'feet'
/toːθiː/: [toːθi] → /toːθiː/: [tøːθi]	'teeth'

The next change involves a change in the phonemic status of the front rounded vowels. Although these vowels themselves did not then change phonetically in any way, there was a general rule of apocope at this stage in the history of the language, which deleted the final /-i/ marking the plural. Thus:

/foːtiː/: [føːti] → /føːt/: [føːt]	'feet'
/toːθiː/: [tøːθi] → /tøːθ/: [tøːθ]	'teeth'

This loss of the conditioning vowel therefore resulted in the existence of minimal pairs between back and front rounded vowels, with the back rounded form occurring in the singular and the front rounded form occurring in the plural. It is from these two forms that the modern irregular plurals are derived.

It was mentioned in the preceding section that although Motu has undergone a change by which /t/ developed a new allophone of the form [s] before a front vowel, this did not introduce any new phonemic contrasts in the language. Now, there is a tendency among younger Motu speakers to drop word final vowels. So, we find alternative pronunciations such as the following:

[lasi	~ las]	'no'
[sinagu	~ sinag]	'mother'
[oiemu	~ oiem]	'your'
[namo	~ nam]	'good'
[mase	~ mas]	'dead'
[lata	~ lat]	'long'

Let us imagine that in two generations' time, this change becomes general, and that all word final vowels following consonants were lost by the rule:

$$V \rightarrow \emptyset /C_____ \#$$

Minimal pairs such as:

/lati/:	[lasi]	'no'
/lata/:	[lata]	'long'

which are now phonemically distinguished by the final vowel, would then come to be distinguished solely by the difference in the consonants. So, we could imagine a new minimal pair with the following forms:

/las/:	[las]	'no'
/lat/:	[lat]	'long'

(b) Foreign Loans

When words from one language are borrowed into another, they are normally phonetically reinterpreted so that they fit the patterns of the language they are being adopted into. For instance, English words borrowed into Motu are normally made to fit the Motu CV syllable structure by deleting consonants and adding vowels to avoid the consonant clusters of English, e.g.:

ENGLISH	MOTU	
gʌvəmənt	gavamani	'government'
bɔtl	botolo	'bottle'

When the influence of the foreign language becomes strong enough, there is less pressure for the words to conform to the phonological structures of the receiving language, and the words are likely to be pronounced much closer to the pronunciation of the source language. If there are sufficient numbers of such borrowings, and speakers of the language no longer feel them to be foreign words, this can influence the phonemic interpretation of existing sounds.

So, let us look at the overall impact of English borrowings on the phonemic system of Motu. Words such as the following have been borrowed into Motu to express new cultural concepts: 'shirt', 'market', 'tin', 'soup' and so on. In the early days of cultural contact, these words were borrowed into Motu with the following forms:

[sesi ~ sedi]	'shirt'
[makesi ~ makedi]	'market'
[sini]	'tin'
[tupu]	'soup'
[topu]	'soap'

and these pronunciations can still be heard today from the very old Motu-speakers. Speakers who have these pronunciations have in fact fully assimilated these English words to the phonemic system of Motu, in either of two ways:

(a) they have borrowed the *phonemes* /t/ and /s/ of English, but given them the regular Motu *allophones* of [s] before front vowels and [t] elsewhere

(b) between vowels, they have substituted the phoneme /d/, which does not have any noticeable allophonic variation.

The fact that there are alternative pronunciations indicates that, for the older generations, speakers really feel that these words involve some sort of phonological 'problem' (even though they would not be able to express what it is).

For the more recent generations however, we are more likely to find pronunciations such as the following:

[seti]	'shirt'
[maketi]	'market'
[tini]	'tin'
[supu]	'soup'
[sopu]	'soap'

In these forms, there is phonetic [t] followed by front vowels, and phonetic [s] followed by non-front vowels. This is in direct violation of the allophonic rules of the language. Speakers have therefore introduced a contrast between the sounds [t] and [s]. So, although the [t] and [s] have themselves not changed in any way phonetically, their phonemic status is being changed from being in complementary distribution to being in contrastive distribution, i.e. with two distinct phonemes.

(c) Change of Structural Pressure

A final possible explanation for the change in status of a sound from being an allophone of a phoneme to being a completely independent phoneme in its own right is a change in the overall structure of the phoneme inventory.

You should all be aware that phonetic sequences of more than one sound are often treated as a single phoneme, depending on the syllable structure of the language. For instance, in Fijian, phonetic sequences of [mb] are treated phonemically as /b/. The reasons for this are that:

(a) [b] occurs only in this environment and nowhere else in the phonology of the language.

(b) the only consonant clusters in the language are those of the type represented by [mb] so we would complicate the syllable structure of the language if we allowed phonemic consonant clusters.

84

The /b/ phoneme in Fijian derives from earlier phonemic consonant clusters of the form /mb/ and /mp/, as the following examples show:

FIJIAN

*tumbu	→	tubu	'grow'
*ləmbut	→	lobo-lobo	'soft'
*ləmpit	→	lobi	'fold'
*kampit	→	kabi	'fasten'

However, although there has been a phonemic change of /mb/ to /b/, there has been no phonetic change at all in the medial sounds in the first two examples given above. How, then, has this phonemic change taken place? The answer is that in the original language, there was a different phonetic distribution of sounds, and this distribution was lost in Fijian. Firstly, there *was* a sound [b] occurring independently of [m], unlike Fijian. This independent [b] changed to [v] in Fijian, leaving [b] occurring only after [m], e.g.:

FIJIAN

*batu	→	vatu	'stone'
*bulan	→	vula	'moon'

Secondly, there *were* consonant clusters in the language other than those of the type represented by [mb]. There were, for instance, contrasting [mp] clusters, as shown in the examples given above. In this original language therefore, /b/ clearly had to be distinguished phonemically from /mb/, unlike in modern Fijian. So, while [mb] has not changed phonetically in Fijian its phonemic status has changed from /mb/ to /b/ because changes which took place elsewhere in the phonology altered the structural pressures and brought about a phonemic reanalysis.

READING GUIDE QUESTIONS
1. What is allophonic change?
2. What is phonemic loss?
3. What is the difference between partial and complete loss?
4. What is rephonemicisation?

5. What is phonemic shift? How does it differ from allophonic change?
6. What is phonemic merger?
7. What is the difference between complete and partial phonemic merger?
8. What is phonemic split?
9. Explain in what ways a sound can change phonemically without changing phonetically.

EXERCISES

1. There are some phonemic differences between the Motu vernacular, and the pidginised form Hiri Motu that is used as a lingua franca in many parts of the Papuan area, at least with some speakers. These differences can be represented by the following examples:

	MOTU	HIRI MOTU	
1.	gado	gado	'language'
2.	hui	hui	'hair'
3.	kehoa	keoa	'open'
4.	γau	gau	'thing'
5.	hahine	haine	'woman'
6.	haginia	haginia	'build it'
7.	boga	boga	'belly'
8.	maγani	magani	'wallaby'
9.	tohu	tou	'sugarcane'
10.	γatoi	gatoi	'egg'
11.	heau	heau	'run'
12.	sinagu	sinagu	'my mother'

Assume that the vernacular Motu forms represent the original form of the language. What kinds of phonemic changes would you say had taken place in terms of what we have been talking about in this chapter?

2. Uneducated speakers of some regional dialects of Tok Pisin change some of the sounds used by speakers of the standard dialect. Imagine somebody speaking the following extremely non-standard regional dialect. How have they changed the phonemic system of the standard language in terms of the kinds of changes we have been looking at in this chapter?

	STANDARD TOK PISIN	REGIONAL TOK PISIN	
1.	ples	feret	'village'
2.	poret	foret	'frightened'
3.	mipela	mifara	'us'
4.	larim	rarim	'leave'
5.	kisim	kitim	'take'
6.	lotu	rotu	'church'
7.	sarip	tarif	'grass knife'
8.	popaia	fofaia	'miss'
9.	sori	tori	'concerned'
10.	belo	bero	'bell'
11.	sapos	tafot	'if'
12.	kirap	kiraf	'get up'
13.	gutpela	gutfara	'good'

3. In the Lakalai forms in Data Set 5, describe the various changes that have taken place as either merger, loss or shift.

4. Examine the Mbabaram forms in Data Set 3. Describe how the changes that have taken place have affected the phonemic system.

5. Compare the English forms below and the Tok Pisin forms that are historically derived from them. What are the main kinds of changes that have taken place which affect the phonemic system of the language?

	ENGLISH	TOK PISIN	
1.	bridʒ	bris	'bridge'
2.	haus	haus	'house'
3.	mætʃez	masis	'match'
4.	bəli:v	bilip	'believe'
5.	ha:f	hap	'half, area'
6.	gra:s	gras	'grass, hair'
7.	tʃi:ki	siki	'cheeky'
8.	fɪʃ	pis	'fish'
9.	ʃɪp	sip	'ship'
10.	pi:nʌt	pinat	'peanut'
11.	dog	dok	'dog'
12.	gəta:	gita	'guitar'
13.	məʃi:n	masin	'machine'
14.	ɛndʒən	ensin	'engine'

	ENGLISH	TOK PISIN	
15.	said	sait	'side'
16.	tʃɪzəl	sisel	'chisel'
17.	dʒækət	saket	'jacket'
18.	woːdə	woda	'warder'
19.	toːk	tok	'talk'
20.	krai	krai	'cry
21.	trʌk	trak	'truck'
22.	fæʃən	pasin	'way, method'
23.	fʌni	pani	'funny'
24.	pæsɪdʒ	pasis	'passage'
25.	klʌb	klap	'club'

6. How would you characterise the various changes that have taken place in Burduna (Data Set 11)?

FURTHER READING

1. Lehmann, Winifred P. *Historical Linguistics: An Introduction,* (Chapter Ten 'Change in Phonological Systems'), pp. 147-176.

2. Anttila, Raimo *An Introduction to Historical and Comparative Linguistics,* (Chapter Four 'Sound Change'), pp. 57-87.

Chapter Five

THE COMPARATIVE METHOD

5.1 Sound Correspondences and Reconstruction

Up to now, we have been giving examples of changes in languages from an earlier form marked with the asterisk * to a later form. But we have not said how we actually found out what these earlier forms were — so far, this has all simply been done on trust! The use of the asterisk is intended to mark the words as unrecorded, never actually seen or heard by anybody around now. Did we just guess at these forms, and hope that we were more or less right, or is there some special method by which we can deduce what the forms were like? How can we 'undo' the changes that have taken place in languages?

While we would have to admit that there is a certain amount of guesswork involved in working out these forms, we can also say that it is not blind guesswork, but intelligent guesswork. How then, do we go about finding out about earlier forms of languages that have never been permanently recorded?

We have already discussed the idea of languages being genetically related in families, all of which are descended from a single ancestor, which we call the proto-language. This model of language evolution looks like this:

PROTO-
LANGUAGE
↙ ↘
LANGUAGE   LANGUAGE
A   B

Even if we have no written records of the proto-language, it is often possible to RECONSTRUCT some of the aspects of the proto-language from the REFLEXES in the daughter languages by using the COMPARATIVE METHOD. When we use the term 'reconstruct', we mean that we make some kind of estimation about what a proto-language might have been like. We are in a sense 'undoing' the changes that have taken place. To do this, we examine what we call 'reflexes' of forms in the original language in the various daughter languages, which means that we look for forms derived from a *common* original form. When we find two forms like this, we say that they are COGNATE with each other, and that both are reflexes of the same form in the proto-language. In carrying out reconstruction, we use the so-called comparative method. What this means is that we compare cognate forms in two (or more) related languages and work out some original form from which these cognates could reasonably be derived, keeping in mind our knowledge of what kinds of sound changes are likely and what kinds of sound changes are unlikely. (It is necessary to keep in mind the survey of types of sound change that we looked at in Chapter Two, when doing reconstruction work of this kind.)

Having introduced some of the basic terminology necessary before learning how to reconstruct the history of languages, let us now go on to look at an actual linguistic situation, and see what we can make of it. We will look at some data from four Polynesian languages: Tongan, Samoan, Rarotongan (spoken in the Cook Islands, a New Zealand dependency) and Hawaiian.

	TONGAN	SAMOAN	RAROTONGAN	HAWAIIAN	
1.	tapu	tapu	tapu	kapu	'taboo'
2.	pito	pute	pito	piko	'navel'
3.	puhi	feula	pu?ı	puhi	'blow'
4.	tafa?aki	tafa	ta?a	kaha	'side'
5.	ta?e	tae	tae	kae	'faeces'
6.	taŋata	taŋata	taŋata	kanaka	'man'
7.	tahi	tai	tai	kai	'sea'
8.	malohi	malosi	ka?a	?aha	'strong'
9.	kalo	?alo	karo	?alo	'dodge'
10.	aka	a?a	aka	a?a	'root'
11.	?ahu	au	au	au	'gall'
12.	?ulu	ulu	uru	po?o	'head'
13.	?ufi	ufi	u?i	uhi	'yam'
14.	afi	afi	a?ı	ahi	'fire'
15.	faa	faa	?aa	haa	'four'
16.	feke	fe?e	?eke	he?e	'octopus'
17.	ika	i?a	ika	i?a	'fish'
18.	ihu	isu	putaŋio	ihu	'nose'
19.	hau	sau	?au	hau	'dew'
20.	tafuafi	si?a	?ika	hi?a	'firemaking'

	TONGAN	SAMOAN	RAROTONGAN	HAWAIIAN	
21.	hiku	siʔu	ʔiku	hiʔu	'tail'
22.	hake	aʔe	ake	aʔe	'up'
23.	huu	ulu	uru	komo	'enter'
24.	maŋa	maŋa	maŋa	mana	'branch'
25.	maʔu	mau	mau	mau	'constant'
26.	maa	mala	mara	mala	'fermented'
27.	naʔa	faʔaŋa	maninia	naa	'quieten'
28.	nofo	nofo	noʔo	noho	'sit'
29.	ŋalu	ŋalu	ŋaru	nalu	'wave'
30.	ŋutu	ŋutu	ŋutu	nuku	'mouth'
31.	vaka	vaʔa	vaka	waʔa	'canoe'
32.	vaʔe	vae	vae	wae	'leg'
33.	laho	laso	raʔo	laho	'scrotum'
34.	lohu	lou	rou	lou	'fruit-picking pole'
35.	oŋo	loŋo	roŋo	lono	'hear'
36.	ua	lua	rua	lua	'two'

Assuming that there was once a language, that we can now call proto-Polynesian, what do we have to do to reconstruct this language?

There is a number of steps that we have to follow. The first step is to sort out those forms which appear to be cognate from those which do not. If two words are not cognate, it means that they are derived from different original forms, and are not reflexes of the same original form. In deciding whether two forms are cognate, we need to consider how similar they are in both form and meaning. If they are similar enough that we could assume that they were derived from a single original form with a single original meaning, then we say they are cognate.

So, we can begin by excluding from the list above, words such as /tafuafi/ in Tongan meaning 'firemaking'. The words to express the same meaning in the other three languages are /siʔa/ in Samoan, /ʔika/ in Rarotongan and /hiʔa/ in Hawaiian. These last three forms are all quite similar phonetically, as well as being identical in meaning, and could well be reflexes of a single original word. The Tongan word /tafuafi/, although having the same meaning, is so different phonologically, that we must assume it has a totally different history altogether. (Similarly, the Samoan word /iʔa/ and the

91

Hawaiian word /hiʔa/, although phonologically very similar, are not considered to be cognate because their meanings are so different. In Samoan, /iʔa/ means 'fish', while in Hawaiian /hiʔa/ means 'firemaking'.)

From the data in the table, we would want to exclude a number of other forms expressing the same meaning as being non-cognate because they are phonologically so different. In the Samoan data, we would probably want to exclude the following:

2.	pute	'navel'
3.	feula	'blow'
27.	faʔaŋa	'quieten'

In Rarotongan, we need to exclude the following forms which are apparently not cognate with forms in the other languages expressing the same meaning:

18.	putaŋio	'noise'
27.	maninia	'quieten'

and similarly in Hawaiian, we need to exclude:

12.	poʔo	'head'
23.	komo	'enter'

Example number eight presents us with a particular problem. The words for 'strong' are given as:

TONGAN	SAMOAN	RAROTONGAN	HAWAIIAN
malohi	malosi	kaʔa	ʔaha

It is clear that the Tongan and Samoan forms on the one hand are cognate, and that the Rarotongan and Hawaiian forms on the other hand are cognate. It is equally likely that the form for 'strong' in the proto-language was similar to either form. The other form must then have had a different, but similar, meaning, which has changed in some languages to mean 'strong'. We might expect to find forms in other related languages which indicate which of these two cognate sets reflects the original situation in the proto-language. With the data we have at our disposal however, we are not able to decide.

Therefore, we cannot reject either of these cognate sets. We must include them both.

Example number four also presents us with another particular type of problem. The forms given for 'side' are:

TONGAN	SAMOAN	RAROTONGAN	HAWAIIAN
tafaʔaki	tafa	taʔa	kaha

It seems clear that the first two syllables of the longer Tongan word are cognate with the words in the remaining Polynesian languages. The second two syllables of the Tongan form, however, do not have any cognate forms in the other languages. We therefore assume that in Tongan, at some stage in its history, an extra morpheme was added. What was originally regarded as being a morphologically complex word then came to be regarded by speakers as morphologically simple. That is to say, some other morpheme came to be REANALYSED as part of the root. In carrying out comparative reconstruction, we must also ignore such cases of reanalysis, and consider *only* those parts of words which are actually cognate. We can therefore set out the cognate forms in these four languages in this case as:

TONGAN	SAMOAN	RAROTONGAN	HAWAIIAN
tafa-	tafa	taʔa	kaha

in which the /-ʔaki/ that has been added in Tongan is ignored, along with all other non-cognate forms.

Having completed the first step, we can now move on to step two. The second step is to set out the complete set of SOUND CORRESPONDENCES. When we talk about a sound correspondence, what we mean is that we try to find the sounds that appear to be descended from the same original form. So, if we take the first word in the list we have given, we find the following correspondences between the sounds:

Tongan	t	a	p	u
Samoan	t	a	p	u
Rarotongan	t	a	p	u
Hawaiian	k	a	p	u

We say that we have an initial correspondence of /t/ in Tongan to

93

/t/ in Samoan, to /t/ in Rarotongan and to /k/ in Hawaiian. With regard to the /a/ in Tongan, this corresponds to an /a/ in all the remaining three languages. Similarly, there is a correspondence of /p/ in all four languages, and finally, there is a correspondence of /u/ in all four languages. What we have to do is list *all* such sound correspondences for the whole of the data.

Actually, a quick examination of the vowel correspondences reveals that the vowels are identical in all four languages in all words. Let us concentrate only on the consonant correspondences, as this is where the differences are to be found. The correspondence sets for consonants actually work out to be as follows:

TONGAN	SAMOAN	RAROTONGAN	HAWAIIAN
p	p	p	p
f	f	ʔ	h
t	t	t	k
k	ʔ	k	ʔ
h	s	ʔ	h
ʔ	ø	ø	ø
h	ø	ø	ø
m	m	m	m
n	n	n	n
ŋ	ŋ	ŋ	n
v	v	v	w
l	l	r	l
ø	l̤	r	l

One brief note that we should make before going on concerns the use of the zero symbol ø. This is used to express correspondences like the following in the word for 'faeces':

Tongan	t	a	ʔ	e
Samoan	t	a		e
Rarotongan	t	a		e
Hawaiian	k	a		e

In these forms, the /ʔ/ in Tongan corresponds to the absence of any sound in the other three languages. Similarly, in the word for 'gall' given on the next page, we find that there are sounds in Tongan corresponding to nothing in the other languages:

94

TONGAN	SAMOAN	RAROTONGAN	HAWAIIAN
p	p	p	p
m	m	m	m
n	n	n	n

In the first consonant correspondence given above, we ask ourselves the question: what phoneme could reasonably be expected to produce a /p/ in all the daughter languages? The obvious answer is /p/, so we reconstruct */p/. We apply the same kind of reasoning to the vowel correspondences and to the other consonant correspondences that we just listed.

The next thing we should do is look at sound correspondence sets that only have slight differences between the various daughter languages, and try to reconstruct original phonemes from the evidence of these. So, from the correspondence sets we listed earlier, we could now go on to look at:

TONGAN	SAMOAN	RAROTONGAN	HAWAIIAN
t	t	t	k
ʻŋ	ŋ	ŋ	n

In these two cases, only one language, Hawaiian, differs from the other three languages. Presumably, in the first case, we could reconstruct either */t/ or */k/. Which is the best solution? We would be more likely to suggest */t/ as the original form and that this changed to /k/ in Hawaiian. To suggest */k/ as the original form would mean that we would have to have had */k/ changing to /t/ in three separate languages. So, when we reconstruct a phoneme from a sound correspondence set, we usually reconstruct as the original form the sound that has the widest distribution in terms of the number of daughter languages. Using the same kind of argument, we can reconstruct */ŋ/ for the second correspondence set presented above.

We now have to go on to deal with those correspondences which have a greater amount of variation in the reflexes of the original phoneme. Where we have greater variation, it is going to require greater consideration on the part of the person doing the reconstruction. Let us take the correspondence:

TONGAN	SAMOAN	RAROTONGAN	HAWAIIAN
k	ʔ	k	ʔ

Here we have two instances of /k/ and two of /ʔ/, so we cannot use the principle just mentioned of using the form with the widest distribution in the daughter languages. Presumably, it would be possible to reconstruct either /k/ or /ʔ/. How do we decide? We have to consider the sounds we have already reconstructed. The evidence we have already looked at provides for the reconstruction of the following original consonant phonemes (as well as five vowel phonemes):

$$*p \quad *t$$
$$*m \quad *n \quad *\eta$$

As you know, languages tend to operate in terms of balanced systems, and they tend to avoid gaps in their phoneme inventories. Since the proto-language was presumably a language like any other, it must have behaved in the same way. So, we would expect to find a */k/, parallelling the */ŋ/, if there was a */p/ and a */t/. We could argue, therefore, that this correspondence should be reconstructed as coming from a */k/ rather than a */ʔ/. A second consideration that we could take into account is the nature of the sound changes we would need to recognise. With an original */k/, we would need to say that:

$$k \quad \rightarrow \quad ʔ$$

in Samoan and Hawaiian. This is a well known sound change of lenition or weakening. However, if we reconstructed */ʔ/ for this correspondence, we would need to say that:

$$ʔ \rightarrow k$$

in Tongan and Rarotongan, which seems to be against the tendencies that we noted earlier. These two arguments together strongly support the reconstruction of */k/ instead of */ʔ/ as the original form for these sounds in the four languages.

Let us now take the next problematic correspondence:

TONGAN	SAMOAN	RAROTONGAN	HAWAIIAN
f	f	ʔ	h

This correspondence is in fact less problematic than the one we just looked at, because there is a greater number of /f/ reflexes of this original phoneme than the other sounds. It would seem reasonable, therefore, to reconstruct an */f/ wherever this correspondence occurs.

Now, we will consider the correspondences involving the liquids:

TONGAN	SAMOAN	RAROTONGAN	HAWAIIAN
l	l	r	l
∅	l	r	l

We now appear to face real problems. We have to reconstruct two different phonemes to account for the two different sets of correspondences, but there is very little difference between the reflexes. Three of the four languages are identical in their reflexes of these sounds, and in both sets of correspondences, /l/ is the most common reflex. Since we have to reconstruct two phonemes, we will presumably have to choose */l/ for one and */r/ for the other. But which will we assign to which correspondence set? It is fairly arbitrary which we say. However, we could argue that a change of the form:

$$r \rightarrow \emptyset$$

is possibly slightly more likely to occur than a change of the form:

$$r \rightarrow l$$

so we could suggest */l/ for the first correspondence and */r/ for the second correspondence. Therefore, we would need to say that Rarotongan underwent a change of:

$$l \rightarrow r$$

Samoan and Hawaiian underwent a change of:

$$r \rightarrow l$$

and Tongan underwent a change of:

$$r \rightarrow \emptyset$$

97

But with this last pair of reconstructions, we are *really* on shaky ground. It is in cases like this that we really *are* operating with guesswork.

We have reconstructed the following consonant inventory for proto-Polynesian so far:

$$
\begin{array}{lll}
\text{*p} & \text{*t} & \text{*k} \\
\text{*m} & \text{*n} & \text{*ŋ} \\
\text{*f} & & \\
& \text{*l} & \\
& \text{*r} &
\end{array}
$$

Now we will turn to the correspondences involving glottal sounds:

TONGAN	SAMOAN	RAROTONGAN	HAWAIIAN
ʔ	∅	∅	∅
h	∅	∅	∅

In fact, Tongan is the only language to have any reflexes of these two phonemes. All the other languages have simply lost them altogether. It is not too difficult to argue, therefore, that we should reconstruct */ʔ/ and */h/ respectively wherever we find these correspondences, especially since /ʔ/ and /h/ are sounds that are very commonly lost in languages. We have yet to consider the following correspondence however:

TONGAN	SAMOAN	RAROTONGAN	HAWAIIAN
h	s	ʔ	h

Here, all languages except Samoan reflect a glottal sound, and /h/ is the most common. However, we have already reconstructed an */h/ for one of the correspondences we have just looked at. Similarly, */ʔ/ is not a possibility because we have already reconstructed this to account for a different correspondence set. The only possibility left seems to be to reconstruct */s/. This is actually quite reasonable. Changes of the type:

$$s \rightarrow h \rightarrow ʔ$$

are quite common in languages of the world, and can be considered

98

as examples of weakening or lenition. Furthermore, we would otherwise have a gap in the phoneme inventory, and by reconstructing an */s/, we are filling the voiceless alveolar fricative slot:

*p *t *k *ʔ
*m *n *ŋ
*f *s   *h
   *l
   *r

It could perhaps be argued instead that the two correspondences involving /h/ discussed earlier need to be re-examined:

TONGAN	SAMOAN	RAROTONGAN	HAWAIIAN
h	∅	∅	∅
h	s	ʔ	h

According to the principles we established earlier, we should reconstruct as the phoneme in the proto-language, the form that has the widest distribution in the daughter languages. We might therefore want to reconstruct instead of */s/ for the second of these correspondences, the phoneme */h/. This is phonetically quite reasonable, but it creates problems for our handling of the first correspondence, for which we have already reconstructed */h/. This problem could be overcome by suggesting a separate original phoneme altogether for this correspondence, perhaps the voiceless velar fricative */x/. Although this would be phonetically reasonable too, we could argue against this solution on the grounds that we should not introduce new phonemes in the proto-language unless it is shown to be absolutely necessary from the evidence in the daughter languages. *None* of the daughter languages *anywhere* has a /x/, so we should be automatically suspicious of a solution that suggests an /x/ in the proto-language. On the basis of this kind of argument, we should reject the revised solution, and stick with the original solution.

Finally, we have the correspondence:

TONGAN	SAMOAN	RAROTONGAN	HAWAIIAN
v	v	v	w

While we would predict */v/ as the most likely original form for this correspondence on the basis of the distribution of its reflexes, by doing so we would create an uneven phonemic system. As it stands, there is no voiced/voiceless contrast in the stop or fricative series (all being voiceless), and to introduce a single voiced sound would seem rather odd. Another odd thing about this phoneme inventory is the lack of semi-vowels. We would therefore probably be more justified in reconstructing*/w/ than */v/. The original phoneme inventory as we have reconstructed it is therefore something like this:

```
*p  *t  *k   *ʔ
*f  *s       *h
*m  *n  *ŋ
    *l
    *r
*w
    *i  *u
    *e  *o
      *a
```

Having arrived at the phoneme inventory of proto-Polynesian by comparing the daughter languages, we can now move on to the comparatively simple task of reconstructing the forms of the actual words. To do this we need to list off the sound correspondences, together with the original phoneme that they are derived from. So:

	TONGAN	SAMOAN	RAROTONGAN	HAWAIIAN	
1.	i	i	i	i	*i
2.	e	e	e	e	*e
3.	a	a	a	a	*a
4.	o	o	o	o	*o
5.	u	u	u	u	*u
6.	p	p	p	p	*p
7.	f	f	ʔ	h	*f
8.	t	t	t	k	*t
9.	k	ʔ	k	ʔ	*k
10.	h	s	ʔ	h	*s
11.	ʔ	ø	ø	ø	*ʔ
12.	h	ø	ø	ø	*h
13.	m	m	m	m	*m

14.	n	n	n	n	*n
15.	ŋ	ŋ	ŋ	n	*ŋ
16.	v	v	v	w	*w
17.	l	l	r	l	*l
18.	ø	l	r	l	*r

Let us try to reconstruct the word for 'four'. The reflexes in the daughter languages of the original word we are trying to reconstruct are:

Tongan	f	a	a
Samoan	f	a	a
Rarotongan	ʔ	a	a
Hawaiian	h	a	a

We therefore have a word containing three sound correspondences which indicates that the original word must have had three original phonemes. What were those original phonemes? The f = f = ʔ = h correspondence, if you check from the list we just gave, goes back to an original */f/. (Note that we have just used a slightly different way of expressing sound correspondences using the = symbol. This is quite common in text books on comparative linguistics.) The two a = a = a = a correspondences point to an original */a/. So, the proto-Polynesian word for 'four' is reconstructed as */faa/.

Looking new at a second example, take the word for 'dodge':

Tongan	k	a	l	o
Samoan	ʔ	a	l	o
Rarotongan	k	a	r	o
Hawaiian	ʔ	a	l	o

Again referring to our list of correspondences above, we find that the K = ʔ = k = ʔ correspondence points to an original */K/, a = a = a = a to */a/, l = l = r = l to */l/ and o = o = o = o to */o/. So, we reconstruct the original word as */kalo/.

Although reconstruction of the vocabularly is relatively simple and straightforward, there are some situations where we cannot be sure of the original form. If we go back to the following example, it should be clear why this is so:

5.1 Sound Correspondences and Reconstruction

	TONGAN	SAMOAN	RAROTONGAN	HAWAIIAN	
8.	malohi	malosi	kaʔa	ʔaha	'strong'

Here, we have two cognate sets, and both could equally well be derived from the word for 'strong' in the proto-language. The Tongan and Samoan forms would suggest an original form */malosi/, while the Rarotongan and Hawaiian forms would suggest an original form */kasa/. All we can do in such cases is reconstruct *both* forms, and indicate that one of them probably meant 'strong' while the other presumably meant something different, but still similar in meaning (perhaps 'hard' or something like that). But which of the two was the original form for 'strong' is impossible to say.

Another problem that we sometimes face in reconstructing vocabulary comes when we have 'incomplete' sound correspondences that we are not able to fill. For instance, let us imagine that we only had the forms below.

	TONGAN	SAMOAN	RAROTONGAN	HAWAIIAN	
9.	"?"	ʔalo	karo	ʔalo	'dodge'

If we did not have a cognate in Tongan (either because the meaning 'dodge' is expressed by a completely different form, or because the data itself may be lacking the appropriate form) then we will not be able to reconstruct a single original form for 'dodge'. This is because the correspondence:

SAMOAN	RAROTONGAN	HAWAIIAN
l	r	l

could point equally well to the reconstruction of */l/ *or* */r/. To be able to decide whether the form should be reconstructed as having */r/ or */l/, we would therefore need to have a Tongan cognate. We can represent the ambiguity in such reconstructions by reconstructing *both* possible phonemes, separated in a word by a slash. So, we would give:

$$*kar/lo$$

which means that the original form was either */karo/ or */kalo/. (As it is however, if you refer back to the earlier list, the Tongan form actually *is* cognate, and the form is /kalo/. This indicates that the reconstructed form is unambiguously */kalo/.)

EXERCISES
1. For each of the remaining sets of words given in the four Polynesian languages above, reconstruct the form in proto-Polynesian.
2. Write formal rules expressing the sound changes that have taken place in each of the four languages and state whether they are conditioned or unconditioned. Also, state whether they are examples of phonemic loss/addition/shift/split/merger.
3. Look at the Suena and Zia (Morobe Province) data in Data Set 6, and state what the sound correspondences are. (Do not attempt to do any reconstruction at this stage.)
4. Look at the data in Data Set 7 from the Korafe, Notu and Binandere languages of Oro Province, and do the same for these languages. (Again, do not attempt to do any reconstruction.)
5. Examine the data from the northern and southern dialects of Paamese (Vanuatu) in Data Set 8 and state the full set of correspondences. (Do not attempt to do any reconstruction.)
6. Examine the data in Data Set 10 from the coastal Sepik languages Sepa, Manam, Kariru and Sera. Take the language pairs Sepa and Manam, and Sepa and Kariru, and say which pairs of words you think are cognate.

5.2 Reconstruction of Conditioned Sound Changes

When you write the rules for the changes from proto-Polynesian into the various daughter languages, you will find that all of the changes that have taken place are unconditioned sound changes. That is to say that an original */s/ always becomes /ʔ/ in Rarotongan, or an original */r/ always becomes /l/ in Hawaiian. There are no conditioned sound changes which have taken place in only certain environments and not others. How does it affect our technique of reconstruction if there are conditioned sound changes involved as well as unconditioned sound changes?

Let us look at some additional data from another Polynesian language. The language we will add is the Maori language of New Zealand, and the words we will consider are:

5.2 Reconstruction of Conditioned Sound Changes

	TONGAN	SAMOAN	RAROTONGAN	MAORI	HAWAIIAN	
8.	kafa	ʔafa	kaʔa	kaha	ʔaha	'strong'
13.	ʔufi	ufi	uʔi	uhi	uhi	'yam'
14.	afi	afi	aʔi	ahi	ahi	'fire'
15.	faa	faa	ʔaa	ɸaa	haa	'four'
16.	feke	feʔe	ʔeke	ɸeke	heʔe	'octopus'

If we ignore the Maori data (as we did before), we find that there is a single regular correspondence of the following form:

TONGAN	SAMOAN	RAROTONGAN	HAWAIIAN
f	f	ʔ	h

and we reconstruced this as going back to an original phoneme */f/. However, if we include the Maori data, we find that there are in fact two separate sets of sound correspondences:

TONGAN	SAMOAN	RAROTONGAN	MAORI	HAWAIIAN
f	f	ʔ	h	h
f	f	ʔ	ɸ	h

Must we therefore reconstruct two separate phonemes for these two correspondence sets? If we do, they will certainly need to be phonetically very similar, as their reflexes are so similar (differing only in Maori). Perhaps we could retain */f/ for the first correspondence, and suggest another sound, maybe */ɸ/, for the second correspondence. So, our reconstructions for the words we are looking at would be:

*kafa	'strong'
*ʔufi	'yam'
*afi	'fire'
*ɸaa	'four'
*ɸeke	'octopus'

However, if we examine the distribution of the reconstructed sounds */ɸ/ and */f/ in proto-Polynesian, we find that they are in fact in complementary distribution. The sound */ɸ/ only occurs word initially, while the sound */f/ only occurs medially. If we assume that for each separate sound correspondence, we need to reconstruct a separate phoneme, we *may* come to the wrong conclusions. What we must look for, therefore, is complementary distribution between phonetically similar correspondence sets. The correspondence f = f = ? = h = h only occurs medially, while the correspondence f = f = ? = ϕ = h only occurs initially. We therefore need to reconstruct only a *single* phoneme for these two correspondence sets. Presumably, we do not need to modify our original reconstruction of */f/, as there is no need to reconstruct a */ϕ/. We find that Maori has undergone a conditioned sound change of the form:

$$f \rightarrow \begin{cases} \phi \ / \ \# \underline{\hspace{1cm}} \\ h \ / \ V \underline{\hspace{1cm}} V \end{cases}$$

which accounts for the fact that there are two correspondence sets in the daughter languages when Maori is considered.

Therefore, after we have set out our sound correspondences between the daughter languages, we *must* also do the following:

(a) Firstly, we must look for sound correspondences that involve phonetically similar sounds, and

(b) Secondly, for each of these phonetically 'suspicious' pairs of sound correspondences, we should try to see whether or not they are in complementary or contrastive distribution.

This is therefore very similar to analysing the phonemes of a language, and we are in fact doing just that. We are trying to analyse the phonemes of the proto-language, using the sound correspondences as the 'phonetic' material. We then have to decide which sound correspondences are phonemically distinctive in the original language, and which are just positional variants (or 'allo-correspondences' of 'correspondence-emes').

Let us look at another very simple situation that we are already familiar with to see what has happened. We are already aware of the fact that in Motu, there has been a palatalisation of */t/ to [s] before the front vowels /i/ and /e/, while elsewhere it remained as [t]. We wrote this rule formally as:

$$t \rightarrow s \ / \underline{\hspace{1cm}} \begin{array}{l} \text{front} \\ \text{vowel} \end{array}$$

Rather than work from the proto-language to the modern language, let us instead work from Motu and one of its sister languages and work *back* to the proto-language. The sister language we will look at is Sinaugoro, and the data we will consider is as follows:

105

SINAUGORO	MOTU	
tama	tama	'father'
tina	sina	'mother'
taγi	tai	'cry'
tui	tui	'elbow/knee'
γita	ita	'see'
γate	ase	'liver'
mate	mase	'die'
natu	natu	'child'
toi	toi	'three'

So let us apply the technique we have just worked out. Firstly, you will remember, we had to sort out the cognate forms from the non-cognate forms. This has already been done for us, and all the forms given are in fact cognate. The second step then, was to set out the sound correspondences. Since we are only interested at this stage in the history of [t] and [s], let us restrict ourselves only to correspondences involving these two sounds. (There are many other correspondences in the two languages where the two sounds are identical, and there is also a correspondence of Sinaugoro /γ/ to Motu /φ/). The correspondences we find are:

SINAUGORO	MOTU
t	t
t	s

There are therefore two sound correspondences here. Does this mean that we should reconstruct two separate phonemes in the original language? If we did, these would presumably be */t/ for the first correspondence and */s/ for the second.

However, since the t = t and t = s correspondences both involve very similar sets of sounds, we should first of all look for complementary distribution. What we find is that the t = s correspondence occurs only when there is a following correspondence of front vowel = front vowel, whereas the t = t correspondence occurs before all other kinds of vowel correspondences. If two (or more) correspondences are in complementary distribution in this way, then we reconstruct only a single original phoneme for both correspondences, and we again say that a conditioned sound change must have taken place. We would therefore want to reconstruct a */t/ using the principle that we normally reconstruct the form with the widest distribution. We then need to say that a conditioned sound change took place in Motu, whereby *[t] became [s] before front vowels, as we saw earlier. The original forms from which the Sinaugoro and Motu forms were derived can therefore be reconstructed as below (with the γ = ø correspondence coming from */γ/ presumably):

PROTO-SINAUGORO /MOTU	
*tama	'father'
*tina	'mother'
*taγi	'cry'
*tui	'elbow/knee'
*γita	'see'
*γate	'liver'
*mate	'die'
*natu	'child'
*toi	'three'

Now that we know that we are to always check phonetically similar sets of sound correspondences for complementary or contrastive distribution, we should go back and check our Polynesian correspondences as well. Which correspondences should we test for distribution because of their phonetic similarity? The first obvious pair of correspondences we should test are the correspondences involving the liquids, for which our earlier reconstructions were given below:

TONGAN	SAMOAN	RAROTONGAN	HAWAIIAN	
l	l	r	l	*l
ø	l	r	l	*r

Are these phonetically similar sets of correspondences in complementary or contrastive distribution? We will list the forms in which they both occur so we can test this easily:

	TONGAN	SAMOAN	RAROTONGAN	HAWAIIAN	
*l	l	l	r	l	
9.	kalo	ʔalo	karo	ʔalo	'dodge'
12.	ʔulu	ulu	uru	—	'head'
29.	ŋalu	ŋalu	ŋaru	nalu	'wave'

107

33.	laho	laso	ra?o	laho	'scrotum'
34.	lohu	lou	rou	lou	'fruit-plucking pole'
*r	ø	l	r	l	
23.	huu	ulu	uru	—	'enter'
26.	maa	mala	mara	mala	'fermented'
35.	oŋo	loŋo	roŋo	lono	'hear'
36.	ua	lua	rua	lua	'two'

We need to test all possible conditioning environments. You should remember from your study of phonology, that when we are looking for possible conditioning factors for allophones, we need to consider the following:

(a) the nature of the sound or sounds which follow
(b) the nature of the sound or sounds which precede
(c) the nature of the syllable (i.e. whether open or closed)
(d) the position in the word (i.e. whether initial, medial or final)

Let us consider these possible conditioning factors to see if these two sets of correspondences are in complementary or contrastive distribution.

Firstly, let us look at the nature of the following sound. Immediately following the first correspondence (i.e. l = l = r = l), we have the following correspondences:

$$u = u = u = u$$
$$a = a = a = a$$
$$o = o = o = o$$

and after the second correspondence (i.e. ø = l = r = l) we have:

$$u = u = u = u$$
$$a = a = a = a$$
$$o = o = o = o$$

There does not appear to be any complementary distribution involving the nature of the following correspondence, so let us try to find out if the nature of the preceding correspondence acts as a conditioning factor. Before the first correspondence we have:

$$u = u = u = u$$
$$a = a = a = a$$

108

and before the second correspondence we have:

$$u = u = u = u$$
$$a = a = a = a$$

Again, there is no complementary distribution. The third possibility (i.e. the nature of the syllable) is of little use because all syllables in the data are open. Finally, we should check the position in the word. We find that *both* sets of correspondences appear both initially and medially. We conclude therefore, that these two correspondences are in contrastive rather than complementary distribution, and that we were correct in the first place in reconstructing two separate phonemes.

In fact, we can present sub-minimal pairs of sets of sound correspondences to back up our statement. Compare the forms for 'head' and 'enter':

TONGAN	SAMOAN	RAROTONGAN	HAWAIIAN	
ʔulu	ulu	uru	—	'head'
huu	ulu	uru	—	'enter'

Between correspondences in which all four languages have /u/, we find *both* correspondences occurring; thus, Tongan has the sequence /ulu/ contrasting with /uøu/. So, we can conclude that there was a phonemic distinction in the original language that goes back to an original sub-minimal pair, i.e.:

$$*ʔulu \quad \text{'head'} \quad *huru \quad \text{'enter'}$$

In conclusion, therefore, we have described a means of reconstructing the phonological system of a proto-language and also its lexicon, and we call this means of reconstruction the comparative method. The comparative method involves *carefully* carrying out *all* of the following steps:

1. Sort out those forms which appear to be cognate. Ignore non-cognate forms.

2. Using only cognate forms, write out the full set of correspondences between the languages you are looking at (including correspondences where the sounds are identical all the way through). Be careful to note correspondences where a sound in

one language corresponds to ø (or the absence of a sound) in another language.

3. Group together all correspondences that have reflexes that are phonetically similar.
4. Look for complementary and contrastive distribution between these suspicious pairs of correspondences.
5. For each correspondence set that is *not* in complementary distribution with any other correspondence set, assume that it goes back to a single original phoneme.
6. Make a guess about the original form of the phoneme using the following criteria:
   (a) the suggested original phoneme must be 'reasonable', meaning that the changes from it to the reflexes in the descendent languages must fit our knowledge about what kinds of sound changes actually occur in langauages
   (b) the sound which has the widest distribution in the daughter languages is most likely to be the original phoneme
   (c) a sound corresponding to a gap in the reconstructed phoneme system of the proto-language is also likely to be a possible reconstruction
   (d) do not reconstruct an original sound that does not occur in any of the daughter languages unless you have to.
7. For each group of correspondence sets that are in complementary distribution, assume that they all go back to a single phoneme. Use the same criteria for reconstruction given in step (6) above.

READING GUIDE QUESTIONS

1. What do we mean when we say that one form is a 'reflex' of another form?
2. What are cognate forms?
3. What is the comparative method?
4. What is linguistic reconstruction?
5. What do we mean by 'sound correspondences' when applying the comparative method?
6. What kinds of factors must we consider while reconstructing the phonemes of proto-language from the sound correspondences in the daughter languages?
7. How can we reconstruct a phoneme if a conditioned sound change has taken place?

EXERCISES
1. Check all of the phonetically similar sets of sound correspondences in the Polynesian data we looked at in this chapter for
   complementary and contrastive distribution. Were the reconstructions we made in the first place valid or not?
2. Look at the Yimas and Karawari forms in Data Set 4. How do
   you think the original forms given on the left for the proto-
   language were arrived at? Do you think they are reasonable
   reconstructions to make on the basis of the evidence you have?
3. Look at the Suena and Zia data in Data Set 6. Using your earlier
   statement of the sound correspondences:
   (a) try to find any examples of complementary distribution
       among correspondence sets
   (b) try to find any examples of minimal pairs between corres-
       pondences
   (c) try to suggest a reasonable phoneme in the proto-language
       for each of the groups of correspondence sets
   (d) reconstruct the actual words in the proto-language
   (e) state the changes that both of the two languages have
       undergone.
4. Look at the Paamese date in Data Set 8. Using the comparative
   method, reconstruct the original forms in Paamese and say what
   changes have taken place.
5. Look at the Korafe, Notu and Binandere data in Data Set 7.
   What do you think were the original forms of these words?
   Why?
6. Examine the data below from the Murut and Dusun languages
   of Sabah in Malaysia. Reconstruct the original *initial* consonants. (Ignore all other phonemes.)

		MURUT	DUSUN
1.	make	baal	waa
2.	reeds	baang	waang
3.	female tambaran	babalian	bobohiyan
4.	rice	bagas	wagas
5.	wash hands	baguʔ	wouʔ
6.	wild pig	bakas	bakas
7.	small basket	balait	baayit
8.	buy	bali	bohi
9.	boundary	balit	wohit

10.	backbone	baluntud	bountud
11.	measure body	bangal	wanga
12.	crow	bangkaak	bangkaak
13.	body	bangkay	bangkay
14.	bedbug	bangking	wongking
15.	log	batang	watang
16.	stone	batu	watu
17.	weave	batug	watuʔ
18.	carry	bauang	bouvang
19.	footprint	bayaʔ	vazaʔ
20.	life	biag	wiyaw
21.	small snail	bilid	biid
22.	stomach	bituko	bituko
23.	dumb	bobow	bobow
24.	tame pig	bogok	wogok
25.	neighbour	bokon	wokon
26.	dew	bolobow	bohobow
27.	voice	bolos	boos
28.	blind person	bolow	bohow
29.	crocodile	buayo	buayo
30.	young man	buayoy	buwayoy
31.	moon	bulan	wuhan
32.	fur/feather	bulu	wuhu
33.	flower	busak	wusak
34.	tortoise	buu	buu
35.	untie	buyad	wuyad
36.	bamboo	buluʔ	vuhuʔ

7. Examine the pairs of cognate forms in Abau and Idam (West Sepik Province). Make an attempt to reconstruct the form in the proto-language, and state what changes have taken place.

		ABAU	IDAM
1.	centipede	ɑnɑn	anan
2.	place	ɑm	am
3.	talk	ɑk	ak
4.	snake	sɑk	sak
5.	lake	hɑuk	ɸɑuk
6.	sago jelly	sɑuk	sɑuk
7.	bangle	kwɑl	kwal
8.	get	nɑnɑk	nanak
9.	tree branch	nɑukɑn	nɑukan

10. taro	hɑu	ϕɑu
11. *bilum*/string bag	ɑuk	ɑuk
12. dry tree	nɑusɑm	nɑusam

8. Try to reconstruct the original forms from which the Ndao and Sawu forms (Eastern Indonesia) are derived, and state what changes have taken place in both languages.

	NDAO	SAWU
1. pig	haha	wawa
2. wear *laplap*	silu	hilu
3. nine	ʈeo	heo
4. one	əʈi	əhi
5. tongue	heʔo	weʔo
6. breast	saʔu	haʔu
7. climb	ʈaʔe	haʔe
8. moon	həru	wəru
9. sea	dəsi	dəhi
10. give	hei	wei
11. receive	səmi	həmi
12. axe	hela	wela

9. Examine the cognate forms below from the Aroma, Hula and Sinaugoro languages of Central Province. Use the comparative method to reconstruct what you think to be the forms for all of these words in the proto-language. Do not forget to look for complementary distribution among phonetically similar correspondence sets to avoid reconstructing too many phonemes in the proto-language. (Note that the data has been slightly regularised to make the problem more workable.)

	AROMA	HULA	SINAUGORO
1. pigeon	pune	—	pune
2. skin	opi	kopi	kopi
3. stone	vau	vau	vatu-
4. chop	—	pai	bati
5. father	ama	ama	tama
6. mother	ina	ina	tina
7. cry	aγi-	aγi	taγi
8. sew	uli	uli	tuli
9. bowels	inaγe	inaγe	tinaγe
10. knee	ui	ui	tui
11. grandparent	upu	upu	tubu
12. see	ia	γia	γita

13.	louse	uu	ɣuu	ɣutu
14.	liver	ɣae	ae	ɣate
15.	octopus	ulia	ɣulia	ɣulita
16.	milk	laa	laa	lata
17.	die	mae	–	mate
18.	child	nau	nau	natu
19.	egg	ɣaoi	aoi	ɣatoi
20.	short	upa	kupa	–
21.	ashes	–	kavu	kaɣu
22.	left hand	auli	kauli	kauli
23.	chest	–	kopa	koba
24.	sand	one	–	kone
25.	tie	wau	kʷau	–
26.	hit	–	kʷari	kʷari
27.	die	wareɣa	kʷarea	–
28.	cough	–	kʷamo	kʷamo
29.	lip	pipiɣa	pipiɣa	bibiɣa
30.	night	poɣi	poɣi	boɣi
31.	belly	–	poka	boga
32.	big	–	para	bara
33.	sky	–	kupa	guba
34.	right hand	ripa	ripa	diba
35.	head	repa	repa	deba
36.	sago	lapia	lapia	labia
37.	finger	riri	–	didi
38.	back	roɣe	–	doɣe
39.	voice	karo	karo	garo
40.	smoke	kovu	–	goɣu
41.	hand	ima	ɣima	ɣima
42.	alive	mauli	maɣuli	maɣuli
43.	bird	manu	manu	manu
44.	fat	mona	mona	mona
45.	brain	mina	mina	mina
46.	eye	maa	–	mata
47.	tongue	maδa	maa	maa
48.	boy	–	melo	melo
49.	house	numa	numa	numa
50.	dream	nivi	nivi	nivi
51.	coconut	niu	niu	niu
52.	mosquito	nemo	nemo	nemo

53. *kunai* grass	leγi	leγi	leγi
54. wind	δaγi	aγi	aγi
55. wallaby	waγi	waγi	waγi
56. urinate	meγi	meγi	meγi
57. wife	arawa	γarawa	γarawa
58. wing	vane	vane	vane
59. hair	vui	vui	γui
60. how many	vira	vira	vira
61. moon	vue	vue	γue
62. woman	vavine	vavine	vavine
63. fruit	vua	vua	γua-
64. full	vonu	vonu	γonu
65. new	valivu	—	valiγu
66. fly	lovo	lovo	loγo
67. plant	varo	—	varo
68. four	vaivai	vaivai	—
69. name	δara	ara	ara
70. lahara	δavala	avala	avala
71. breadfruit	unu	γunu	γunu
72. pot	ulo	γulo	γulo
73. *buai*/betelnut	uria	γuria	γuria
74. eat	γaniγani	aniani	γaniγani
75. mountain	—	oro	γoro·
76. sing	mari	mari	mari
77. dirty	milo	milo	milo
78. sea	rawa	rawa	rawa
79. sail	lala	laa	laγa
80. vine	walo	walo	walo
81. water	wai	wai	wai
82. widow	wapu	—	wabu

5.3 The Reality of Proto-languages

At the beginning of this chapter on the comparative method we said that
the method involved a certain amount of guesswork, but that this guesswork was intelligent rather than blind guesswork. But what do our
reconstructions actually represent? Do they represent a real language as it
was actually spoken at some earlier time, or do our reconstructions only
give an approximation of some language?

One point of view we can take is that we are not actually trying to reconstruct the facts of a language, as it was actually spoken, when we are applying the comparative method, nor should we even try to do this. Many linguists argue that we should not try to suggest any phonetic form of reconstructed original phonemes deduced from the evidence of sound correspondences between daughter languages. Rather, what we should do is to simply deduce that in such and such a word, there *was* a phoneme, that was distinct from all other sounds, but that we do not know what its phonetic form was. According to this point of view, a 'proto-language' as it is reconstructed is not a 'language' in the same sense as any of its descendants, or as the 'real' proto-language itself. It is merely an abstract 'statement of correspondences'.

It would be logical, holding this point of view, to devise totally arbitrary symbols to express the original phonemes in the proto-language for each of the sets of sound correspondences in the descendant languages. So, we could for instance, say that the Polynesian t = t = t = k correspondence should be reconstructed as $, the a = a = a = a correspondence as @, the p = p = p = p correspondence as $\sqrt{}$ and the u = u = u = u correspondence as &. So the original form that produced:

TONGAN·	SAMOAN	RAROTONGAN	HAWAIIAN	
tapu	tapu	tapu	kapu	'taboo'

would be reconstructed as *$@ $\sqrt{}$ &, which says nothing at all about the phonetic form of the word; all it says is that there was a word containing four different phonemes, which behaved in four different ways in the daughter languages.

Other linguists, while not going as far as this, have stated that while languages that are related through common descent are derived from a single ancestor language, we should not necessarily assume that this language really existed as such. The assumptions of the comparative method that we should arrive at an entirely uniform proto-language is likely to give us a distorted or false view of the proto-language. In some cases, the comparative method may even allow us to reconstruct a proto-language that never existed historically. For instance, we can reconstruct various proto-languages between Latin and the modern languages Spanish, French, Portuguese, Italian and Rumanian (i.e. proto-Spanish, proto-French and so on) from which all of the modern dialects of these languages are supposed to have descended. Historically however, we know that these proto-languages never existed. Innovation from Latin took place in local areas from the time that Latin was spoken in the areas in the first place. There was no period of uniform change from Latin to proto-French in the area of modern France, with a subsequent split into the multitude of modern French dialects. We must therefore be careful about assuming that proto-languages ever existed, and that there was ever a speech community to go along with that proto-language.

As far as the phonological reality of the proto-languages we are reconstructing is concerned, most linguists do try to make their reconstructions with a view to estimating something about the phonetic form of the language they are reconstructing. We all realise that there are times when we simply cannot be sure what the original phonetic forms were. A good case is the difference between the Polynesian l = l = r = l and ø = l = r = l correspondences we looked at earlier. We reconstructed */l/ for the first correspondence and */r/ for the second correspondence. However, it is quite possible that we are wrong. In cases such as this, we would be wiser to regard */l/ and */r/ not so much as reliable phonetic indications of the original forms, but simply as indications that there *was* a phonemic distinction of *some* sort (probably involving liquids).

It is sometimes possible to check on the accuracy of our guesses about the phonetics of a proto-language. One possibility is to use older written records of a proto-language, if these are available. In chapter one, we looked at the development of Latin into the modern Spanish, French, Italian and Rumanian languages. We can check on the validity of the comparative method in this case by trying to reconstruct *back* from the modern languages, to see if what we end up with coincides with the actual written Latin records. There are, in fact, many things that the comparative method cannot tell us about Latin. For instance, look at the following forms in these languages:

SPANISH	FRENCH	ITALIAN	RUMANIAN	
naso	ne	naso	nas	'nose'
kabo	ʃɛf	kapo	kap	'head'
kabra	ʃɛ:v ʁ	kapra	kaprə	'goat'
aba	fɛ:v	fava	faw	'bean'

117

(Although the French forms are phonetically quite different from the other languages, they are still cognate.) Because of this wide variation in the range of variation and the small number of examples we have got to deal with, we cannot really attempt any valid reconstructions. We could, however, guess that the original word for 'nose' might have been something like */naso/, the word for 'head' */kapo/, the word for 'goat' */kapra/ and the word for 'bean' */faba/. Now, since we have written records of Latin, we can check the accuracy of our reconstructions. The written records give us the following forms:

nasum	'nose'
caput	'head'
capram	'goat'
fabam	'bean'

We know that 'c' in Latin represented the phoneme /k/. However, the written records do *not* provide us with the same forms as the comparative method does. The comparative method does not enable us to reconstruct a feature of a language when *all* of the daughter languages have *lost* that feature. We can only reconstruct when some traces of an original form are left. In the examples we have just looked at, the final consonant has been lost in all of the daughter languages. The final */u/ has also changed to /o/ or has been dropped in all of the daughter languages, so this cannot be reconstructed either.

A second possibility for checking on the validity of our reconstructions is to look at loan words. It is often possible to find that words were borrowed from a proto-language into some other language, and they have been retained in the language up till the present time without losing some of the original features of its pronunciation at the time it was borrowed. The form in which they were borrowed can tell us something about their pronunciation in the earlier stage of the language we are studying. For example, we have reconstructed a series of changes from Latin */k/ to the later forms [t ʃ] and [ts] in languages descended from it, and modern forms [ʃ] and [s]. What evidence do we have for these different stages? In German, a number of words have been borrowed from Latin since the time of the Roman Empire. For instance, the Latin word for 'emperor' was /kaesar/, and this was borrowed into German as /kaizer/ (now known in names like Kaiser Wilhelm and so

118

on). The word was borrowed again several hundred years later as /tsɛ:zar/, indicating that the [k] had shifted to a [ts] sound. In a similar way, we can tell something about the pronunciation in the past of the sound spelt 'ch' in French. Nowadays, this is pronounced [ʃ] though earlier it must have been pronounced as [t ʃ]. We can say this, because there are words in English borrowed from earlier times which have a [t ʃ] pronunciation instead of [ʃ]. In fact, there are even examples where English has 'reborrowed' the same word from French at different times with different pronunciations and different meanings. One such example is the word 'chief' and the word 'chef'. The first form is the earlier borrowing with [t ʃ] while the second form is the modern borrowing with [ʃ].

READING GUIDE QUESTIONS
1. In what situations is the comparative method unable to recon-struct a proto-language correctly?
2. How can we check on the accuracy of our historical recon-structions?

EXERCISES
1. Modern French has the following words:
    ekut   'listen to'
    etʁã3   'foreign'
    eta   'state'
    which were borrowed in the past into English as 'scout' (one who listens), 'strange' (something which is foreign) and 'state'. At a later stage, English reborrowed the last two words as 'estrange' (as in 'estranged wife') and 'estate'. From the form of these borrowings into English, what can you suggest about the history of the three French words given above?
2. Many linguists use the evidence provided in rhyming poetry to justify reconstructions of earlier stages of languages. What do you think the following famous nursery rhymes can tell us about the history of English?
    1. Ride a cock-horse
        To Banbury Cross
        To see a fine lady
        Upon a white horse
        Rings on her fingers
        And bells on her toes
        She shall have music
        Wherever she goes

2. Jack and Jill
    Went up the hill
    To fetch a pail of water
    Jack fell down
    And broke his crown
    And Jill came tumbling after

3. Old Mother Hubbard
    Went to the cupboard
    To get her poor doggie a bone
    But when she got there
    The cupboard was bare
    So the poor doggie had none

4. Hickory dickory dock
    The mouse ran up the clock
    The clock struck one
    The mouse ran down
    Hickory dickory dock

FURTHER READING

1. Langacker, Ronald W. *Language and its Structure* (Chapter Eight 'Genetic Relationships'), pp. 207-19 is an excellent easy-to-read summary of how to apply the comparative method of reconstruction.

2. Anttila, Raimo. *An Introduction to Historical and Comparative Linguistics* (Chapter Eleven 'The Comparative Method [The Central Concept]'), pp. 229-65.

3. Bloomfield, Leonard. *Language* (Chapter Eighteen 'The Comparative Method'), pp. 297-321.

4. Lehmann, Winfred P. *Historical Linguistics: An Introduction* (Chapter Five 'The Comparative Method'),pp. 83-89.

Chapter Six

PROBLEMS WITH THE COMPARATIVE METHOD

The comparative method that we talked about in the preceding chapter was developed mostly in the eighteen hundreds, by scholars who were mostly from Germany. This method may seem very simple to apply if we just follow the steps that were set out in chapter five, but in fact, it is often very difficult indeed to apply the method. In this chapter, we will look at some of the problems that historical linguists face in applying the method. We will begin by looking at the historical development of the comparative method, and its refinement by the Neogrammarians of the preceding century, and some of the problems that they recognised themselves. We will then go on to look at some more fundamental objections to a strict application of the comparative method.

6.1 The Neogrammarians

The comparative method that we described in the previous chapter was first developed in Europe, mostly by German scholars, and it was first applied to the languages of the Indo-European family. This family includes all of the languages first recognised by Sir William Jones in 1786 as being descended from a common ancestor. It was perhaps most natural that European scholars should investigate their own languages first, as these are languages with a very long history of writing. This made it possible to start our reconstructions further back in time than we can with languages that are unwritten, or which have only recently been written. A long history of writing also enables us to check on the accuracy of reconstructions made from the present.

After the period of European exploration and colonisation, scholars came into contact with a wide range of languages previously unknown in Europe. Word lists were compiled in various languages, for people to see the similarities and differences between them. Before the nineteenth century, a field of study called ETYMOLOGY had become quite well established. This term is currently used to refer simply to the study of the history of words though in earlier times the history of 'words' and the history of 'languages' was often confused. Many of the early attempts at etymology would be regarded as childish by modern standards. One French scholar called Etienne Guichard in 1606 compiled a comparative word list in Hebrew, Chaldaic, Syrian, Greek, Latin, French, Italian, Spanish, German, Flemish and English, in which he tried to show that all languages can be traced back to Hebrew! The kind of evidence he presented to support his hypothesis was the existence of similarities between words like the following:

Hebrew	*dabar*
English	*word*
Latin	*verbum*

Scholars who followed were more sceptical of these kinds of methods, and Voltaire, a famous French philosopher, described etymology at the time as the science in which: '. . . the vowels count for little and the consonants for nothing'.

As we found in chapter one, the statement by Sir William Jones in 1786 about Sanskrit opened the eyes of European scholars to a whole new field of linguistic data, as well as profoundly altering their perception of the nature of language relationships. Jones emphasised the similarities in the 'structure' of the Indo-European languages rather than individual similarities between words, as was the practice of etymologists such as Guichard. This led to a new intellectual climate in the study of language relationships, as scholars turned to looking for grammatical similarities between languages to determine whether or not they should be considered to be related. Lexical similarities, it was argued, were poor evidence of genetic relationship, as practically anything could be related to practically anything else with enough effort.

So, for instance, we find one of the famous nineteenth century scholars, Rasmus Rask, in 1818, investigating the history of the Icelandic language on the basis of its grammatical similarities to other Germanic languages (such as Norwegian, German and English), rather than its lexical similarities.

Rask also argued, however, that while individual lexical similarities were not good evidence of linguistic relationship, *repeated* occurrences of sound correspondences between words could not be due to chance, so these *were* evidence of genetic relationship. By recognising only repeated occurrences of sound correspondences as valid evidence in the study of the history of language, it was possible to exclude chance similarities such as those noted above by Guichard for Hebrew, English and Latin.

In 1822, Jakob Grimm described a series of sound correspondences that he had noticed between Sanskrit, Greek, Latin and the Germanic languages (which include the now extinct Gothic language, as well as English). For instance, he noticed that very often where Sanskrit, Greek and Latin had a /p/, the Germanic languages had an /f/, e.g.

GREEK	LATIN	GOTHIC	ENGLISH
pous	pes	fotus	foot

and where Sanskrit, Greek and Latin had a /b/, the Germanic languages had a /p/, e.g.

GREEK	LATIN	GOTHIC	ENGLISH
turbe:	turba	thaurp	thorp (an old word for 'village'

and finally, where Sanskrit had a /bh/, the Germanic languages had a /b/, e.g.

SANSKRIT	ENGLISH
bhra:ta:	brother

(Note that we are considering only the underlined sounds. The remaining correspondences are clearly far less obvious than these.) The full set of correspondences noticed by Grimm is set out below:

SANSKRIT	GREEK	LATIN	GERMANIC	PROTO-INDO-EUROPEAN
p	p	p	f	*p
t	t	t	θ	*t
k	k	k	x	*k
b	b	b	p	*b
d	d	d	t	*d
g	g	g	k	*g
bh	ph	f	b	*bh
dh	th	f	d	*dh
gh	kh	ø	g	*gh

So, Germanic voiceless fricatives correspond to voiceless stops in the other languages, and voiceless stops correspond to voiced stops.

Germanic voiced stops correspond to voiced aspirated stops in Sanskrit and voiceless aspirated stops in Greek. (The Latin correspondences are rather odd in this case.) According to the methodology described in the previous chapter, using the principle that the forms with the widest distribution in the daughter languages are the most likely original forms, and also the principle that sound changes are more likely to be 'natural' than 'unnatural', then we can suggest that these correspondences go back to the proto-Indo-European phonemes presented above. (Sanskrit is therefore the most conservative of these languages, having undergone no changes from the proto-language. Germanic is the language group that has undergone the greatest number of innovations.)

No scholar at the time thought to distinguish between sound correspondences that were without exception and those which appeared to be sporadic (i.e. applying in some words but not in others). In fact, while the correspondences that Grimm noted were found to be true for very many words, there were at the same time many words in which these correspondences were not found, and other correspondences were found instead. There were, for instance, many voiceless stops in Sanskrit, Greek and Latin that corresponded to voiceless stops in Germanic, instead of voiceless fricatives, e.g.:

LATIN	GOTHIC	
sp̱uo	speiwan	'spit'
est̠	ist̠	'is'
nok̠tis	nax̠ts	'night'

The Gothic forms were not /sfeiwan/, /isθ/ and /naxθs/ as we might expect if the correspondences noted by Grimm were to be completely general. It was, however, soon realised that the two sets of correspondences:

SANSKRIT/GREEK/LATIN		GERMANIC
voiceless stops	=	voiceless stops
voiceless stops	=	voiceless fricatives

were in fact in complementary distribution. In the previous chapter, we saw that when a conditioned sound change takes place in any of the daughter languages, the result is that the sound correspondence sets themselves are in complementary distribution. So, once we have set out the full range of correspondence sets, we must check to see whether phonetically similar correspondence sets are in complementary or contrastive distribution, and if they are in complementary distribution, we need only reconstruct a single original phoneme that has undergone a conditioned sound change. The first of the two correspondences above was found only when Gothic had a preceding fricative, whereas the second correspondence was found elsewhere. We could therefore reconstruct both correspondences as going back to a single voiceless stop series, and say that there has been a conditioned sound change of the following form in the Germanic languages:

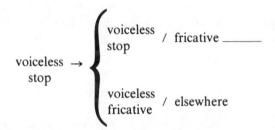

More and more sound correspondences came to be recognised as being due to the influence of phonetic factors of some kind, such as the nature of the preceding and following sounds, or the position of stress or the position of the sound in the word (i.e. whether initial, medial or final). By taking into account other phonetic factors, Hermann Grassmann was able to account for a further set of consonant correspondences in these languages. It had been noticed that some voiced stops in Germanic corresponded with aspirated stops in Sanskrit and Greek (as covered by Grimm's statement as we saw earlier), while some corresponded with unaspirated stops. We have, once again, a double set of correspondences. Grassmann was able to show that these two correspondences were in complementary distribution, and that both Sanskrit and Greek had undergone a conditioned sound change. Note the following forms in these two languages:

GREEK		SANSKRIT	
do:so:	'I will give'	a-da:t	'he gave'
di-do:mi:	'I give'	da-da:mi	'I give'

125

GREEK		SANSKRIT	
the:so:	'I will put'	a-dha:t	'he put'
ti-the:mi:	'I put'	da-dha:mi	'I put'

The first two forms in these two languages indicate that there is a regular morphological process of reduplication of the initial syllable. In Greek, this expresses a change from future to present tense, while in Sanskrit, it expresses a change of third person past tense to first person present tense. When a syllable containing an aspirated stop is reduplicated, the reduplicated syllable contains an unaspirated stop. In chapter two, this kind of change was described as dissimilation at a distance. Grassmann related this kind of morphological alternation in these two languages to certain unpredictable sound correspondences between these two languages and Germanic languages. e.g.:

SANSKRIT	GREEK	GOTHIC	
b̲o:dha	p̲ewtho	b̲ewda	'bid'

We would expect Sanskrit to have /bh/ and Greek to have /ph/ wherever Germanic languages have /b/ according to the correspondences noted by Grimm. Grassmann noted that Sanskrit and Greek must originally have had these forms, but later underwent dissimilation under the influence of the aspirated stop in the following syllable.

In 1875 , Carl Verner was able to dispose of yet another set of apparently irregular forms according to Grimm's statement of correspondences. Compare the following set of forms:

LATIN	GOTHIC	
pater	fadar	'father'

Where Latin has /t/, we would normally expect Germanic languages to have /θ/. Whereas in this (and other) words, there is instead /d/. Verner collected a full set of such irregular forms and showed that the correspondences of t=d and t=o were in complementary distribution. It was shown that the reflex of the original */t/ as either /θ/ or /d/ in the Germanic languages depended on the position of the stressed syllable (i.e. whether the following syllable was stressed or unstressed).

Grimm had stated earlier that:

the sound shifts succeed in the main, but work out completely only in individual words, while others remain unchanged.

He stated this because of the large number of forms which did not fit his generalisations. However, with the discoveries of Grassmann, Verner and others, most of these irregularities were eventually eliminated. Towards the end of the nineteenth century, scholars like Brugmann and Leskien made the famous statement that: 'sound laws operate without exception.' The sound correspondences of Grimm, Verner and Grassmann were restated as 'laws' to emphasise the fact that they could not be 'broken'. Newtonian physics gave them a model of a closed system in which there could be no exceptions, like the laws of gravity. Darwinian biology offered them a model of organisms developing according to unbendable laws of chance (i.e. survival of the fittest). This was the birth of the NEOGRAMMARIAN school, often called the JUNGGRAMMATIKER [yuŋgramaːtikər] in German. The Neogrammarians argued that these phonetic laws operated without exception in a language, and they further argued that the only conditioning factors that could affect the direction a particular sound would take were purely *phonetic* factors. They therefore excluded grammatical or semantic factors from being involved in sound change applying in words referring to trees and plants for example, without applying to all other words. The only factors that could condition a sound change were purely phonetic, i.e. the nature of the preceding and following sounds, the position in the word and so on.

This was a very significant innovation for historical linguistics. Once it was acknowledged that sound change was a regular process, operating without exceptions, then it became possible for the study of etymology, or the study of the history of words (and therefore also of languages) to become SCIENTIFIC (i.e. rigorous and open to proof). Scholars now had a way of arguing scientifically against proposals like those of Etienne Guichard, who tried to relate all languages to Hebrew as we saw earlier. A sound correspondence or similarity between two languages is of *no* value for reconstruction unless it is SYSTEMATIC or REGULAR.

In working out the history of languages, we therefore need to make the important distinction between a SYSTEMATIC or REGULAR SOUND CORRESPONDENCE and an ISOLATED or SPORADIC SOUND CORRESPONDENCE. This is a distinction that we did not make in the previous chapter dealing with the comparative method, and it is very important. We therefore need to introduce between steps two and three of the comparative method as summarised at the end of section 5.2, a further step, which says:

> Separate those correspondences which are systematic from those which are isolated (i.e. occurring in only one or two words) and ignore the isolated correspondences.

Let us look at an example of what we mean by this. In addition to the forms given in Tongan, Samoan, Rarotongan and Hawaiian in chapter five to illustrate the application of the comparative method, let us also add the cognate forms below:

TONGAN	SAMOAN	RAROTONGAN	HAWAIIAN	
paaʔi	paʔi	paki	paʔi	'slap'

If we were to set out the sound correspondences that are involved in this cognate set, then we would have:

$$p = p = p = p$$
$$aa = a = a = a$$
$$ʔ = ʔ = k = ʔ$$
$$i = i = i = i$$

If we compare these correspondences with the correspondences we had already set out at the end of 5.1, then we find that there are actually two completely new correspondences i.e.

$$aa = a = a = a$$
$$ʔ = ʔ = k = ʔ$$

According to step five of the comparative method described in chapter five, we are to assume that each set of correspondences that is not in complementary distribution with any other correspondence must be assumed to go back to a separate original phoneme. However, these correspondences are found in only a single word, so we should ask ourselves the question: is it reasonable to reconstruct new phonemes for these correspondences, which occur in just a single word? Rather than complicate the statement of the phonemes of the original language, what we do is simply *ignore* such isolated correspondences and reconstruct only on the basis of the evidence provided by systematic sound correspondences. We therefore reconstruct the word for 'slap' on the basis of the Samoan, Rarotongan and Hawaiian evidence only, which is quite regular. These forms point to the original form */paki/. We must then state that in Tongan, there have been unpredictable changes of the form:

$$a \rightarrow aa$$
$$k \rightarrow ʔ$$

These changes have taken place in just this single word.

According to the Neogrammarian hypothesis that sound change is without exception, there *must* be an explanation for such 'irregularities' as these irregular Polynesian correspondences. What the Neogrammarians said was that instead of recognising the existence of irregularities, such correspondences must involve some other factors. It could simply be a matter of 'undiscovered regularity'. There may in fact be a regular phonetic conditioning factor which nobody has yet been able to discover. Also, correspondences that seem to be irregular could be explained in other ways too however, and these will be discussed in the following sections.

6.2 Analogy

The term ANALOGY is used in a non-technical sense to mean that we find similarities between things that are not ordinarily regarded as being similar. In presenting an argument, we often 'draw an analogy' to illustrate a new concept, by taking a concept that our audience is already familiar with, and showing how it is similar to the new concept.

For example, if we were explaining the unfamiliar concept of the complementary distribution' of allophones of a phoneme to a beginning student of phonology, we could use an analogy. We might say that complementary distribution can be compared to the relationship between formal and non-formal education. Formal education is carried out only in certain contexts by certain people (i.e. by recognised teachers in schools). Non-formal education is also carried out only in certain contexts (i.e. by our parents, village elders, big-men[1], *didiman*[2] and *didimeri*[2] and so on, and always outside the schools). Similarly, certain allophones of phonemes may occur only in certain phonetic contexts and other allophones in other contexts. Although there is nothing else in common between education and phonemes, we can use the similarity that does exist to illustrate the point.

Analogies can be represented by the formula:

$$A : B :: C : D$$

which is read as:

$$A \text{ is to } B \text{ as } C \text{ is to } D$$

or:

the relationship between A and B is the same as
the relationship between C and D

Using this formula, we can represent the analogy we just presented above as:

formal education	.	informal education	::	one allophone	.	another allophone

or:

the relationship between formal and informal education is the same as the relationship between two allophones of a phoneme

Using the same formula we can express other concepts by means of analogies, i.e.

$$3 : 6 :: 8 : 16 \quad \text{(the concept of 'double')}$$

---

[1] Melanesian men of high social standing within their own communities.

[2] Respectively, male and female agricultural extension officers, employed by the PNG Department of Primary Industry, to improve agricultural production at the village level.

> man : woman :: boy : girl   (the concept of 'sex')
>
> quick : quickly :: good : well   (the concept of 'manner')

(a) Analogical Change by Meaning

Analogy is a very powerful force in language change, and this fact was recognised by the Neogrammarians. Speakers of a language often perceive a partial similarity between two forms on the basis of their *meaning* alone, even when there is no *formal* similarity. To then force the two forms to become phonetically more similar as a result of semantic similarity is change that is brought about by analogy. This can be expressed in terms of the formula we have been using as:

$$\text{meaning}_a : \text{meaning}_b :: \text{form}_a : \text{form}_b$$

Ordinarily, we would expect there to be no relationship between form_a and form_b, even though they are expressing two related meanings, because, as we know, the linguistic sign is arbitrary rather than iconic or natural. However, sometimes similarities in meaning *do* cause words to change so that the forms end up being phonologically closer to each other than before. Let us examine the history of the words for 'four' and 'five' in Latin:

	LATIN	
*kwetwo:res →	kwattwor	'four'
*penkwe →	kwinkwe	'five'

If */penkwe/ had changed regularly in Latin, we would have expected to find /pinkwe/ instead of /kwinkwe/. Why then did */p/ irregularly change to become /kw/? The answer is that on the basis of the similarity in meaning of the two words (i.e. both refer to numbers, one after the other), a similarity is perceived, and speakers of Latin changed one of the forms so that they became more similar in form as well as in meaning. So, on the analogy of */kw-/ initially in the word for 'four, */p-/ became /kw-/ initially in the word for 'five'.

(b) Analogical Change by Form

Analogy need not just take *meaning* as the basis for comparing two forms as is the case in the example we have just looked at. Analogical change can also operate by the perception of partial similarities in *form*, without reference to similarities in meaning. For instance, there was an earlier word *ewt* meaning a kind of lizard in English, which has irregularly become *newt*. It is not a regular change in English for *n-* to be added before a word initial vowel, so we need to find an explanation for this change. Again we can quote analogy as the responsible factor. Look at the following:

name : a name :: ewt : an ewt

On the basis of the similarity in form between 'a name' and 'an ewt' (i.e. there is *n* following the indefinite article in both cases, though this is part of the next word in one case and part of the same word in the other), there has been an analogical change. The result has been that the similarity in the form with the indefinite article (i.e. with the *n*) has been carried over to the form without the indefinite article by adding an *n* before 'ewt'. Thus:

name : a name :: newt : a newt

So, an original partial similarity on the basis of form has been made into a more general similarity.

(c) Folk Etymology

Another kind of analogy that we will consider is often referred to as FOLK ETYMOLOGY or POPULAR ETYMOLOGY. Etymology, as we saw earlier, is the study of the history of words. When we speak of 'folk' etymology, we mean that people who speak a language often make their own guesses about what the history of a word is on the basis of partial similarities to some other words (and in doing this, they obviously have no interest in what the professional etymologist might have to say about the history of the word!). Speakers of the language may then actually *change* the word so that its pro-nunciation comes more into line with their proposed history of the word.

Folk etymology tends to take place in words that are relatively long and in some sense felt to be unusual by speakers of the language. Speakers may then take part of this word, or all of it, and change it so that it looks more like a word they already know, and one that may also be related in meaning in some way. For instance, the word 'crayfish' in English was originally borrowed from the French word *crévisse*. Ordinarily, a word of this form in French would probably have been borrowed into English as something like *creviss* [krɛvəs], and not *crayfish* [krɛfiʃ]. Although this form was a single morpheme, English speakers felt it was long enough and unusual enough in its sound that it must 'really' be two morphemes. Speakers at the time also noted a partial similarity in meaning between *crévisse* and 'fish' (both living in the water), as well as a partial similarity between *-visse* and 'fish'. So, they changed the word *crévisse* to 'crayfish' so that the new pronunciation reflected what they felt to be the history of the word (though professional etymologists deny that the word 'fish' originally had anything to do with this word!).

Other folk etymologies can be seen taking place in the minds of speakers when they make certain 'mistakes' in pronunciation. For example, note the following:

asphalt	ashfelt (for *kolta* or bitumen)
watercress	water grass

While these are nothing but errors at the present, it is possible that they may eventually become accepted right through the English-speaking community, and become fully standardised.

6.3 Spelling Pronunciation

Another factor that can be involved in the creation of irregular sound correspondences is SPELLING PRONUNCIATION. Not all languages that are written have writing systems that accurately reflect the pronunciation, and English is a good example of such a language. We are all aware of the different pronunciations of *gh* in the words 'rough', 'night', 'bough' and 'aghast'. It is possible sometimes for people to pronounce a word according to its spelling, rather than pronouncing it as we would predict from its history. For instance, in English */sy/ sequences have regularly become /ʃ/ by a process of phonological fusion, as shown by words such as the following:

ENGLISH

*syuə	→	ʃoː	'sure'
*syʊgə	→	ʃʊgə	'sugar'

Earlier, words like 'suit', 'consume', 'sue' and so on were also (as we would expect) pronounced with /ʃ/. However, we now pronounce these with /s/ because of the influence of the spelling system. This has therefore produced an irregular set of reflexes in English of earlier */sy/ sequences.

6.4 Borrowing

Linguistic borrowing can also cause sound correspondences to appear irregular or unpredictable. It is possible for a language to borrow a cognate form from another language which has undergone different sound changes. If this happens, it sometimes becomes difficult to establish what the sound correspondences should be. When loan words come from very different languages, this causes few problems as they are usually sufficiently different to be easily recognised. It is when there is borrowing from closely related languages, or even dialects of the same language, that problems arise. In the history of English, this kind of situation has arisen. The regular reflex of */sk/ in English is /ʃ/. The /ʃ/ in words like 'shirt' and 'ship' comes alongside the words 'skirt' (meaning 'dress') and 'skiff' (a kind of sailing boat) in English. Does this mean that */sk/ sporadically became /sk/ in English, while usually becoming /ʃ/? The answer is that */sk/ in fact regularly became /ʃ/, while the /sk/ forms were reintroduced at a later date from Danish (of nearby Denmark) which did not undergo this change. We would therefore need to exclude such words as 'skirt' and 'skiff' if we were trying to reconstruct the phonology of the language from which modern English is derived. The fact that we have a sk = ʃ correspondence between English and Danish as well as a sk = sk correspondence does *not* point to an original new phoneme.

Let us look at another example of the same kind of thing, this time with the examples coming from two languages of Central Province where there are no written records to back up our guesses. The data to be considered is given below:

SINAUGORO	MOTU	
γita	ita	'see'
γutu	utu	'lice'
γate	ase	'liver'
γulita	urita	'octopus'

Sinaugoro	MOTU	
tuliɣa	turia	'bone'
ɣatoi	ɣatoi	'egg'
leɣi	rei	*'kunai* grass'

We can recognise two correspondences involving /ɣ/ in Sinaugoro and Motu:

SINAUGORO	MOTU
ɣ	∅
ɣ	ɣ

Clearly, however, we should be suspicious of the ɣ = ɣ correspondence as we have only a single example. Presumably it would be wiser to regard this as an irregular sporadic correspondence and to ignore it in our reconstruction. Its irregularity could easily be explained by saying that Motu borrowed the Sinaugoro word /ɣatoi/ for 'egg' instead of keeping its own original word /atoi/, which no longer exists in the language.

6.5 Opposition to the Neogrammarian Hypothesis

The basic hypothesis of the Neogrammarians, as we have seen, was that sound changes operate without exception, and that they are subject only to phonetic conditioning factors. Once we exclude irregular sound correspondences caused by analogical change, spelling pronunciation and borrowing, we have the raw materials with which we can scientifically apply the comparative method.

However, the Neogrammarian Hypothesis upon which the comparative method rests, has never been free from attack. Even at the time that it was most forcefully expressed by Brugmann and Leskien in the 1870s, there were opponents in the field of historical linguistics, who claimed that their position was overstated. Even today, the comparative method is generally accepted and applied by historical linguists with results that seem to be fairly realistic and convincing, but there are some scholars who claim that some of the basic assumptions that underlie our application of the comparative method are simply wrong. It is argued that a strict application of this method will not always produce accurate results.

One of the criticisms that the Neogrammarians faced very early on related to their view of how languages diverge. In chapter nine,

135

we speak of SUBGROUPS of languages within larger families. What this means is that we can actually draw family TREES of languages, which may look something like this:

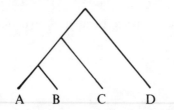

What this diagram means is that languages A and B are more closely related to each other than either of these languages is related to C or D. Similarly, language C is more closely related to languages A and B than it is to D.

This model of language change is essentially the model that we have inherited from the Neogrammarians. It suggests that languages undergo sudden splits into two (or more) quite different daughter languages, and that once these splits have taken place, there is no longer any contact between the new languages. Each new language, it is assumed, then continues completely on its own, undergoing its own completely individual set of changes.

However, many scholars have pointed out that this model of language change is nothing but an unrealistic, highly idealised picture of how languages actually do change. It has been pointed out that languages do not split suddenly. Generally, what happens is that a language develops two closely related dialects, which only very gradually diverge into separate languages. While these dialects are slowly becoming more and more different, there is usually some degree of contact between the two speech communities, often with some kind of influence between the two dialects. Even when the two dialects finally end up as distinct languages (i.e. when speakers have to learn the other speech variety as a separate system in order to be able to understand it), there is often mutual influence.

The Neogrammarian model would also suggest that there are quite discrete or separate areas of linguistic uniformity within language or dialect areas. In reality however, this is almost always not true. Languages are in fact very "un-uniform", and there are often no distinct boundaries between languages or dialects at all. A detailed study of any language area (even very small ones) will generally reveal the existence of a number of DIALECTS, or local varieties of the language. However, dialect boundaries are also often very indistinct. In fact, it is often impossible to say where one dialect begins and the other ends.

We will now look at a particular example to show what we mean. On the island of Paama in Vanuatu, the people speak a single language, the Paamese language, of which there is something like 4,000 speakers. The island itself is quite small, being only about ten kilometres from north to south, and four kilometres from east to west. The total number of villages on the island is twenty. Even within this speech community, which is extremely small by world standards, there is dialect variation. Speakers of the language themselves recognise two dialects, a northern and a southern variety. Some of the differences between these two dialects are illustrated by forms given in Data Set 8. A more detailed statement of the dialect differences can be covered by the observations below:

(a) Sequences of /ei/ and /ou/ in the north correspond to /ai/ and /au/ in the south, e.g.:

NORTH	SOUTH	
eim	aim	'house'
keil	kail	'they'
oul	aul	'maggot'
moul	maul	'alive'

(b) The south often has /l/ where the north has /i/ or zero, e.g.:

NORTH	SOUTH	
amai	amal	'reef'
a:i	a:l	'stinging tree'
tahe	tahel	'wave'
mea	mela	'get up'

(c) The south has initial /g/ and /d/, where the north has initial /k/ and /r/, e.g.:

NORTH	SOUTH	
raho	daho	'he is fat'
rei	dai	'he chopped it'
kea	gela	'he crawled'
keih	gaih	'he is strong'

(d)   The north often has /a/ when the following syllable contains an /a/, where the south has /e/ in the first syllable and /a/ in the second syllable, e.g.:

NORTH	SOUTH	
atau	letau	'woman'
namatil	nematil	'I slept'

(e)   The south has /m/ and /v/ when the north has /mʷ/ and /vʷ/, e.g.:

NORTH	SOUTH	
mʷail	mail	'lefthand side'
mʷeatin	meatin	'man'
vʷe:k	ve:k	'my sleeping place'
vʷakora	vakora	'coconut shell'

In addition to these phonological differences between the two dialects, Paamese speakers are also able to point to numerous lexical and grammatical differences between the northern and southern varieties of the language.

However, the picture is not nearly as simple as this. While the extreme north and the extreme south of this small island *do* differ in the ways that are shown, it is in fact *impossible* to draw a single line that marks the boundary between the two dialects. At this stage, we need to introduce the term ISOGLOSS. An isogloss is a line drawn on a map that marks two areas that differ in one particular linguistic feature. On a map of Paama, it is possible to draw isoglosses for each of these linguistic features. If we do this, we find that while the northern and southern ends of the island *do* have the features we have indicated, the villages of the centre of the island actually share features from both the north and the south. So, for example, the isogloss dividing the features listed under (a), (c) and (e) above is located as follows:

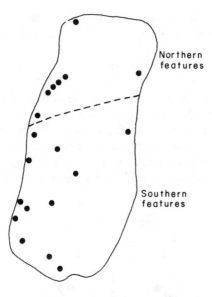

(with each of the dots representing the location of a village), and the isogloss dividing the features listed under (b) and (d) is located as follows:

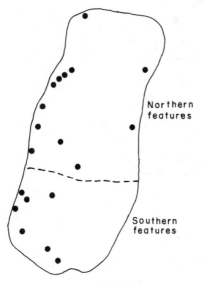

There is therefore clearly no single boundary that can be drawn between the northern and the southern dialects, as the isoglosses do not run together.

The situation is actually even more complicated than this however. In many cases, words seem to behave individually with respect to the phonological features that were mentioned earlier. For instance, the correspondences stated above between southern bilabial consonants and northern labiovelar consonants are grossly oversimplified. The reality of the situation is better shown by breaking these larger areas into much smaller areas. So, on the map below, we can draw isoglosses dividing the island up into six areas, as shown.

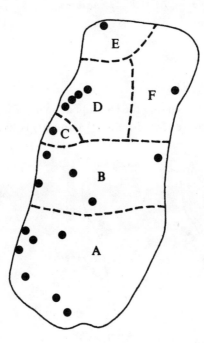

These areas are each characterised by the following facts:

Area A: There are no words containing labiovelar sounds. All words contain only biliabials.

Area B: There are some words with /m^w/, but none with /v^w/. The only words that are consistently pronounced with /m^w/ are:

m^{w}eatin	'man'
m^{w}eahos	'male'

Area C: There are some more words with /m^w/, and a few words with /v^w/. These words include those listed for Area A, and also include the following:

am^{w}e	'married man'
ti:m^{w}e	'friend'
v^{w}e:k	'my sleeping place'

Area D: There are some words with /m^w/, and several more with /v^w/. These include:

m^{w}eas	'dust'
rom^{w}eite	'top of tree'
um^{w}e:n	'work'
v^{w}eav^{w}e	'type of tree'
v^{w}aila	'footprints'

Area E· More words again contain these two sounds. E.g.

m^{w}ail	'lefthand side'
v^{w}alia	'spider'
v^{w}eihat	'coastal rocks'
v^{w}aiteh	'door'

Area F: Yet more words again contain these sounds, which correspond to ordinary bilabials in all of the other areas. E.g.

m^{w}ai	'he straightened it'
v^{w}akora	'coconut shell'
av^{w}e	'bell'

What all of this means is that the simple isogloss we drew earlier, separating the areas that have labiovelars from the areas that do not have labiovelars, represents a gross oversimplification. It can be seen that the labiovelars are in a sense "creeping in", being highest in number in Area F, and lowest in Area A. Which words will have the labiovelars in any particular area is quite unpredictable. Each word, in fact, seems to have its own behaviour. These facts could therefore be set out in the form of separate lexical correspondences between these six "dialects", as shown below:

A	B	C	D	E	F	
meatin	m^{w}eatin	m^{w}eatin	m^{w}eatin	m^{w}eatin	m^{w}eatin	'man'
ame	ame	am^{w}e	am^{w}e	am^{w}e	am^{w}e	'married man'
meas	meas	meas	m^{w}eas	m^{w}eas	m^{w}eas	'dust'
mail	mail	mail	mail	m^{w}ail	m^{w}ail	'lefthand side'
mai	mai	mai	mai	mai	m^{w}ai	'he straightened it'

On the basis of the earlier statement that there was a dialect with words containing labiovelar consonants corresponding to bilabial consonants in the other dialect, we would have suggested, quite reasonably, that the proto-language contained labiovelar consonants in contrast to bilabial consonants. However, if we were to strictly apply the comparative method to the data we have just looked at, we would need to reconstruct for proto-Paamese a separate phoneme for each of the following sound correspondences between the six "dialects":

$$m = m^w = m^w = m^w = m^w = m^w$$
$$m = m = m^w = m^w = m^w = m^w$$
$$m = m = m = m^w = m^w = m^w$$
$$m = m = m = m = m^w = m^w$$
$$m = m = m = m = m = m^w$$
$$m = m = m = m = m = m$$

This would lead us to the ridiculous conclusion that, in addition to the ordinary bilabial consonants represented by the straightforward correspondence:

$$m = m = m = m = m$$

we would also have to reconstruct five other labial nasal phonemes in proto-Paamese!

This brings us to the point where we should mention the French dialectologist Gilliéron, who opposed the point of view of the Neogrammarians late last century, when he said: 'every word has its own history'. What he meant was that sound changes are *not* determined by purely phonetic factors, as the Neogrammarians insisted. Instead, it seems that some words undergo a particular change, while others do not. Which words actually undergo a change can in fact be quite arbitrary, as we have just seen with the Paamese example. This view is therefore totally incompatible with a strict application of the comparative method, which considers only sound correspondences that operate generally in the vocabularies of two (or more) languages.

This model of linguistic change is often referred to as the WAVE MODEL, in contrast to the FAMILY TREE MODEL. The wave model implies that instead of sharp linguistic splits, linguistic changes take place like waves spreading outward from the place where a stone is dropped into water, travelling different distances in different words, and crossing with waves from other stones. So, instead of the tree-type diagram presented earlier, this model can be represented in the following form:

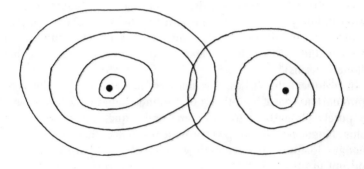

That is to say, a change may apply in some words to a certain distance from the starting point of the dispersal, and it may apply to a smaller set of words further from the dispersal point. In the Paamese case we have been looking at, the dispersal point is very clearly Area F. This is the area in which there is the greatest number of words with the labiovelar sounds, while as we move further and further from this area, the number of words containing these sounds decreases, until we get to Area A, in which there are no labiovelars at all.

Another criticism of the Neogrammarian Hypothesis has been made in more recent decades, and this criticism is of a quite different kind to the criticism we have just looked at, involving questions of dialect geography. Linguists in the first half of the twentieth century inherited from the Neogrammarians a belief in the "strict separation of levels" in linguistic analysis. That is to say, when we are looking at phonology, the only facts that linguists should be allowed to deal with are purely phonetic facts. Considerations from other 'levels' such as grammar and semantics should be excluded, and considered irrelevant in the statement of the distribution of the allophones. According to linguists who hold this view, historical sound changes should be described only with phonetic conditioning factors. Sound changes could never be conditioned by grammatical, or semantic factors, it was claimed. This view of phonology is often called AUTONOMOUS PHONEMICS, because phonemics is supposed to be completely autonomous, or independent of all kinds of facts except facts from its own 'level'.

Recently, linguists have questioned the strict separation of levels insisted upon by earlier linguists. In particular, it makes it much easier in many cases to state the distribution of allophones of phonemes if we are allowed to use terms like 'morpheme boundary' or 'word boundary' (which are clearly grammatical terms rather than phonetic terms).

In historical linguistics, this question has also caused the Neogrammarians' basic hypothesis that sound changes are conditioned by purely phonetic factors to come under question. It seems that some languages do in fact provide evidence that some sound changes do apply only in certain word classes (or "parts of speech") and not in others. If this is the case, then we very clearly have an example of grammatical conditioning of sound change rather than purely phonetic conditioning of sound change.

We can give Paamese again, as an example of a language that has undergone a grammatically conditioned sound change. We mentioned earlier the correspondence of southern Paamese /l/ to northern Paamese /ø/ or /i/. The southern varieties directly reflect the forms in proto-Paamese with respect to this feature, with the northern areas having undergone the following changes:

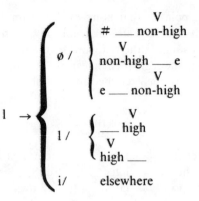

That is:

(a) */l/ was deleted initially before the vowels */e/, */a/ and */o/, and medially between */e/ and any of these vowels, e.g.

		NORTHERN PAAMESE	
*leiai	→	eiai	'bush'
*alete	→	aet	'flat area'
*melau	→	meau	'scrub turkey'

(b) */l/ remained unchanged when it was preceded or followed by a high vowel, in any position of the word, e.g.

		NORTHERN PAAMESE	
*asilati	→	asilat	'worm'
*haulue	→	houlu	'many'
*teilaɲi	→	teilaŋ	'sky'
*ahilu	→	ahil	'hair'
*tahule	→	tahul	'rubbish'

(c) Elsewhere, */l/ changed to /i/, e.g.

		NORTHERN PAAMESE	
*la:la	→	a:ia	'bird species'
*malou	→	maiou	'kava'
*meta:lo	→	meta:io	'European'
*to:lau	→	to:iau	'northeast wind'
*amalo	→	amai	'reef'
*avolo	→	avoi	'mushroom'

145

The interesting point is that none of the examples we have just looked at involve verbs. Verbs, it seems, always retain an original */l/ in initial position (although word medially and finally, */l/ in verbs is subject to the regular changes). So, note the following examples where */l/ has been retained instead of being dropped as we would predict:

	NORTHERN PAAMESE	
*leheie	→ lehei	'he pulled it'
*loho	→ loh	'run'
*la:po	→ la:po	'fall over'

This is therefore a clear example of a sound change that involves grammatical conditioning, as well as phonological conditioning. (We will also see later in chapter ten, that sound changes do not affect all words of a particular phonetic type as the Neogrammarians claimed. Sound changes 'creep' through the vocabulary, affecting some words first, and other words later. The changes involving Paamese labiovelars that we looked at in this chapter also showed this.)

READING GUIDE QUESTIONS
1. What is the basic difference between the study of etymology before the Neogrammarians and the present day?
2. What was the importance of Sir William Jones statement in 1786 for the study of the history of languages?
3. What important contribution did Jakob Grimm make to the study of the history of languages?
4. What was the importance of Verner's and Grassmann's discoveries in the history of the Germanic languages?
5. What was the 'Neogrammarian Hypothesis'? How did the neogrammarian view of language change differ from the view of language change proposed by Grimm?
6. What do we mean by the terms 'systematic sound correspondence' and 'sporadic sound correspondence'?
7. How does the existence of sporadic sound correspondences affect the way we apply the comparative method?
8. What is analogical sound change? How can it affect the way we apply the comparative method?
9. In what way can meaning influence the direction of a sound change?

10. What is folk etymology?
11. What is spelling pronunciation?
12. What is borrowing? How can borrowing cause sound correspondences between languages to become unpredictable?
13. How does the wave model of linguistic change differ from the family tree model?
14. What is an isogloss? What is significant about the fact that isoglosses do not always coincide (and sometimes even cross over each other)?
15. What is autonomous phonemics and what impact did its acceptance have on the way linguists viewed language change?

EXERCISES

1. Papua New Guineans speaking English as a second language have been occasionally making 'errors' like the following in their speech:

hibiscus	hibiscuit
pandanus	panda nuts
lingua franca	lingo franco

(Another example of the same thing, but involving a spelling change rather than a change in pronunciation is:

surname	sir name)

What factor is responsible for these unpredictable phonetic changes in the English of people who might say these things?

2. People for whom English is their mother tongue normally pronounce the words 'gibberish' and 'gesture' as:

dʒɪbərɪʃ
dʒɛstʃə

What factor is responsible for the very common pronunciation of these two words by many Papua New Guineans in the following ways?

gɪbərɪʃ
gɛstʃə

3. The English word 'ambassador', when taken into Tok Pisin, would normally be expected to become *embesada*. Some speakers actually say *embesirep* instead. Why?

FURTHER READING

1. Kenyon, John Samuel. 'Spelling Pronunciation', in Anderson and Stageberg (eds) *Introductory Readings in Language*, pp. 248-254.
2. Nida, Eugene. 'Analogical Change', in Anderson and Stageberg (eds) *Introductory Readings in Language*, pp. 86-92.
3. Bloomfield, Leonard. *Language* (Chapter 23 'Analogic Change'), pp.404-424.
4. Bynon, Theodora. *Historical Linguistics* (Chapter 4 'The Neogrammarian Postulates and Dialect Geography'), pp. 173-197.
5. Bynon, Theodora. *Historical Linguistics* (Chapter 6 'Contact between Languages'), pp. 217-239.
6. Jespersen, Otto. *Language: Its Nature, Development and Origin* (Chapters 1-4 'History of Linguistic Science'), pp. 19-102.

Chapter Seven
INTERNAL RECONSTRUCTION

In chapter five, we learned how to apply the comparative method to reconstruct an earlier unrecorded language, by comparing the forms in the various daughter languages that are descended from this original language. In chapter six we introduced a number of refinements to our application of the method, so that we could recognise (and exclude from consideration) various 'irregular' or problematic forms.

The comparative method is not the only method, however, which we can use to reconstruct linguistic history. There is a second method, called INTERNAL RECONSTRUCTION, which allows us to make guesses about the history of a language as well. The basic difference between the two methods is that in the case of internal reconstruction, we reconstruct only on the basis of evidence *within* a *single* language, rather than on the basis of evidence from *several* separate languages (or dialects) as in the comparative method. With the comparative method, we arrive at a proto-language, from which two languages or dialects are derived, while with the internal method of reconstruction, we simply arrive at an earlier stage of the language, between a reconstructible proto-language and the descendant languages. We can call this reconstructed language a PRE-LANGUAGE.

The internal method of reconstruction clearly does not take us as far back in time as the comparative method. Before going on to look at how to apply this method, we should perhaps look at the kinds of situations in which we might want to use it:

(a) Sometimes, the language we are investigating may be an ISO-LATE, i.e. it may not be related to any other language (and is therefore in a family all of its own). In such a case, there is no possibility of applying the comparative method (as there is nothing to compare it with). Internal reconstruction is therefore the only possibility that is available.

(b) A very similar situation to this would be one in which the language we are studying is so distantly related to its sister languages that the comparative method is unable to reveal very much about its history.

(c) We may want to know something about changes that have taken place *between* a reconstructed proto-language and its descendant languages.

(d) Finally, we may want to try to reconstruct further back still from a proto-language that has been arrived at by the comparative method. There is no reason why we cannot apply the method of internal reconstruction to a proto-language, the same as any other language, to go back even further in time.

The Dutch linguist van der Tuuk once said: 'All languages are something of a ruin'. What he meant was that as a result of changes having taken place, some 'residual' forms are often left to suggest what the original state of affairs might have been. Applying the method of internal reconstruction is in some sense similar to the science of archaeology. In archaeology we use the evidence of the present (i.e. buried remains of earlier times) to reconstruct something of the past. Archaeology does not enable us to reconstruct *everything* about the past - only those facts which are suggested by the present-day 'ruins' from the past.

Let us look at an example of a linguistic change that has taken place in a language and see what sorts of 'ruins' it leaves in the modern language. The language we will look at is Samoan. This is a language that has verbs which appear in both intransitive and transitive forms. The intransitive form (used when there is no following object noun phrase) is expressed by using the bare root of the verb, while the transitive form (used when there is a following object noun phrase) is expressed by adding a suffix to the root.[1] This

---

[1] The function of this suffix in Samoan has actually been the subject of a great deal of debate among linguists. Some have suggested that it should be called instead a passive suffix, while others have said that its function is to indicate some specific control that the subject has over the object. For our purposes the *function* of this particular suffix is not important, as we are only considering its *form*.

situation parallels the situation in Tok Pisin where intransitive verbs use the root form and transitive verbs take the suffix /-im/, e.g.

> *Kar bilong mi i*   *bagarap*
> car of   I verb marker   broken down
> 'My car is broken down.'

> *Husat i*   *bagarapim*   *kar bilong   mi*
> who verb marker break down-trans car of   I
> 'Who damaged my car?'

In Hiri Motu too, the same function is marked on verbs by the suffix /-a/, e.g.

> Ṭura, oi   aniani
> friend you eat-reduplication
> 'Friend, have something to eat.'

> *Biku   lau ura   ania*   *lasi*
> Banana I   want eat-trans not
> 'I don't want to eat banana.'

In Samoan, different verbs take different suffixes to mark the transitive form, as shown by the following examples:

INTRANSITIVE	TRANSITIVE	
inu	inu-mia	'drink'
ŋau	ŋau-sia	'break'
mataʔu	mataʔu-tia	'fear'
taŋi	taŋi-sia	'weep'
alofa	alofa-ŋia	'love'
fua	fua-tia	'weigh'
ole	ole-ŋia	'cheat'
sila	sila-fia	'see'

The fact that modern Samoan has a variety of suffixes to mark the same function, i.e. /-mia/, /-sia/, /-tia/, /-ŋia/ and /-fia/, is a result of a sound change having taken place between pre-Samoan and modern Samoan. From comparative evidence, we know that the verb roots of Samoan originally mostly ended in consonants, and that the transitive form of the verb was marked by simply adding /-ia/ (which is very similar to the /-a/ suffix of Motu, a language which is related to Samoan). The final consonants of Samoan were then all lost by regular sound change of the form:

$$C \rightarrow \emptyset / \underline{\hspace{2cm}} \#$$

The forms of the original final consonants in some of the intransitive verbs given above is clearly indicated by the cognate forms in Bahasa Indonesia, where the final consonants were retained:

SAMOAN	BAHASA INDONESIA	
inu	minum	'drink'
mataʔu	takut	'fear'
taŋi	taŋis	'weep'

In early Samoan, the consonants were still to be found in word final position, and the transitive suffix was simply /-ia/. When the word final consonants were lost, they disappeared in the intransitive verb forms, but were retained in the transitive verb forms, because, with the addition of the suffix /-ia/, the consonants were now in the middle of the word rather than at the end. Now that in Samoan there were no longer any word final consonants, the consonants that were retained in the transitive forms came to be reanalysed as part of the suffix instead of being part of the root. So, what was originally a single suffix has now developed a wide range of different forms, or ALLOMORPHS, as a result of a sound change having taken place. These allomorphs are morphologically conditioned allomorphs, which means that each verb must be learnt with its particular transitive suffix.

This change can actually be reconstructed without reference to any of the other languages that are related to Samoan, i.e. it can be reconstructed entirely on internal evidence. What we do when we apply the method of internal reconstruction is to look at cases of morphological alternants (or ALLOMORPHS of MORPHEMES), and we work on the assumption that unusual or complex distributions of allomorphs of morphemes may well go back to a simpler state of affairs, and that the complexity we see is a result of sound change having taken place. The distribution of the differing forms of the transitive suffix in Samoan is extremely complex (and every intransitive verb must simply be learned along with its transitive counterpart as there are no general rules that can be used), so we could assume that in pre-Samoan, the language was more 'learnable' and that this earlier system has 'broken down' because of some sound change having taken place. The unpredictability lies not in the vowel of the transitive suffix as this is always /-ia/: it is therefore the preceding consonant that needs explanation. If we assume that the consonants were originally part of the root, and that there was a later loss of final consonants, then this gives a very simple picture of pre-Samoan morphology, with a very natural sound change having taken place (i.e. loss of final consonants). So earlier in Samoan, the intransitive/transitive pairs would have looked like this:

INTRANSITIVE	TRANSITIVE	
*inum	*inum-ia	'drink'
*ŋaus	*ŋaus-ia	'break'
*mataʔut	*mataʔut-ia	'fear'
*taŋis	*taŋis-ia	'weep'
*alofaŋ	*alofaŋ-ia	'love'
*fuat	*fuat-ia	'weigh'
*oleŋ	*oleŋ-ia	'cheat'
*silaf	*silaf-ia	'see'

A comparison of the statements of the rule for deriving the transitive form of the verb from the intransitive form at the two stages of the history of the language clearly shows that the reconstructed pre-rule is much less complex:

I.   Pre-Samoan: add suffix /-ia/ to intransitive form
II.   Modern Samoan: add one of the following suffixes, according to the class of the particular verb:
-mia, -sia, -tia, nja or -fia

153

7. Internal Reconstruction

Let us look again at some German data, relating to the change of final devoicing that we looked at in chapter two. In modern German, the plural of certain nouns is formed by adding the plural suffix /-ə/. With other nouns, the plural is formed by:

(a) adding /-ə/
(b) changing final voiceless consonants to voiced consonants

Thus:

SINGULAR	PLURAL	
laut	laut-ə	'sound'
boːt	boːt-ə	'boat'
taːk	taːg-ə	'day'
hunt	hund-ə	'dog'

Here again, we have a case of complexity in the morphological alternations, and we should ask ourselves if this complexity could reasonably be derived from an earlier more simple way of forming the plural. The suffix /-ə/ is common to all forms, so we can assume this to be original. We note, however, that some plurals have voiced consonants and some have voiceless consonants, while the singular forms have only voiceless consonants. If we assume that the plural roots represent the original roots, then we can say that the singular forms have undergone a change of final devoicing:

$$\begin{matrix} C \\ \text{voiced} \end{matrix} \rightarrow \begin{matrix} C \\ \text{voiceless} \end{matrix} / \underline{\hspace{1cm}} \#$$

Clearly, the consonants in the plural would have been 'protected' from this rule by the presence of the following plural suffix.

It should be pointed out that not *all* cases of morphological alternation can be reconstructed as going back to a single original form that 'split' as a result of sound change taking place. The important point to keep in mind is that the modern alternations must be derivable from the reconstructions by means of reasonable kinds of sound changes. So, while we might want to reconstruct the /-s/, /-z/ and /-əz/ markers of the plural of English nouns as going back to

154

a single original form of their phonetic similarity, we would be unlikely to reconstruct irregular plurals such as the following as being derived from the same original suffix (whatever we may reconstruct it as):

SINGULAR	PLURAL
foot	feet
goose	geese
man	men
woman	women
child	children
louse	lice

These must presumably be reconstructed as going back to irregular forms even in pre-English.

READING GUIDE QUESTIONS

1. What is the difference between the comparative method and the method of internal reconstruction?

2. When might we want to use internal reconstruction instead of the comparative method?

3. What is a language isolate?

4. What sort of data do we take as the basis for applying the method of internal reconstruction?

5. What assumption do we operate under when we apply the internal method of reconstruction?

6. Can all cases of morphological alternation be reconstructed as resulting from sound changes having taken place?

EXERCISES

1. The comparative method and the method of internal reconstruction appear to be quite different. Can you find any *similarities* between the two methods?

2. Examine the following forms in southern Paamese (Vanuatu) and use the method of internal reconstruction to recreate the original root forms of the words below, and state what changes have taken place.

	FREE FORM	THIS X	ONLY X	
1.	aim	aimok	aimos	'house'
2.	ahat	ahatuk	ahatus	'stone'
3.	molatin	molatinek	molatines	'person'
4.	ahin	ahinek	ahines	'woman'
5.	atin	atinuk	atinus	'aibika /bush vegetable'
6.	atas	atasik	atasis	'sea'
7.	metas	metasok	metasos	'spear'
8.	ahis	ahisik	ahisis	'banana'
9.	ahis	ahisuk	ahisus	'rifle'

3. Examine the data below from Bislama (Vanuatu Pidgin). In Bislama, there are two forms of adjectives, one called the "attributive" form, which is used when it precedes a noun in a noun phrase. e.g.

> *Hemi i   wan bikfala   man*
> he   verb marker indef big-attributive man
> 'He is a big man.'

and the other is called the "predicative" form, which is used when the adjective is used as an adverb or in a predicate. e.g.

> *Hemi   i   singaut bikwan*
> s/he   verb marker shout   big-predicative
> 'S/he shouted loudly.'

> *Haus blong hem i   bikwan*
> house of   s/he verb marker big predicative
> 'Her/his house is big.'

The attributive and predicative forms differ in that they are marked by different suffixes, as the following examples show.

156

	ATTRIBUTIVE	PREDICATIVE	
1.	bikfala	bikwan	'big'
2.	sotfala	sotwan	'short'
3.	smolvala	smolwan	'small'
4.	retfala	retwan	'red'
5.	gutfala	gutwan	'good'
6.	niuvala	niuwan	'new'
7.	yangvala	yangwan	'young'
8.	naisfala	naiswan	'nice'

Using the method of internal reconstruction, can you reconstruct the form of the attributive suffix in pre-Bislama?

4. The plural in English is regularly expressed by adding one of the following suffixes:

(a) /-s/ after nouns ending in voiceless non-sibilants, e.g. 'cake', 'ship', 'death', 'dock', 'gift'.

(b) /-z/ after nouns ending in voiced non-sibilants, e.g. 'sin', 'fever', 'piano', 'cab', 'dog', 'wave'.

(c) /-əz/ after nouns ending in sibilants, e.g. 'bus', 'dish', 'wage', 'stitch'.

What do you think the regular plural marking in pre-English might have been and why?

5. Examine the following Huli (Southern Highlands) numerals, given in their unsuffixed form used in counting, and their ordinal forms (i.e first, second, third ...). Reconstruct the original ordinal suffix and the changes that have taken place.

	BASE	ORDINAL	
1.	tebo	tebone	'3'
2.	ma	mane	'4'
3.	dau	dauni	'5'
4.	waraga	waragane	'6'
5.	ka	kane	'7'

    6.   hali   halini   '8'
    7.   di   dini   '9'
    8.   pi   pini   '10'
    9.   hombe(a) hombe (a)ne '11'

6. Use the method of internal reconstruction to reconstruct the original roots and the active and passive prefixes from the data below in Bahasa Indonesia.

	ACTIVE	PASSIVE	
1.	membuka	dibuka	'open'
2.	mendapat	didapat	'get'
3.	meɲjelaskan	dijelaskan	'explain'
4.	meŋgosok	digosok	'rub'
5.	memerlukan	diperlukan	'need'
6.	menanam	ditanam	'plant'
7.	meɲerahkan	diserahkan	'surrender'
8.	meŋaraŋ	dikaraŋ	'compose'
9.	meɲurus	diurus	'arrange'
10.	meŋeja	dieja	'spell'
11.	meɲambil	diambil	'take'
12.	meɲikat	diikat	'tie'
13.	meɲerikan	diŋerikan	'give a fright'
14.	meŋhapuskan	dihapuskan	'wipe'

7. Examine the following data from Huli (Southern Highlands) and reconstruct the original roots and the original pronominal suffixes and state what changes have taken place.

	present	past	plural imperative	
I	ebero	ibiru		
you	ebere	ibiri	ibidaba	'come'
he	ibira	ibiya		
I	laro	laru		
you	lare	lari	ladaba	'speak'
he	lare	laya		

I	wero	wiru		
you	were	wiri	widaba	'put'
he	wira	wiya		

I	homaro	homaru		
you	homare	homari	homadaba	'die'
he	homara	homaya		

I	biraro	biraru		
you	birare	birari	biradaba	'sit'
he	birara	biraya		

8. In the Muruwari language of northwestern New South Wales, nouns which are functioning as the subject of a transitive verb take the following suffixes:

1. gudařa-ŋgu   'child'
2. mayɲd̪u   'person'
3. gaṇ-ḍu   'snake'
4. gandal-u   'dog'
5. gula-ŋgu   'kangaroo'
6. guyu-ŋgu   'fish'
7. duři-ŋgu   'sun'
8. waɲiɲ-ḍu   'lightning'

Can you suggest a reasonable original form (or forms) for the suffix that would account for |the diversity of the allomorphs in Muruwari?

FURTHER READING

1. Lehmann, Winfred P. *Historical Linguistics: An Introduction* (Chapter 6 'The Method of Internal Reconstruction'), pp. 99-106.

2. Anttila, Raimo. *An Introduction to Historical and Comparative Linguistics* (Chapter 12 'Internal Reconstruction'), pp. 264-73.

Chapter Eight

GRAMMATICAL AND SEMANTIC CHANGE

So far in this textbook, we have been dealing almost entirely with questions to do with sound change. There is more to a language than sounds however. We also have to consider the grammar of the language, i.e. the ways in which units of meaning are put together to make up larger units of meaning. Grammar is traditionally divided into morphology (i.e. the ways in which words are made up of smaller grammatical elements — morphemes) and syntax (i.e. the way words are combined with other words to form larger elements — sentences). The grammatical rules of a language are what link sounds to meanings. In talking about a language, we must also talk about the kinds of meaning that are expressed, i.e. the semantic system. Just as languages change in their sound systems, they can also change in their grammatical systems and their semantic systems. It is the purpose of this chapter to introduce the kinds of changes that take place in morphology, syntax and semantics.

In this textbook, there is a heavy concentration on the study of sound change, with comparatively little emphasis on grammar and semantics. This is no accident. The study of sound change has a long history, going back to before the Neogrammarians, over 150 years ago. Scholars have therefore had lots of time to gather all kinds of information on sound change. Not only this, but it is probably inherently easier anyway to study the changes to the sound system of a language compared to its grammatical and semantic systems. The number of individual phonemes in a language ranges from around about a dozen or so in some languages, to seventy or eighty at the very most in other languages. The range of possible variations and changes in the phonology is much more restricted than in the grammatical system of a language, where there may be dozens and dozens (or even hundreds) of grammatical categories; not only that, we also have to consider the existence of thousands of particular syntactic constructions for any language. Also, when considering the semantic system of a language, the number of semantic relations that hold between different items in the lexicon would be so huge that it would be almost uncountable. So, it is not really surprising that we know more about phonological change than we know about grammatical and semantic change.

161

8.1 Grammatical Change

Languages of the world can be classified according to their grammatical TYPOLOGY. A typological classification of languages is one that looks for certain features of a language and groups that language with another language that share the same features. A typological classification differs fundamentally from a genetic classification of languages. The two may coincide in some particular case, but this will not always be so. In the following chapter, we talk about subgrouping of languages, and we will see that some similarities between languages are not the result of genetic relationship at all, but may be the result of the two languages having both undergone the same kind of change. The result of this is that two languages may share the same feature, yet they are not genetically of the same group. However, if they share the same feature, then we *can* say that they belong to the same typological group.

Typological groupings of languages can be quite independent of genetic groupings as we have just said. A language can belong to only one genetic group, but it can belong to different typological groups, depending on what particular features we are looking at. For instance, English and Tolai belong to the same typological group if we consider the shared feature of basic word order, i.e. SUBJECT + VERB + OBJECT. Tolai and Motu however (though they are genetically both Austronesian languages), belong to different typological groups, as Motu has the basic word order SUBJECT + OBJECT + VERB. If we look at a different feature however, we can group Tolai and Motu together typologically, with English belonging to a different typological group. For instance, both Tolai and Motu have pronominal suffixes to mark possession on noun phrases, whereas in English possession is marked by free form pronouns. So, we find Tolai forms as:

> *bilau-gu*
> nose my
> 'my nose'

and Motu forms as:

> *idu-gu*
> nose my
> 'my nose'

contrasting with the English structure.

Typological groupings of languages can be based on whatever features we want to base them on. Some shared features would seem to be of little significance however, while other shared features are of much greater interest. In the study of grammatical change, what linguists basically do is to look at how languages change from one grammatical typology to another. We will now look at some of the major grammatical typologies, and see how the languages in these typological groups have got to be that way, or how they might change their typology in the future.

(a) Morphological Type

Languages can be grouped typologically according to what we might want to call their MORPHOLOGICAL TYPE, i.e. the way in which the significant features of their grammars are expressed morphologically.

The first type of language that we can talk about is the ISOLATING type of language. An isolating language is one in which there tends to be only one morpheme per word — there are many free morphemes, with very few bound morphemes. A language of this type would be Hiri Motu. If we take the sentence:

Lauegu	*sinana*	*gwarume*	*ta*	*ia*	*hoia*	*Koki*	*dekenai*
my	mother	fish	one	she	buy	Koki	at

'My mother bought a fish at Koki.'

we can see that each word expresses one meaning and one meaning only.

A second type of language is what we call the AGGLUTINATING type. An agglutinating language is one in which a word may contain many morphemes, but the boundaries are clear and easy to recognise. It is as if the bits of the language were simply 'glued' together to make larger words. Each morpheme still expresses a single meaning, but each word has several meanings contained in it. A language like Bandjalang (of northern New South Wales) is agglutinating in its type. So look at the following sentence:

Mali-yu	*baygal-u*	*mala*	*ɖa:ɖam*	*buma-ni-ɖa: ɲ*	:
the actor	man actor	the	child	hit past	really

'The man really hit the child.'

163

The word /bumaniɖa:ŋ/, for instance, expresses three meanings, firstly the idea of 'hitting' in the root /buma-/, secondly the idea that the event took place sometime in the past. i.e. /-ni/, and thirdly the idea that the event really took place, i.e. /-ɖa:ŋ/. These three meanings are expressed by simply attaching the suffixes to the root in sequence.

A third type of language that we can consider is the INFLECTIONAL type. Inflectional languages are those in which there are many morphemes included within a single word, but where the boundaries between one morpheme and another are not clear. So, in inflectional languages, there are many meanings per word, but there is not the clear 'gluing' together of morphemes as is the case with agglutinating languages. An example of an inflecting language is French. Examine the following sentence:

> *Marsɛl ɛm   Sofi*
> Marcel loves   Sophie
> 'Marcel loves Sophie.'

The verb /ɛm/ contains the following four meanings:
- (a)   the idea of 'loving'
- (b)   the fact that the event takes place in the present tense
- (c)   the fact that the subject is in the third person
- (d)   the fact that the subject is singular

If any of these meanings were to be changed, the verb would take a different form from this, e.g.

> *Vuz ɛmǝre   Sofi*
> you will love   Sophie
> 'You will love Sophie.'

In this sentence, the difference in the verb arises because the following meanings are expressed:
- (a)   the idea of 'loving'
- (b)   the fact that the event will take place in the future
- (c)   the fact that the subject is in the second person
- (d)   the fact that the subject is plural

However, we cannot draw boundaries between the various 'bits' of the verb form /ɛmǝre/. Although there is clearly an extra /-ǝre/ in the second example, this suffix expresses the ideas in (b), (c) and

(d) all together. We cannot say that the idea of (b) is expressed by the initial schwa of the suffix for example.

There is a tendency for languages to change typologically according to a kind of cycle. Isolating languages tend to move towards agglutinating structures. Agglutinating languages tend to move towards the inflectional type, and finally, inflecting languages tend to become less inflectional and more isolating. 'This cycle can be represented by the following diagram:

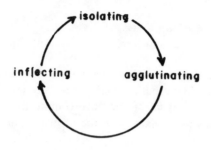

Isolating languages become agglutinating in structure by a process of PHONOLOGICAL REDUCTION. Free form grammatical markers may become phonologically reduced to unstressed bound form markers (i.e. suffixes or prefixes). If we look at modern Tok Pisin for example, as it is spoken rather than as it is written, we can see that a number of grammatical changes appear to be taking place. Firstly, we find that the prepositions *long* and *bilong* are tending to be pronounced nowadays as prefixes to the following noun phrases. The forms of these prefixes are:

> lo-/blo- before consonants
> l-/bl- before vowels

So, we find forms like the following:

> *Em kar bilong mi*
> that car of   I

which becomes:

Em kar blomi
'That is my car.'

and:

Em stap long aus
s/he is in   house

which becomes:

Em stap laus
'S/he is at home'

Not only are the prepositions being phonologically reduced in this way, but also the verbal auxiliaries *save* 'do habitually', *laik* 'want to/is going to' and *bai* 'future' are coming to be attached to the following verb as prefixes, with the forms *sa-*, *la-* and *ba-* respectively, e.g:

Em no   save   waswas
S/he not   habitual wash

becomes:

Em no sawaswas
'S/he never washes.'

and:

Yu laik   go we?
you are going go where

becomes:

Yu lago we?
'Where are you going to go?'

Languages which belong to the agglutinating type tend to change towards the inflectional type. By the process of MORPHOLOGICAL FUSION, two originally clearly divisible morphemes in a word may change in such a way that the boundary is no longer clearly recognisable. We could exemplify this process of morphological fusion by looking at the following example from Paamese (spoken in Vanuatu). The original marker of a first person singular subject on verbs can be reconstructed as */na-/, and the second person singular subject marker can be reconstructed as */ko-/, and these are the forms still found in Paamese, e.g:

> *na- lesi- ɸ*
> I   see   it
> 'I see it'

> *ko- lesi- nau*
> you see me
> 'You see me.'

Other tenses, as well as the negative, are expressed by adding prefixes and suffixes in sequences, e.g.

> *ko- va-   ro- lesi- tei- nau*
> you are going not see not me
> 'You are not going to see me.'

The future tense was also originally marked in this way, by a prefix of the form */i-/, which appeared after the subject marker. This future tense marker has fused morphologically with the preceding subject marker in the modern language however, so we now get the form /ni-/ to mark the first person singular future form, and /ki-/ marks the second person future form, e.g:

> *ni-lesi-ɸ*
> 'I will see it'

> *ki-lesi-nau*
> 'You will see me'

We cannot divide the /ni-/ and the /ki-/ into a subject marker and a future tense marker as we can in the other examples we looked at, because the forms /n-/ or /k-/, and /i-/ do not occur elsewhere in the language as recognisable morphemes. We must therefore speak of indivisible morphemes that express two meanings at once (which we call PORTMANTEAU morphemes). This situation has arisen as a result of the fusion of two originally separate morphemes into one. When this kind of fusion affects the grammar of the language in a major way, then the language can be said to have changed from an agglutinating type to an inflectional type.

Finally, languages of the inflectional type tend to change to the isolating type, and the process that is involved is MORPHOLOGICAL REDUCTION. Very commonly in languages, inflectional morphemes tend to become more and more reduced, until they disappear altogether. The resulting forms once again consist of a single morpheme. The functions that were originally expressed by the inflectional suffixes then come to be expressed by word order or by free form morphemes. Latin was a highly inflectional language. So many ideas were contained in a single word that there was no need for word order to be fixed. Words could occur in any order because the one that was doing an action and the one that was receiving an action was marked on the noun phrase itself. So:

> *Markellus   amat Sofiam*
> Mark-doer love Sophie-receiver
> 'Mark loves Sophie'

could be expressed equally well as:

> *Amat Sofiam Markellus*

or:

> *Sofiam amat Markellus*

or even:

> *Sofiam Markellus amat*

To indicate the fact that the roles are reversed in this situation, we need to change the marking on the nouns. So:

> *Sofia   amat Markellum*
> Sophie-doer loves Mark-receiver
> 'Sophie loves Mark'

This can also be expressed in the following ways without changing the basic meaning:

Sofia Markellum amat
Amat Sofia Markellum
Markellum Sofia amat

Latin evolved into modern Italian, and in the process lost a lot of its original inflections. (The language therefore moved towards the isolating type.) Nouns are no longer marked to indicate whether they are performing an action or receiving an action, as they do not change in form like they did in Latin. To express the first meaning in Italian, we can only say:

Marcello ama   Sofia
Mark   loves Sophie
'Mark loves Sophie.'

Whereas in Latin, we could change the order of these words without changing the basic meanings, this is not possible in Italian. If we change this sentence to:

Sofia ama Marcello
Sophie loves Mark

we change the meaning to:

'Sophie loves Mark.'

It is now word order which marks the difference between the subject and the object of a verb, whereas before it was the presence of a particular inflection on the noun.

This typological cycle, and the processes involved in this transition from one type to another, are presented in the following diagram:

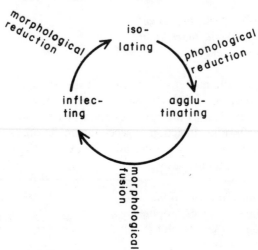

(b) Accusative and Ergative

Languages of the world can be grouped typologically according to the way they mark the basic subject and object noun phrases in a sentence. In a language like English, we speak of the SUBJECT of a verb, and the OBJECT. The subject is the noun phrase that comes before the verb, and which causes the verb to choose between the '-s' singular form and the '-ø' plural form in the third person present tense. The object is the noun phrase that comes after the verb, and it does not affect the verb whether it is singular or plural. So, we have sentences like these:

The Vice-Chancellor	*likes*	{ *the student* { *the students*
SUBJECT(singular)	VERB(singular)	OBJECT
The Vice-Chancellors	*are praying*	
SUBJECT(plural)	VERB(plural)	

There are other languages however, which differ from English in the way the subject and object noun phrases are marked. Look at the following sentences in Bandjalang:

Mali-yu   baygal -u   mala   ḍa:ḍam buma-ni
the   man   the   child hit   past
'The man hit the child.'

Mala baygal gaware   -:la
the   man   run away   present
'The man is running away.'

Mali-yu ḍa:ḍam-bu mala baygal ɲa:-ni
the   child   the   man   see past
'The child saw the man.'

You will see that the noun /baygal/ 'man' actually appears in two separate forms, either /baygalu/ with the suffix /-u/, or just as /baygal/, with no suffix. (Note that the accompanying word for 'the' also varies in its form, and it appears as either /maliyu/ or as /mala/). The form with the suffix /-u/ is found when the noun is the subject of the transitive verb /buma/ 'hit'. When the noun is the subject of the intransitive verb /gaware/ 'run away', the noun /baygal/ has the same form as when it is the object of the transitive verb /ɲa:/'see'.

If you compare English and Bandjalang, what you will find is that there are three basic grammatical functions that are being expressed in both languages, but in different ways in both cases. In English, we have:

intransitive subject
transitive subject

being marked in the same way, and being distinguished from:

transitive object

while in Bandjalang, we have:

intransitive subject
transitive object

being marked in the same way, and being distinguished from:

transitive subject

171

With such different types of languages, we obviously cannot really use terms like 'subject' because it will mean different things depending on what type of language we are looking at. So, we have special terminology. The English 'subject' is called the NOMINATIVE, and the object is called the ACCUSATIVE. The Bandjalang transitive subject is called the ERGATIVE, while the remaining functions can be referred to as the ABSOLUTIVE. English can be referred to as an 'accusative' language, while Bandjalang can be referred to as an 'ergative' language.

It is possible for languages to change grammatically with respect to accusativity and ergativity. That is, an accusative language can change typologically to become an ergative language, and an ergative language can change typologically to become an accusative language.

How might these changes come about? Australian languages are mainly of the same type as Bandjalang; that is, they are ergative rather than accusative. Some linguists have argued in the past that they were originally accusative and that they changed to become ergative. The original language is supposed to have had constructions like these:

> *wati   ŋina-ŋu
> man-nominative sit   past
> 'The man was sitting'

> *wati   yipi-ku   paka-ŋu yuku-ŋku
> man-nominative woman-accusative hit-past stick-
>   instrument
> 'The man hit the woman with a stick'

which are clearly accusative in type. Just as English has a passive construction, so too did this reconstructed Australian language. This passive construction would have looked like this:

> *yipi   wati-ŋku   paka-li -ŋu
> woman-nominative man-instrument hit-passive past
> 'The woman got hit by the man'

where the verb is marked as passive by the presence of the suffix */-li/, and the performer of the action is marked in the same way

172

as the instrument in the preceding example. It is then argued that the passive sentences eventually 'took over' from the active sentences, and the active sentences were no longer used at all, and ceased to be part of the grammar of the language. The sentence that we just saw would then have become the normal way of saying:

'The man hit the woman.'

So, the performer of an action (i.e. the transitive subject) would always be marked differently from the intransitive subject or the transitive object. (Note that this hypothesis has been challenged for the history of Australian languages and there are few linguists who take it very seriously now. However, the suggestion does indicate how a language *could* change its typology.)

(c) Basic Word Order

Languages can also change their grammatical typology by changing the order in which the basic constituents of the sentence are placed. Most languages of the world have the order SUBJECT + VERB + OBJECT (SVO). The next most frequently found word order is SUBJECT + OBJECT + VERB (SOV). The only other commonly found word order is VERB + SUBJECT + OBJECT (VSO). It is possible for a language to change from one of these basic types to another.

For example, most of the Austronesian languages of the Pacific region are SVO languages. The Tolai language of Rabaul, for instance, is of this type, as shown by the following example:

A	*pap*	*i*	*gire*	*tikana*	*tutana*
noun marker	dog	3sg	see	one	man
S		V		O	

'The dog saw a man'

The Austronesian languages of Central Province and Milne Bay however, are generally of the SOV type. For example, the same sentence in Motu would be expressed as:

Sisia	*ese*	*tau*	*ta*	*eitaia*
dog	doer	man	one	it-saw-him
S		O		V

These languages appear to have changed from the earlier SVO order to the SOV structure. Some scholars have argued that this change took place when the ancestor language from which Motu was derived first came into contact with the non-Austronesian languages of the area, which are SOV languages. For instance, in the non-Austronesian Koita language, which is spoken by the neighbouring group to the Motu, the sentence we have just given for Tolai and Motu would be expressed as:

Tora	*ata*	*be*	*eraɣanu*
dog	man	one	saw-him
S		O	V

The suggestion is that the proto-language from which Motu is derived changed its basic word order in the direction of the word order in a language that was similar to modern Koita.

(d) Verb Chains

While there are many grammatical facts that we could consider when setting up language typologies, the final example of typological change that we will look at is the development of what is called in some languages VERB CHAINS or SERIAL VERBS.

In many languages of Melanesia, especially the non-Austronesian languages, we find that a whole series of verbs can be strung together, often in just a single phonological word, with just a single subject and a single object. For instance, in the Alamblak language of the East Sepik, we find sentences such as these:

Wifèrt	*fɨr*	*gëñNgɨ-më*		*-t*	*-a*
wind	blow	cold	remote past	it	me

'The wind blew me and I got cold' (i.e. 'the wind blew me cold')

Languages of this type often allow three or four (or more) verbs to be chained together in single words of this type. For instance, in the Yimas language, which is a close neighbour of Alamblak, we find such complex examples as this:

Na-bu-wul-ɨay pra-kiak
him they afraid try come remote past
'they tried to frighten him as he came'

In languages that have these kinds of constructions, it is often possible to show that these chains of verbs originate from much simpler constructions in which each verb has its own set of subject and object markers. For instance, the complex Alamblak structure that we have just seen could be derived from the Alamblak equivalents of:

'The wind blew me'

and:

'I got cold'

respectively. Languages which develop verb chains of these types are generally SOV languages. This is actually not surprising, as this allows speakers to simply state the subject and the object once at the beginning and then the string the verbs together one after the other following these noun phrases. It is then a relatively small step for these chained verbs to be 'collapsed' into a single word.

In all of these different examples of grammatical change that we have looked at, we can recognise three general factors that seem to be involved. These factors are REANALYSIS, ANALOGY and DIFFUSION.

Reanalysis in grammatical change refers to the process by which a form comes to be analysed in a different way grammatically. What happens is that a particular form may be structurally ambiguous in some of the contexts in which it occurs, i.e. it may have more than one possible grammatical analysis. What then happens is that one of these analyses 'takes over' from the original analysis in the minds of the speakers of the language. This new analysis may then become the basic form for a whole new paradigm. For instance, the original word for 'I' has been reconstructed for Australian Aboriginal languages as */ŋay/. When this pronoun was used as the subject of a transitive verb, it added an ergative suffix, which had the form */-ɖu/ after the final glide of the pronoun, producing a contrast between the intransitive subject form */ɲay/ and the transitive subject form */ŋayɖu/ (which then became phonologically reduced to */ŋaɖu/). The transitive subject form then in some cases 'took over' the intransitive subject */nay/ form, and so it came to be reanalysed as the root. Some languages then added to this reanalysed root a *new* eragative marker. There are now Australian languages like Walbiri which have the intransitive subject form /ŋaɖu/ and the transitive subject form /ŋaɖulu/, in which the /-lu/ is the allomorph of the ergative suffix that is found on stems that end in vowels!

Some Austronesian languages of the Pacific area have also undergone grammatical reanalysis with respect to what were originally noun markers. In languages like Tolai, common noun phrases must be preceded by a marker of the form /a/, which simply has the function of indicating that what follows is a noun phrase. So, we find forms such as this:

a vat   'stone'
a vavina   'woman'
a pal   'house'

This /a/ is in fact inherited from the proto-language, where it had a very similar function. However, in the Paamese language of Vanuatu, this original */a/ has become part of the root of the noun itself, and the two cannot be separated, e.g.

		PAAMESE	
*batu	→	ahat	'stone'
*tansik	→	atas	'sea'
*niu	→	ani	'coconut'

We therefore need to say that the noun marker has lost its noun marking function, and it has simply become part of the following noun root.

A final example of grammatical reanalysis comes in the morpheme *-burger* that is creeping into the English language in words like:

hamburger
cheeseburger
eggburger
fishburger

The word *hamburger* was originally the only one of these four words to be used in English. Its derivation was from the name of the city *Hamburg,* with the suffix *-er.* However, there was ambiguity between splitting the word into *hamburg-er* (on the basis of the name of the city) and *ham-burger* (on the basis of the fact that there is a meat filling to the bread roll), and it was the second analysis that won out over the first one, thus creating a new morpheme *-burger* meaning 'toasted bread roll with a certain kind of filling with salad'. This suffix then came to be attached to other nouns referring to different kinds of fillings, such as *cheese, egg* and *fish.*

There is another kind of reanalysis, which is known as BACK FORMATION. An example of this process is involved in the change of

176

the English word *cherry.* This word was originally borrowed from French, where there is a word /seriz/, which is the same in the singular and the plural. When /seriz/ was borrowed into English however, speakers of English analysed the word as being plural because it ended with /-z/, the same ending which marks the plural of many English nouns. What they did then was to drop this /-z/ to make the singular form *cherry,* with the regular plural *cherries.* If the English speakers had not reanalysed this root, we would now have the singular form *one cherries,* and the plural form *two cherrieses!*

Another powerful force in grammatical change in addition to reananlysis is analogy. We saw in Chapter Six that analogy can influence the direction of a sound change in individual words in a language. In grammatical change, analogy is one of the most significant factors in determining the direction of the change.

Grammatical systems operate in terms of general patterns. Patterns, however, tend to have exceptions (or: special 'sub-patterns' that are used in only a small, unpredictable set of situations). For instance, to form the plural of nouns in English, we regularly add a morpheme which has the following variants or allomorphs:

-əz   after sibilants
-s   after voiceless non-sibilants
-z   after voiced non-sibilants

There are, however, a few irregular plural forms, including the following:

singular	*plural*
man	men
woman	women
child	children
foot	feet
mouse	mice
ox	oxen

Anybody who makes a mistake and says *mans* for *men,* or *foots* for *feet* (as a child might) would be operating under the influence of analogy. While such forms are clearly regarded by English-speakers as mistakes, there are some forms that started out as mistakes, but have become fully standardised. For instance, the word *shoe* originally had an irregular plural *shoen*, this has of course now become completely regularised to *shoes*.

Analogy can also operate in the opposite direction. Instead of creating more regularity, it can also cause regular forms to become irregular on the basis of patterns that exist in their regular forms. For instance, in most dialects of English, the verb *dive* is quite regular in its past tense and people simply say *dived*. In American English however, it is quite acceptable to say *dove*, on the analogy of the irregular pair *drive:drove*.

The final factor that influences that direction of grammatical change is diffusion. This basically means that one language may influence another language in its grammatical structure when there are enough people who speak both languages. We have already seen one example where it has been suggested that one language changed its basic word order from SOV under the influence of a neighbouring language with the SOV order.

It is in fact possible for languages that are genetically quite diverse to influence each other to such an extent that they look quite similar to each other. Structural features of languages that are shared because these features have diffused or spread from one language to another are called AREAL FEATURES. When a group of genetically diverse languages share a large number of areal features, we have what is called a LINGUISTIC AREA, or sometimes also a SPRACHBUND [ʃpraxbunt], from the German word for the same thing. For instance, the Balkan area of Europe has had a long period of influence between its various languages, with the result that these languages are now quite similar in structure, whereas in the past, they were quite different. Other well known linguistic areas are the Indian subcontinent, and southeast Asia.

It is usually pointed out that languages borrow lexical items quite easily because the lexicon is not highly structured like the grammar. While it is easy to borrow a word without changing the entire system of the language, a new pronoun or a new suffix of some kind *will* cause some kind of dramatic change to the grammatical system as a whole because it contains less items to begin with. The question of the diffusion of grammatical features is particularly important for a discussion of the linguistic history of Melanesia, because there too we have a high degree of multilingualism. Linguists have argued that historical origins of languages have in fact been obscured by continual borrowing of grammatical features.

8.2 Semantic Change

We mentioned earlier that phonological change in language has been fairly well studied. Grammatical change is less well studied, but it is an area that is receiving a lot of attention from linguists at the present. Semantic change, however, seems to be the area of language change that is least well understood, perhaps because semantics is still the weak point in synchronic language study. However, there are still some observations that we can make as to the kinds of semantic change that occur in languages and the forces that are involved in bringing these changes about.

Changes in meaning can perhaps be divided into four basic types. The first of these kinds of semantic change can be called BROADEN-ING. What this means is that a word changes in meaning so that, in addition to the meaning it originally had, it comes to have other meanings. The original meaning, however, is still included within the new meaning. For instance, many of the semantic changes that have taken place in the history of Tok Pisin involve this concept of broadening. The English word 'pigeon' has come into Tok Pisin as *pisin*. In Tok Pisin, however, this word refers not to just pigeons, but to any kind of bird at all.

The second kind of meaning change that we can recognise is the exact opposite of this, and that is NARROWING. Semantic narrowing takes place when a word comes to refer to only part of the original meaning. It is harder to find good examples of semantic narrowing. One example would be the change of English 'dry' to Tok Pisin *darai*. The term *darai* in Tok Pisin refers specifically to a dry coconut that can be used for scraping out the flesh to get the milk for cooking (in contrast to a green coconut, which is called *kulau*, and which is used mainly for drinking the water inside). Another example of semantic narrowing would be the term 'favour' in Papua New Guinea English. To 'favour' something in standard English means that you prefer it over something else, but in Papua New Guinea English, it is generally used to indicate that you are sexually 'favouring' someone.

A third type of semantic change can be called semantic SPLIT, or sometimes BIFURCATION. This term describes the change by which a word acquires another meaning that relates in some way to the original meaning. For instance, if we take the phrase 'pitch black' in English, we will find that some people do not realise that the

179

word 'pitch' comes from the name of the very black substance like tar or *kolta*. These speakers of English would simply regard 'pitch' in this example as meaning 'very' or 'completely'. If you ever hear anybody saying 'pitch blue' or 'pitch yellow', then you will know that for them, the original meaning of 'pitch' has split into two quite different meanings.

The final type of semantic change that we will consider is semantic SHIFT, where a word completely loses its original meaning and acquires a new meaning. In all of the cases we have just looked at, at least something of the original meaning is retained, but this is not the case with semantic shift. An example of semantic shift would be where the English word 'monkey' has become the Tok Pisin word *mangi*, meaning a young unmarried man or boy.

It is also possible for a semantic change to fall into more than one of these categories at once. If we look at the semantic changes that took place when the English word 'medicine' was taken into Tok Pisin as *marasin,* we will see what is meant by this. In English, the word 'medicine' refers to any substance that is used in the treatment of disease, as long as it is drunk, swallowed or injected. Medicine must be taken inside the body; anything this is applied to the surface of the body (for example lotions and ointments) is not 'medicine'. Medicines in English can be manufactured, or may occur naturally. We can therefore talk about medicinal herbs, and leaf medicines that were used by people before the arrival of manufactured European medicines. In Tok Pisin however, the word *marasin* can be used to refer to any of the following things: hair shampoo, dettol, toilet disinfectant, hair dye, rat killer, sun-tan oil, fly spray, Pretty Hair louse killing powder, malaria tablets, cough mixture and a variety of other things. The term *marasin* seems to refer to any manufactured substance that acts to improve our physical situation in some way. In fact, some speakers even refer to beer as *marasin* because of the benefits they gain from it! The term *marasin* would therefore seem to involve a fair degree of semantic broadening from the original meaning of 'medicine'. However, while there has been some broadening of meaning, there has been at the same time a narrowing of the meaning too. There are some things that are covered by the term 'medicine' which cannot be called *marasin.* Substances that occur naturally and are not manufactured cannot be called *marasin,* even if they are used in the treatment of disease. For instance, leaves and bark that have medicinal qualities are simply called *lip-diwai* 'tree leaf' and *skin-diwai* 'tree skin' respectively. The English term 'leaf medicine' cannot be translated literally into Tok Pisin.

When talking about semantic change, we can recognise a number of different forces that seem to be operating to influence the directions that the semantic changes acutally take. These forces include METAPHOR, EUPHEMISM, HYPERBOLE and INTERFERENCE.

A metaphor is an expression in which something is referred to by some other term because of a partial similarity between the two things. For example, if you say:

'He is a pig'

you do not mean he is literally a pig, but that there are certain things about his appearance or his behaviour that remind you of a pig: perhaps he eats a lot, or perhaps he is an extremely dirty and untidy person. Sometimes the metaphoric use of a word can cause the original meaning to change in some way. The word 'insult', for instance, originally meant 'to jump on'; presumably, if you insulted somebody, it was as though you had jumped on them. This meta-ophoric use of the word then completely took over the original meaning, and a semantic shift had taken place.

A euphemism is a term that we use to avoid some other term which has some kind of unpleasant associations about it, or a term which is completely taboo. For instance, in colonial Papua New Guinea, people were often call 'natives' by Europeans. As Papua New Guineans became more aware of the connotations of the word 'native' (as it implies a certain backwardness, similar to the Tok Pisin word *bus-kanaka*), people had to find a new word to talk about Papua New Guineans that was not so offensive. This is how the expression 'a national' became the accepted expression to replace a 'native'. The term 'national' has therefore undergone semantic broadening in Papua New Guinea English under the pressure of euphemism.

Some words in languages are felt to express meanings in a much 'stronger' way than other words which express more or less the same thing. For instance, of the two words 'good' and 'fantastic', it is the second word which has the greater impact. Stronger words can often change to become more neutral if the form is used often enough. This force in semantic change is referred to as hyperbole, which means that an originally strong connotation of a word is lost because of overuse. The English expression 'buggered up' is quite forceful, and is even insulting in some contexts. When this was taken into Tok Pisin as *bagarap*, it lost all of its force and became a neutral term, and simply means 'not functioning properly'.

A final force that operates in semantic change is interference. Sometimes one of a pair of two similar words, or identical words with two different meanings (i.e. homonyms) can undergo semantic change of one kind or another to avoid the possibility of interference between the two meanings. For example, Americans very rarely use the word 'cockroach', and they prefer to just call cockroaches 'roaches'. The reason for this is that someone might misunderstand the term 'cockroach', and think that they heard the taboo word 'cock'. The word 'gay' at the moment is undergoing semantic change in English. This word originally meant 'happy'. Then, it underwent a semantic split and acquired a second meaning, that of 'defiant and proud homosexual'. When the heterosexual majority of the English-speaking population became aware of this new meaning of the word 'gay' they tended to avoid the word altogether. People now are not very likely to say:

'I am feeling very gay today.'

in case somebody thinks that they are declaring themselves to be homosexual. In this case, we can see that semantic interference from this homonym is causing the word 'gay' to lose its original meaning of 'happy'.

READING GUIDE QUESTIONS
1. What is the difference between a genetic grouping and a typological grouping of languages?
2. What is an isolating language?
3. What is an agglutinating language?
4. What is inflectional language?
5. How can phonological reduction cause a language to change its grammatical typology?
6. What is morphological fusion? What sort of typological change can result from this kind of change?
7. What is morphological reduction? What kind of grammatical type results from this kind of change?

8. What is meant by the terms ergativity and accusativity with respect to language typology? How can a language change its type from one to the other?
9. How can languages change their basic word order?
10. What are verb chains? How can these develop in languages?
11. What is meant by the term grammatical reanalysis?
12. What is back formation?
13. How can analogy cause grammatical change?
14. What is grammatical fusion?
15. What is a lingusitic area?
16. What is semantic broadening?
17. What is semantic narrowing?
18. What does the term bifurcation mean with respect to semantic change?
19. What is semantic shift, and how does this kind of change differ from the other kinds of semantic change mentioned in this chapter?
20. How can metaphor influence the direction of a semantic change?
21. What is euphemism? How can it influence semantic change?
22. What is meant by hyperbole, and how is this involved in semantic change?
23. What is meant by interference when speaking of change of meaning?

EXERCISES
1. Many speakers of Tok Pisin express a relative clause by simply putting the relative clause inside another clause without any special marking at all, as in:

Dispela man **ol paitim**	'The man **who got beaten**
em asde i dai pinis	**up yesterday** has died'

However, many speakers of Tok Pisin, especially (but not exclusively) people from the Highlands, are coming to mark relative clauses by adding *longen* at the end of the relative clause, e.g.:

Em i bin draiv long	'He drove on the bridge **that**
bris **i bruk longen**	**was broken.**'
Mi paitim em long diwai	'I hit him with the stick **which**
mi holim longen	**I had been holding.**'

What is the normal function of *longen?* How do you think this new function of *longen* has developed with these speakers of Tok Pisin?

2. Other speakers of Tok Pisin are coming to mark relative clauses in the written form of the language by placing *husat* in front of the relative clause. Here is an example of such a construction that was taken from a student's actual essay written for a Foundation Year course in Tok Pisin:

Bai mi toktok long ol	*'I will discuss the problems*
asua **husat bai i kamap**	**that would arise** *if Tok Pisin*
sapos Tok Pisin i kamap	*were to become the national*
nambawan tokples bilong	*language of Papua New*
Papua Niugini	*Guinea.'*

    How has this innovation come about?

3. There are some speakers of Tok Pisin for whom the transitive verb 'drink' is expressed as *dringim,* e.g.:

    Yu laik dringim sampela bia?

    Most people however, would prefer to say:

    Yu laik dring sampela bia?

    What factor would you say is responsible for bringing about the change from *dring* to *dringim* with those people who use this form?

4. Recently on the NBC, a speaker said in Tok Pisin:

I gat plandepela samting	*'There are numerous*
ol i laik wokim long ples	*things they would like*
bilong ol	*to do in their villages.'*

    Would you say *plandepela?* Why do you think this person did?

5. Can you think of other ways that languages might change their basic word order? For instance, could you imagine a sentence like this in Tok Pisin becoming the basis for a new construction?

    Joni Woka, mi no save laikim; bia, yes!
    'I don't like whiskey, but I *do* like beer.'

6. Some people might say:
    'He drank two gins and tonic'.
    While others might say:
    'He drank two gin and tonics.'
    What is happening here?

7. Compare the following English and Tok Pisin forms. How would you describe the nature of the semantic changes that have taken place?

ENGLISH	TOK PISIN
1. arse	as
2. bed	bet
3. box	bokis
4. garden	gaden
5. grass	gras
6. hand	han
7. cargo	kago
8. copper	kapa
9. cry	krai
10. straight	stret
11. take away	tekewe

8. Compare the meanings of the words in italics in Papua New Guinea English below, with their meanings in standard English. How would you describe the changes that have taken place?

'That guy, he's really *waterproof* ia!'

'Those *boys* were making a lot of *unnecessary* noises the whole night while they were drinking.'

'We were just *spinning* around Four Mile whole day today.'

'He is really *service* in *greasing ladies.*'

'I'm not drinking because I've got no *bucks.*'

'I really don't want to see that *fellow.*'

'Ss, really *hopeless!*'

9. A thesaurus is a book that lists words by meaning, and which makes it possible to find out the synonyms of a word (or, words that have the same or nearly the same meaning). Look up some synonyms for the following in a thesaurus. Then look up a dictionary that goes back a couple of hundred years if possible, and see how these words have changed semantically:

popular
fantastic
style
native
juvenile

FURTHER READING

1. Sapir, Edward. *Language: An Introduction to the Study of Speech* (Chapter 6 'Types of Linguistic Structure'), pp. 120-46.
2. Arlotto, Anthony. *Introduction to Historical Linguistics* (Chapter 10 'Changes in Grammar') pp. 149-64, (Chapter 11 'Semantic Change'), pp. 165-83.
3. Bloomfield, Leonard. *Language* (Chapter 24 'Semantic Change'), pp. 425-43.
4. Bolinger, Dwight. *Aspects of Language* (Chapter 7 'The Evolution of Language: Meanings, Interpretations and Adjustments'), pp. 100-24.

Chapter Nine

SUBGROUPING

By using the comparative method, we can reconstruct a proto-language, and also determine which languages are related to other languages in a family. However, it is possible for some languages in a family to be more closely related to each other than to other members of the family. For instance, let us compare the following six Indo-European languages:

ENGLISH	DUTCH	GERMAN	FRENCH	ITALIAN	RUSSIAN
wʌn	eːn	ains	œ̃	uno	adʸin
tuː	tweː	tsvai	dø	due	dva
θriː	driː	drai	trwa	tre	trʸi
foː	fiːr	fiːr	katr	kwatro	tʃetɨrʸe
faiv	fɛif	fünf	sɛ̃k	tʃinkwe	pʸat

There are enough similarities even here, in the words for 'two' and 'three' for example, that we could probably justify putting these six languages in a single language family. However, there are other similarities that seem to suggest that English, Dutch and German are closer to each other than to the other three languages. Similarly, French and Italian seem to be relatively closely related, while being less closely related to the others. Finally, Russian seems to stand on its own. What we say, therefore, is that we have three SUBGROUPS of the one language family, one containing the first three languages, one containing the next two, and a final subgroup with only a single member.

We can represent subgrouping in a family tree by a series of branches coming from a single point. The family tree for the six languages described above would therefore look something like this:

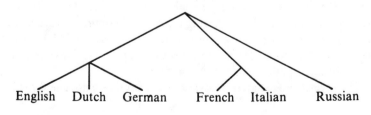

English Dutch German   French Italian   Russian

187

We presume from this diagram that English, Dutch and German are all derived from a common proto-language (which we can call proto-Germanic) that is itself descended from the proto-language that is ancestral to all of the other languages (which we call proto-Indo-European). We can therefore offer a tentative definition of a subgroup by saying that it comprises a number of languages that are all descended from a common proto-language that is intermediate between the ultimate (or highest-level) proto-language and the modern language, and which are as a result more similar to each other than to other languages in the family.

9.1 Shared Innovation and Shared Retention

Clearly, languages that belong to the same subgroup must share some kind of similarities that distinguish them from other languages in the family that do not belong to this subgroup. However, the simple fact that there are similarities does not *necessarily* mean that they belong to the same subgroup.

If we say that two languages belong in the same subgroup, we imply that they have gone through a PERIOD OF COMMON DESCENT, and that they did not diverge until a later stage in their development, However, similarities between languages can be explained as being due to either SHARED RETENTION from the proto-languages, or SHARED INNOVATION since the time of the proto-language. If two languages are similar because they share some feature that has been retained from the proto-language, we cannot use this similarity as evidence that they have gone through a period of common descent. The retention of the particular feature in the two languages is not significant because we expect a large number of features to be retained anyway. However, if two languages are similar because they have both undergone the same innovation or change, then we can say that this is evidence that they have a period of common descent and that they belong to the same subgroup. We can say that shared innovations are evidence for subgrouping because exactly the same change is unlikely to take place independently in two separate languages. By suggesting a period of common descent, we are saying that the change took place only *once* and that other changes then took place later in the individual languages to differentiate one language from another.

However, while shared innovations are used as evidence for subgrouping, it should be pointed out that certain kinds of innovations are likely to be stronger evidence of subgrouping than other kinds. Subgrouping rests on the assumption that shared similarities are unlikely to be due to *chance*. However, some kinds of similarities are in fact due to chance, i.e. the same changes *do* sometimes take place quite independently in different languages. This kind of situation is often referred to as DRIFT or as PARALLEL DEVELOPMENT. One good example of drift is in the Oceanic subgroup of the Austronesian family of languages. In proto-Oceanic, word final consonants were apparently retained from proto-Austronesian. However, many present-day Oceanic languages have since apparently lost word final consonants by a rule of the form:

$$C \rightarrow \emptyset \ / \ \underline{\qquad} \ \#$$

The fact that many Oceanic languages share this innovation is not sufficient evidence to work out subgroups. Loss of final consonants is a very common sort of change that could easily be due to chance. There are in fact other languages that have undergone this change which are well outside the Oceanic area, for example, the Enggano language of southern Sumatra in Indonesia.

We therefore need to avoid the possibility that two innovations are due to drift or parallel development. We can do this by looking for:

(a) particularly unusual changes, or
(b) sets of quite different types of changes both of which occurring together are unlikely to be due to chance.
(c) phonological changes which occur together with grammatical or semantic changes.

For instance, if two languages shared a common sporadic or irregular change, then this would be good evidence of subgrouping, as the same irregular change is unlikely to take place twice independently. One piece of evidence that is often quoted for grouping the Oceanic languages into a single subgroup of Austronesian is the irregular metathesis that has taken place in the proto-Austronesian word */limaw/ 'orange'. On the basis of evidence from the present-day Oceanic languages, we can reconstruct an original form */moli/. We would predict an original */limo/, however, from the earlier proto-Austronesian form we have just seen. There has therefore been irregular metathesis of */limo/ to */moli/ in all of the

Oceanic languages. Such a change is unlikely to be due to chance, so we say that it is evidence that the Oceanic languages have a period of common descent.

The Oceanic subgroup of Austronesian can be further justified by quoting various other changes that have taken place. These include the following:

$$\begin{aligned}
\text{ə} &\to \text{o} \\
\text{b} &\to \text{p} \\
\d{d} &\to \text{d} \\
\text{g} &\to \text{k}
\end{aligned}$$

These changes are all of quite different types, so parallel development is unlikely to be the explanation. We therefore conclude that any Austronesian language having all of these changes is a member of the Oceanic subgroup.

Finally, if we can match phonological innovations with shared grammatical or semantic innovations, then we can argue that we have evidence for sub-grouping. Although grammatical reconstruction of proto-Austronesian is far from certain, there are some linguists who argue that the basic clause structure of Oceanic languages is different from that of proto-Austronesian. If this is true, then this would be further evidence for the existence of an Oceanic subgroup.

9.2 Lexicostatistics and Glottochronology

There is a second technique for subgrouping languages that is often used with languages for which we have only limited amounts of data available, and that is the technique of LEXICOSTATISTICS. Since Melanesia (and Australia) is an area of great linguistic diversity, and comparatively few of these languages are well known to linguists, this is a technique that has been used very frequently in trying to determine the interrelationships among the languages of Melanesia and Australia. We will therefore need to have a good understanding of how linguists apply this technique, and its strengths and weaknesses.

Lexicostatistics is a technique that allows us to determine the degree of relationship between two languages by comparing the vocabularies of the languages and determining the degree of similarity between them. This method operates under two basic assumptions.

The first assumption that underlies this method is that some parts of the vocabulary of a language are much less subject to change than other parts. When we speak of 'change', we do not mean that certain parts of the vocabulary are resistant to various phonological innovations, because, as we saw in Chapter Six, sound changes are not semantically conditioned but phonetically conditioned. What we mean therefore, is that a word is simply *replaced* by a non-cognate form. This may be because the original form changes in meaning so that it comes to refer to something else, or because a word is borrowed from another language to express the meaning and so replaces the original form. If we were to compare the Tok Pisin vocabulary of a couple of generations ago with that of today for example, we would find that the word *limlimbur* has been replaced by the word *raun-raun* or *go raun*.

There is a second part to this first assumption, and that is the fact that this basic 'core' of relatively change-resistant vocabulary is the same for all languages. It includes items like the following: pronouns, numerals, body parts and geographical features. Items like these are unlikely to be replaced by borrowings from other languages because all people, whatever their cultural differences, have eyes and mouths and legs, know about the sky and clouds, the sun and the moon, stones and trees and so on. Other concepts however, may be 'culture-specific', or known only to people of certain cultures. The danger in using such words is that cultural items are very frequently borrowed, along with the names for them. So, while the name for a particular kind of implement may be similar in two languages, it may be because one group borrowed it from the other because originally they did not have that kind of tool. But if two languages have a similar word for 'nose', it is unlikely to be due to borrowing because we assume that all languages will already have a word for 'nose'.

This contrast between the amount of change that takes place in 'core' vocabulary and 'peripheral' (or general) vocabulary can be seen by looking at the vocabulary of English. If we take the dictionary of English as a whole, we find that about 50% of the words are borrowed from words in French, either because English has borrowed directly from French (and there has been massive borrowing over the last 900 years from French to English), or because both French and English have borrowed from some other language, such as Greek or Latin. However, if we restrict ourselves to just the 'core' vocabulary of the two languages, we find that there is much less similarity. The figure for borrowed forms between English and French drops to as low as 6% in fact.

The second assumption that underlies the lexicostatistical method is that the actual *rate* of vocabulary replacement in the core vocabulary is more or less stable, and is therefore the same for all languages at any period of time. (However, in peripheral vocabulary, replacement is not stable, and may be relatively fast or relatively slow, depending on the nature of the cultural contact between two languages.) This assumption has in fact been tested in thirteen languages for which there are written records going back over long periods of time. It has been found that there has been an average vocabulary retention of 80.5% every thousand years. That is to say, after a thousand years, a language will have lost about a fifth of its original basic vocabulary and replaced it with new forms.

If these assumptions are acceptable, then it should be possible to work out the degree of relationship between two languages. If the core vocabulary of two languages is relatively similar, then we can assume the they have diverged relatively recently in time, and that they therefore belong to a lower level subgroup. If, on the other hand, their core vocabularies are relatively dissimilar, then we can assume that they must have diverged at a much earlier time, and that they therefore belong to a much higher level subgroup. Different levels of subgrouping are given names by lexicostatisticians as follows:

Level of subgrouping	cognate percentage in core vocabulary
dialects of a language	81-100%
languages of a family	36-81%
families of a stock	12-36%
stocks of a microphylum	4-12%
microphyla of a mesophylum	1-4%
mesophyla of a macrophylum	0-1%

It should be noted immediately that lexicostatisticians use the term 'family' to mean something very different to the way we have been using it. We have all along been taking it to refer to *all* languages that are descended from a common ancestor language. According to a lexicostatistical classification however, a 'family' simply refers to all languages that share between 36% and 81% of their core vocabularies. Languages in lesser degrees of relationship are not considered to be in the same family, but in the same 'stock' or 'phylum'. A further problem that arises in the use of lexicostatistical figures to indicate degrees of relationship is that different linguists sometimes use different figures. Some users of lexicostatistics often use the following figures instead:

dialects of a language	81-100%
languages of a sub-family	55-80%
subfamilies of a family	28-54%
families of a stock	13-27%
stocks of a phylum	5-12%

Having outlined the assumptions behind lexicostatistics, and the theory behind its application, we can now go on to examine the actual technique we need to follow to use this method. The first problem is to distinguish the so-called 'core' vocabulary from the 'peripheral' vocabulary. We gave some indication earlier about the kinds of things that would need to go into such a list. But how long should it be? Some have argued that we should use a 1000-word list, others a 200-word list, and others a 100-word list. Since lexicostatistics is supposed to be a convenient and easy way of working out subgrouping, it would be awkward to insist on a 1000-word list (especially since for many Melanesian languages, linguists do not even have word lists this long!). A 100-word list is probably a bit short, so the chances of error would be greater. Most linguists tend to operate with a 200-word list, and the most popular is the so-called 'Swadesh' list, named after the linguist who worked it out. This list comprises the following items:

all	bark	blow	clothing	_____	dry
and	because	bone	cloud	dance	dull
animal	belly	breast	claw	day	dust
ashes	big	breathe	cold	die	
at	bird	brother	come	dig	_____
_____	bite	burn	cook	dirty	ear
back	black	_____	count	dog	earth
bad	blood	child	cut	drink	eat
					egg

193

eight	he	louse	rightside	some	tree
eye	head	_____	river	spear	turn
_____	hear	man/male	road	spit	twenty
fall	heart	many	root	split	two
far	heavy	meat/flesh	rope	squeeze	_____
fat/grease	here	moon	rotten	stab/	vomit
father	hit	mother	rub	pierce	_____
fear	hold/take	mountain	_____	stand	walk
feather	horn	mouth	salt	star	warm
few	how	_____	sand	stick	wash
fight	hundred	name	say	stone	water
fire	hunt	narrow	scratch	straight	we
fish	husband	near	sea	suck	wet
five	_____	neck	see	sun	what?
float	I	new	seed	swell	when?
flow	ice	night	seven	swim	where?
flower	if	nose	sew	_____	white
fog	in	not	sharp	tail	who?
foot	_____	_____	shoot	ten	wide
four	kill	old	short	that	wife
freeze	knee	one	sing	there	wind
fruit	know	other	sister	they	wing
full	_____	_____	sit	thick	wipe
_____	lake	person	skin	thin	with
give	laugh	play	sky	think	woman
good	leaf	pull	sleep	this	woods
grass	leftside	push	small	thou	work
green	leg	_____	smell	three	worm
guts	lie	rain	smoke	throw	_____
_____	live	red	smooth	tie	ye
hair	liver	right/	snake	tongue	year
hand	long	correct	snow	tooth	yellow

Even with this list however, there are problems in applying it to Melanesian languages. Firstly, it contains words like 'and' and 'in' which in many languages are not expressed as separate words, but as affixes of some kind. It contains the separate words 'woman' and 'wife', even though in many languages these are the same. It contains words like 'freeze' and 'ice' which are clearly not applicable in most Melanesian languages. Clearly, there are other words which *could* be used in a basic vocabulary list for Melanesian languages, yet which would not be suitable for other languages, e.g. 'bow and arrow', 'spear', *kunai* grass' , 'chicken', 'cuscus', 'snake' and so on.

Once we have decided on a suitable list of core vocabulary, what we have to do is decide how many of the pairs of words are cognate in two languages. Ideally, a cognate pair of words should be decided on by working out the systematic sound correspondences between the two languages. If there are two forms that are phonetically similar, but which show an exceptional sound correspondence, then we assume that they are borrowed and so exclude them. It is very important to exclude such borrowings, as these can make two languges appear to be more closely related than they really are.

However, since we are working with fairly short word lists, there may not be enough data to make generalisations about sound correspondences. Also, we are not likely to know much about the proto-language anyway if we are dealing with languages for which we have limited data, so it will be even more difficult to distinguish genuine cognates from borrowings. In fact, lexicostatistics tends to rely heavily on the so-called INSPECTION METHOD of deciding whether two forms are cognate. This simply involves intelligent guesswork. If two forms *look* cognate, then they are given a 'yes' score for cognate; if not, they are given a 'no' score.

Let us now look at an actual problem. We will use the lexicostatistical method to try and subgroup the following three languages of Central Province: Koita, Koiari and Mountain Koiari. Rather than use a full 200-word list, we will use a shorter 25-word list and assume that it is representative of the fuller list.

	KOITA	KOIARI	MTN KOIARI
1. man	γata (A)	ata (A)	maraha (B)
2. woman	maγi (A)	mavi (A)	keate (B)
3. child	moe (A)	moe (A)	mo (A)
4. boy	γamika (A)	vami (A)	mo ese (B)
5. husband	mobora (A)	mobora (A)	koria (B)
6. wife	mabara (A)	mabara (A)	keate (B)
7. father	mama (A)	mama (A)	mama (A)
8. mother	neina (A)	neina (A)	neina (A)
9. I	da (A)	da (A)	da (A)
10. you (sg)	a (A)	a (A)	a (A)
11. he	au (A)	ahu (A)	au (A)

12. head	omoto (A)	kina (B)	kina (B)
13. hair	hana (A)	homo (B)	numu (C)
14. nose	uri (A)	uri (A)	uri (A)
15. ear	ihiko (A)	ihiko (A)	gorema (B)
16. tongue	meina (A)	neme (B)	neme (B)
17. chin	hata (A)	auki (B)	aura (C)
18. mouth	ava (A)	ava (A)	aka (B)
19. back	dehi (A)	gadiva (B)	inu (B)
20. leg	vasa (A)	vahi (B)	geina (C)
21. sun	vani (A)	vani (A)	fani (A)
22. star	vanumo (A)	koro (B)	didi (C)
23. cloud	gousa (A)	yuva (B)	goe (C)
24. rain	veni (A)	veni (A)	feni (A)
25. wind	nono (A)	hihi (B)	heburu (C)

What we have to do is distinguish cognate forms from non-cognate forms. This can be done by deciding how many cognate 'sets' there are for each form in the three languages. For instance, with the word for 'man', there are two clear sets: Koita and Koiari both have /ata/, while Mountain Koiari has /maraha/. We can therefore label the first set as (A), and the second set (B). On the other hand, the word for 'chin' is quite different in all three languages, so we need to recognise three cognate sets, (A), (B) and (C). Finally, the word for 'sun' is cognate in all three languages, so we recognise only one cognate set, (A).

Now we need to work out the degree to which each pair of languages shares cognates. So, if we first of all examine the pair Koita/Koiari, we find that there are 16 shared forms, as against 9 that are not. We can therefore say that 16/25 of the core vocabulary of these two languages is cognate. Doing this for the remaining pairs of languages, we will get three fractions, which can be set out in the following way:

KOITA[1]

$\frac{16}{25}$ KOIARI

$\frac{9}{25}$ $\frac{10}{25}$ MOUNTAIN KOIARI

196

These figures must now be converted to percentages. Thus:

KOITA
64%   KOIARI
36%   40%   MOUNTAIN KOIARI

Now that we have the figures, we need to interpret them. Clearly, Koita and Koiari are more closely related than either is to Mountain Koirai. We can therefore draw a family tree of the following kind:

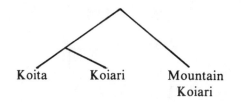

Koita   Koiari   Mountain
                       Koiari

In terms of the degrees of relationship that we looked at earlier, these languages are all contained within a single 'family' (i.e. they share between 36% and 81% of their core vocabularies).

This was a rather simple example however, and the procedures for working out degrees of relationship between a larger number of languages for which lexicostatistical figures have been calculated are rather more complex. Let us take the following lexicostatistical figures for ten hypothetical languages and present an interpretation of the data.

A
91 B
88 86 C
68 62 64 D
67 65 66 63 E
55 51 56 53 55 F
57 53 54 57 56 89 G
23 27 36 31 32 30 29 H
25 28 33 29 27 34 22 88 I
31 22 30 27 28 26 28 86 89 J

Where do we start in trying to draw a family tree for these languages? The first step is to try to find out which languages in the data are most closely related to each other. The procedure is to look for figures that are *significantly higher* than any other figures in the table, which is an indication that these particular languages are relatively closely related to each other. On this table, therefore, the following figures are noticeable in this respect:

```
A
91  B
88  86  C
68  62  64  D
67  65  66  63  E
55  51  56  53  55  F
57  53  54  57  56  89  G
23  27  36  31  32  30  29  H
25  28  33  29  27  34  22  88  I
31  22  30  27  28  26  28  86  89  J
```

Communities A, B, and C, therefore, would seem to belong to a very closely related subgroup. Communities F and G would also seem to belong together, and so too would the three communities H, I and J.

The second step is to try to find out what the next level of relationship is. To make this task easier, we can now treat the subgroups we have just arrived at as single units for the purpose of interpretation. Let us, at this level, relabel the units so that it is clear that we are operating with units at a different level of subgrouping. The new labels that we could use are:

```
A, B, C, . . . . . . . .  I
D   . . . . . . . . . . .  II
E   . . . . . . . . . . . .  III
F, G  . . . . . . . . .  IV
H, I, J   . . . . . . . .  V
```

Now, we need to ask ourselves what is the shared cognate percentage between these different units. In dealing with the first pair on the new table, i.e. the pair I and II, we are immediately faced with a problem as II (i.e. language D) has three different figures for the parts that go to make up I (i.e. languages A, B and C). A and D share 68%, B and D share 62%, while C and D share 64%. The easiest way

around this problem is to simply average out this block of figures
and enter them onto the new table in that way. The average of the
figures just given is about 65%, so we can enter this figure on the
table. We will therefore need to average out the figures in the
following blocks on the original table before we can go on to the
next step:

```
A       ⎫
91 B    ⎬ I
88 86 C ⎭
┌─────────┐
│68 62 64│ D      II
├─────────┼────┐
│67 65 66│63│ E       III
├─────────┼──┴──┬────┐
│55 51 56│53│55│F      ⎫
│57 53 54│57│56│89 G  ⎬ IV
├─────────┼──┴──┼────┴──┐   ⎭
│23 27 36│31│32│30 29│H     ⎫
│25 28 33│29│27│34 22│88 I  ⎬ V
│31 22 30│27│28│26 28│86 89 J ⎭
└─────────┴──┴──┴──────┘
```

Doing this, we come up with the following table:

I

65 II

66 63 III

54 55 55 IV

28 29 29 27 V

    We now treat this as a lexicostatistical table in the ordinary way
and look for the highest cognate figures as an indication of the
closest degree of relationship. It would seem that units I, II and III
are more closely related to each other than any of the other units,
with the figures 65%, 66% and 63%. They therefore belong to a
higher level subgroup. We then combine these into a single unit for
analysis, and relabel the units once again to avoid confusion, to
work out the next degree of relationship. The new labels could be:

I, II, III X

IV. . . . . Y

V . . . . Z

We will once again need to work out the averages of the cognate
percentages in the blocks shown below:

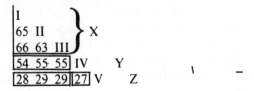

to be included in the new table. Doing this, the new table will look like this:

$$X$$
$$55 \; Y$$
$$29 \; 27 \; Z$$

It is clear from this that units X and Y are more closely related to each other than either is to Z.

We now need to gather together all of these facts and draw a family tree that will clearly indicate the degrees of relationship between the ten original languages. At the lowest level of relationship we discovered that the following units belong together:

A, B, C
F, G
H, I, J

while D and E were on their own. At the next level of relationship, we found that A, B, C, D, and E all belonged together, while the others were on their own. At the next level, we found that F and G could be related to the subgroup consisting of A, B, C, D, and E, with H, I and J as a separate subgroup of their own. This situation can be represented in a tree diagram in the following way:

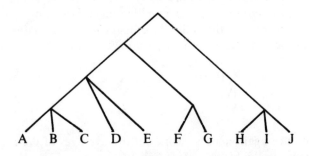

Having dealt in detail with the claim that lexicostatistics enables us to work out degrees of relationship within a language family, we can now go on to discuss a second claim that lexicostatisticians sometimes make, though most linguists are now very cautious about this. If we accept the basic assumptions that we looked at earlier, we should not only be able to work out the degree of relationship between two languages, but also the actual period of time that two languages have been separated. Once the percentage of cognate forms has been worked out, we can use the following mathematical formula to work out the 'time-depth' of the languages:

$$t = \frac{\log C}{2\log r}$$

In this formula, t stands for the number of thousands of years two languages have been separated, C stands for the percentage of cognates as worked out by comparing basic vocabularies, and r stands for the constant change factor mentioned earlier (and the value is .805). The following table gives logarithms for numbers less than 1 for use in this formula.

	.00	.01	.02	.03	.04	.05	.06	.07	.08	.09
.1	2.303	2.207	2.120	2.040	1.966	1.897	1.833	1.772	1.715	1.661
.2	1.609	1.561	1.514	1.470	1.427	1.386	1.347	1.309	1.273	1.238
.3	1.204	1.171	1.139	1.109	1.079	1.050	1.022	.994	.968	.942
.4	.916	.892	.868	.844	.821	.799	.777	.755	.734	.713
.5	.693	.673	.654	.635	.616	.598	.580	.562	.545	.528
.6	.511	.494	.478	.462	.446	.431	.416	.400	.386	.371
.7	.357	.342	.329	.315	.301	.288	.274	.261	.248	.236
.8	.223	.211	.198	.186	.174	.163	.151	.139	.128	.117
.9	.105	.094	.083	.073	.062	.051	.041	.030	.020	.010

So, going back to the earlier problem dealing with Koita, Koiari and Mountain Koiari, if we wanted to know how long it has been since Koiari split off from Koita, we would take the cognate percentage of 64% (as this is the figure given on the table) and convert it to a factor of one (i.e. .64) and apply the formula:

$$t = \frac{\log C}{2\log r}$$

$$t = \frac{\log .64}{2\log .805}$$

$$t = \frac{.446}{2 \times .217}$$

$$t = \frac{.446}{.434}$$

$$t = 1.028$$

This therefore means that Koita and Koiari must have diverged 1028 years ago, or, rounded off to about a thousand years. The Koiari migration from the mountains to the coast therefore should have taken place just before the French invaded England in the famous Battle of Hastings in 1066.

Given this method of dating for languages, which is called GLOTTOCHRONOLOGY, we can also give dates for the 'age' of the different degrees of relationships between languages. Thus:

level of subgrouping	*years of separation*
dialects of language	0-500
languages of family	500-2500
families of stock	2500-5000
stocks of microphylum	5000-7500
microphyla of mesophylum	7500-10000
mesophyla of macrophylum	over 10000

In fact, the following graph can be used to calculate the supposed time depth for any linguistic separation:

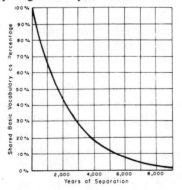

202

This technique of lexicostatistics has not been without its critics however. We have already hinted at a number of practical problems associated with the method. Firstly, there is the problem of deciding on which particular sets of words we should treat as being 'core' vocabulary. Different sets of words may produce slightly differing results. Secondly, there is the problem of distinguishing between genuine cognates and borrowings in languages which we do not know the full history of.

Apart from these practical problems, there are some more basic *theoretical* objections to the method, which destroy the validity of the underlying assumptions we looked at earlier. Firstly, we need to question the validity of the assumption that there is a constant rate of lexical replacement in core vocabulary for all languages over time, and that this rate of replacement is 19.5% every thousand years. This figure was arrived at by testing only thirteen languages with long histories of writing, and of these thirteen, eleven were Indo-European. However, differing cultural factors can affect the speed at which lexical replacement takes place.

For instance, in many cultures of this part of the world, and especially among the Australian Aborigines, there is a very strong tendency to name people after some particularly noticeable everyday thing in the environment at the time of the child's birth. For instance, a child born during a violent thunderstorm might be called 'lightning'. In many of these societies, there is a very powerful social restriction against mentioning somebody's name when they have died. In modern times, this also carries over to hearing the voice of a dead person on tape, or seeing their face in a photograph or a movie-film. Now, if someone is named after some common thing and that person dies, then speakers of that language cannot use the name of that thing either. In situations like this, the easiest way of avoiding the problem is to borrow a word meaning the same thing from a nearby language. Australian Aborigines normally speak more than one language anyway, so this is always quite simple to do.

There is also a similar kind of practice in the West New Britain province of Papua New Guinea. For instance, in the Kabana language, people often have personal names that also refer to everyday objects. In this society, as in many other Melanesian societies, there is a strong restriction against saying the names of one's in-laws. This is true, even if someone is simply using the word in its ordinary meaning, rather than as the name of his or her in-law. To refer to these things in such cases, the language has a set of special words 'on reserve'. These special 'reserve' terms are either words in the Kabana language itself, but with a different meaning, or words borrowed from neighbouring languages with the same meanings. For example, the word in Kabana for a particular kind of fish is /urae/. If someone's in-law is called Urae, this fish must be referred to instead as /moi/, which is usually the word for 'taro'. Also, the word for 'crocodile' in Kabana is /puaea/. This word cannot be used if someone's in-law has the name Puaea, and the crocodile must be called /bagele/. This form /bagele/ is apparently borrowed from a nearby language, where the word for "crocodile" is actually /vaɣele/.

A similar kind of cultural practice is found in Polynesia also. There is custom in Tahiti known as /pii/ which says that the name of a chief, or even a part of the name of the chief cannot be used by ordinary people. So, for instance, during the time that the very powerful chief called Pomare was in power, the words /poo/ 'night' and /mare/ 'cough' became taboo simply because they sounded like parts of the chief's name, and they were replaced by the words /ruʔi/ and /hota/ respectively.

The result of such a situation can be that even basic vocabulary, if given a long enough period of time, will change. If the new words are obtained by borrowing as is the case in Australia, then the change will be in the direction of nearby languages. Two languages which may only be very distantly related, may eventually come to have a very high cognate percentage of shared items even in core vocabulary items.

Having shown that the basic assumption that vocabulary replacement operates at a constant rate for all languages is *wrong*, we cannot *assume* that the method will be applicable for Melanesian languages either. We cannot prove it is wrong either. We can only say that we cannot be sure of its validity.

There is a second problem with lexicostatistics, and that is one of interpretation of the results. Given that change is random within the core vocabulary, it is possible for *some* languages to change the same 19.5% of their vocabulary every 1000 years, and to retain the remaining 80.5% intact over succeeding periods. It is also possible at the other extreme for *some* languages to change 19.5% of their vocabulary every 1000 years as we would predict, yet for the actual items to be different in each successive period. The result of this possible change will be that two languages, while separated by the same period of time, might have dramatically different vocabulary retention figures, depending on which items were actually replaced. Some languages will simply be accidentally conservative, while others will accidentally have a high degree of change. However, we would be forced to recognise these as being fairly distantly related. For instance, after 2000 years, it can be expected that the range of core vocabulary retentions will be as low as 10% in a few languages, and as high as 70% in a few others, while for most it will be around 40% as we would predict from the figures earlier. The languages that have retained 10% and 70% will *look* quite divergent, though they are in fact separated by the same time period. We should not assume, therefore, that simply because two languages share a fairly low figure for cognate percentage that the degree of relationship is particularly distant. This fact makes it impossible to be certain of the correctness of our interpretation of lexicostatistical data.

Finally, perhaps, we can point out that there are often practical difficulties in interpreting lexicostatistical data, for a wide variety of reasons some of which have been mentioned, and some of which may apply in only a particular situation. The data presented earlier as an illustration of subgrouping technique was in fact highly idealised. (You might remember that only hypothetical data was used, and not real data, for this reason.) It is not often that data from actual languages produces a completely consistent picture, without contradictions. A more typical set of lexicostatistical data may look more like this data from a number of languages in Milne Bay, for example:

Mwalakwasia
87 Somwadina
82 86 Biawa
72 71 82 Sigasiga
74 73 76 78 Lomitawa
64 62 84 69 80 Sipupu
59 58 55 52 67 79 Kelologea
62 59 71 66 79 86 78 Meudana
74 72 76 65 74 76 70 71 Kasikasi
73 74 80 67 72 62 55 66 76 Guleguleu

In this data, there do not appear to be many clear 'discontinuities' or 'breaks' between one group and another. The figures seem to generally gradually 'merge' into each other, producing very little hope of drawing a family tree.

It is perhaps appropriate at this point to remind you of something we looked at earlier, in Chapter Six. When we were looking at criticisms of the Neogrammarian Hypothesis, we noted that it is in fact unrealistic to think strictly in terms of a family tree model of language change, with sharp splits between languages. We saw, in fact, that languages often change according to a wave model, with innovations spreading out from one (or more) central points. According to this model, languages and dialects often *do* merge into each other. So, this Milne Bay data that we have just looked at perhaps represents the rule rather than the exception when it come to trying to work out subgroups.

READING GUIDE QUESTIONS
1. What is a subgroup?
2. What is the difference between a shared retention and a shared innovation?
3. Why can similarities between languages due to shared retentions not be used as evidence for subgrouping?
4. What is drift or parellel development? How does this affect the way we go about deciding on subgroups?
5. What sorts of innovations are the best kind of evidence for subgrouping?
6. What is lexicostatistics?
7. What basic assumptions underlie the method of determining linguistic relationships by lexicostatistics?
8. What is the inspection method of determining whether two forms are cognate or not?
9. What is the difference between core and peripheral vocabulary?
10. What is glottochronology?
11. What are some problems associated with lexicostatistics and glottochronology?

EXERCISES
1. Look at the Korafe, Notu and Binandere data in Data Set 7. Make a hypothesis concerning the subgrouping of these languages on the basis of the reconstruction of the changes from proto-language you worked out earlier.

2. Look back at the data from exercise 9 in Chapter Five for Aroma, Hula and Sinaugoro. What subgrouping hypothesis can you make for these three languages on the basis of shared innovations?

3. Look at the following forms in Proto-Gazelle Peninsula, and in the descendant forms of Lunga-Lunga, Nodup, Pila-Pila and Vatom (locations shown on map). What is the subgrouping of these four speech communities, and give your justification for the subgrouping you propose.

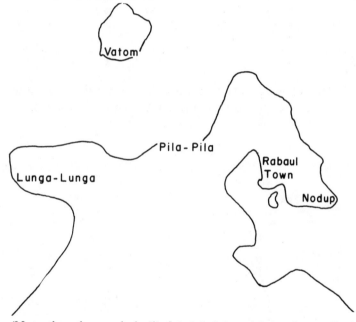

(Note that the symbols [i̥], [e̥], [ḁ], [o̥] and [u̥] refer to final voiceless vowels.)

	PROTO GAZELLE	PILA-PILA	NODUP	VATOM	LUNGA-LUNGA
1. basket	*ratu̥	rat	ratu̥	rat	ratu̥
2. fishtrap	*vupu̥	vup	vuvu	vup	vuvu̥
3. club	*ramu̥	ram	ramu̥	ram	ramu̥
4. sling	*vasiani̥	vaian	vaiani̥	vaian	vasiani̥
5. outrigger	*samani̥	aman	amani̥	aman	samani̥
6. house	*pali̥	pal	pali̥	pal	pali̥
7. fence	*lipilipi̥	liplip	livilivu	liplip	

207

8. axe	*pemu̱	pem	pemu̱	pem	pemu̱
9. ground	*pisa	pia	pia	pia	pisa
10. *kulau*	*tiripu̱	tirip	tirivu	tirip	tirivu̱
11. *kambang/*					
lime	*kabaṉi	kabaŋ	kabaṉi	kabaŋ	kabaṉi
12. yam	*upu̱	up	uvu	–	uvu̱
13. *talis* nut	*talisa	talia	talia	talia	talisa
14. dog	*papi̱	pap	pavu	pap	–
15. cry	*taṉisi̱	taṉi	taṉi	taṉi	taṉisi̱
16. fire	*iapi̱	iap	iavu	iap	iavi̱
17. ground	*pisa	pia	pia	pia	pisa
18. orange	*mulisi	muli	muli	muli	mulisi̱
19. bird	*beso	beo	beo	beo	beso
20. nits	*lisi	li	lia	li	lisi̱
21. small	*sikiliki̱	ikilik	ikiliki̱	ikilik	sikiliki̱
22. sea	*tasi̱	ta	tai	ta	tasi̱

4. The following data comes from four languages spoken in the
   areas of Cape York in northern Queensland as shown below.

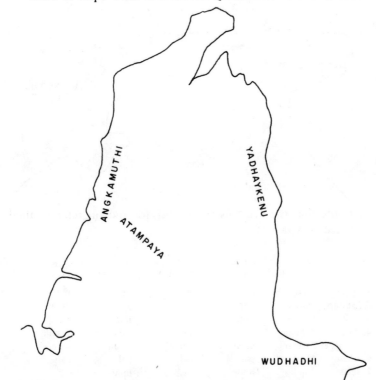

Examine the reconstructed proto-language and the descendant forms, and suggest a subgrouping hypothesis on the basis of shared innovations, and give your reasons.

	ATAMPAYA	AKGKAMUTHI	YADHAYKENU	WUDHADHI
1. *kaʈa 'rotten'	ɣaʈa	aʈa	aʈa	—
2. *kantu 'canoe'	ɣantu	antu	antu	antu
3. *puŋku 'knee'	wuŋku	wuŋku	wuŋku	—
4. *ɲaŋka 'mouth'	naŋka	aŋka	aŋka	aŋka
5. *yuku 'tree'	yuku	yuku	yuku	—
6. *ɲukal ' ot'	nukaw	uka:	uka:	ukal
7. *pinta 'arm'	winta	winta	winta	inta
8. *puɲa 'sun'	wuɲa	wuɲa	wuɲa	uɲa
9. *ʈipa 'liver'	lipa	yipa	yipa	—
10. *wapun 'head'	wapun	apun	apu	apun
11. *wuypu 'bad'	wuypu	uypu	uypu	uypu
12. *uypuɲ 'fly'	uypuɲ	uypuɲ	uypuɲ	uypuy
13. *aypaɲ 'stone'	aypaɲ	aypaɲ	aypaɲ	aypay
14. *ʈalan 'tongue'	lalan	yalan	yala	alan
15. *panʈal 'yam sp'	wanʈaw	wanʈa:	wanʈa:	—
16. *ɾanʈal 'hill'	ɾanʈaw	yanʈa:	yanʈa:	—
17. *pili 'run'	wili	wili	wili	—
18. *ɾuŋka 'cry'	ɾuŋka	yuŋka	yuŋka	uŋka
19. *ɾa 'throw'	ɾa	ya	ya	—
20. *ɾupal 'white'	ɾupaw	yupa:	yupa:	—
21. *ɾuʈu 'dead'	ɾuʈu	yuʈu	yuʈu	uʈu
22. *pilu 'hip'	wilu	wilu	wilu	ilu
23. *pupu 'buttocks'	wupu	wupu	wupu	upu
24. *ŋampu 'tooth'	ŋampu	ampu	ampu	ampu
25. *mayi 'food'	mayi	ayi	ayi	ayi
26. *miɲa 'meat'	miɲa	iɲa	iɲa	iɲa
27. *iwuɲ 'ear'	—	—	iwuɲ	iwuy
28. *ɾapan 'strong'	ɾapan	yapan	yapa	—

5. Look at the following data from six different languages and answer the questions below:

	A	B	C	D	E	F
1. child	mwana	mwana	umwana	bačeh	anak	bataʔ
2. cry	lia	dila	lila	giryeh	triak	iyak
3. drink	ɲwa	nua	nwa	nuʃidan	minuman	inum
4. fire	moto	tiya	umulilo	ateʃ	api	apoy
5. five	tano	tanu	sanu	pænɟ	lima	lima
6. four	nne	ia	ne	čæhær	empat	ampat
7. hill	kilima	mongo	ulupili	tel	bukit	bukid
8. laugh	čeka	seva	seka	xændidan	tertawa	tawa
9. leg	mguu	kulu	ukuulu	saq	kaki	pa
10. lip	mdomo	koba	umulomo	læb	bibir	bibig
11. man	mtu	muntu	umuntu	mærd	oraŋ	tau
12. news	habari	nsangu	ičeevo	xæbær	xabar	balita

Bongabonga
88 Tongariki
32 31 Makatea
57 56 29 Woraviu
57 56 27 91 Sesake
53 53 28 87 86 Nguna
55 54 30 86 86 93 Pwele
56 55 29 88 87 93 94 Siviri
50 50 26 75 75 78 79 78 Lelepa
50 49 30 67 67 69 68 69 72 Pango
47 45 26 60 61 63 64 65 65 86 Eratap
50 48 29 67 67 69 79 70 71 82 76 Eton

9. The basic vocabularies of the following ten languages/dialects
   share the cognate percentages below. According to lexicostatistics, how might you subgroup these languages? Give your
   reasons. How might you account for any of the languages that
   do not seem to fit your hypothesis? (Note that this data is made
   up.)

   A
   89 B
   91 93 C
   87 87 85 D
   73 72 73 74 E
   91 66 68 66 69 F
   65 68 63 62 67 89 G
   51 54 52 50 46 43 54 H
   42 47 43 49 51 41 48 90 I
   43 48 42 49 50 51 75 88 86 J

10. The following made up figures present the shared cognate per-
    centages between ten languages. Draw a family tree to indicate
    the degrees of relationship between these languages. Present
    your arguments.

A
93 B
70 73 C
74 72 91 D
72 75 86 85 E
72 71 88 90 89 F
51 54 58 52 56 51 G
53 56 56 52 52 55 87 H
55 52 51 55 53 56 71 73 I
55 51 51 52 53 57 53 50 55 J

FURTHER READING

1. Lehmann, Winfred P. *Historical Linguistics: An Introduction* (Chapter 7 'Study of Loss in Language: Lexicostatistics'), pp. 107-114.
2. Gudschinsky, Sarah 'The ABC's of Lexicostatistics (Glottochronology)', in Hymes (ed.) *Language in Culture and Society*, pp. 612-623.

Chapter Ten
OBSERVING LANGUAGE CHANGE

10.1 The Traditional View

If you ask a speaker of any language the question 'Can you think of any changes that you can see taking place in your language now?', you will be quite likely to get a positive answer. It seems that people are usually aware of some kinds of changes that are taking place in their language at any particular time.

For instance, if you were to ask somebody what changes are taking place in English, you might get answers like this: 'The word "whom" is being replaced with "who" in sentences like "This is the person whom I saw yesterday".' If you were to ask speakers of Tok Pisin if they can observe any changes taking place at the moment in the language, you will probably find a range of answers, which might include things like:

- some words are being replaced. Instead of *natnat*, people are starting to say *moskito* for 'mosquito' and the word *arapela* for 'other' is being replaced by *narapela*.
- people are shortening some of their words, so *mipela* 'us' is becoming *mipla,* and *bilong* 'of', is becoming *blo.*

We saw in Chapter One that speakers of languages are often aware of changes that are taking place in their languages, and that these changes tend to be regarded as 'corruptions' of the 'correct' or unchanged form of the language. We mentioned specifically the fact that speakers of various Melanesian languages often regret the changes they see taking place in their own languages nowadays, as words from Tok Pisin or other languages are coming to replace some of the original words of the language.

Even though the actual speakers of languages are often quite aware of changes taking place in their languages at a given time, it is rather surprising to find that for a long time, linguists claimed that language change could never be observed. Linguists claimed that all we could do was to study how a language behaved before a change and after a change, and to compare the two. But to study the change actually taking place was impossible. They argued that language change was so slow and so gradual that the differences between the stages of language would be so far apart in time that we could not hope to observe any of the changes taking place. One of the most important linguists of the century after Saussure was the American Leonard Bloomfield, and he stated quite clearly in 1933 that:

> The process of linguistic change has never been directly observed; ... such an observation, with our present facilities, is inconceivable.

Why did linguists say this, ignoring the obvious facts around them that ordinary speakers of any language can very clearly see?

As we mentioned back in Chapter One, Saussure is regarded as the originator of modern linguistics, and one of his major achievements was to divert attention from the purely diachronic study of language to the synchronic study of language. Before him, the Neogrammarians claimed that they had established linguistics as a genuine empirical science, i.e. a field of study based on the observation of physical data, with generalisations that can be tested by referring back to a different (but comparable) set of data. The Neogrammarians were able to point to earlier etymological studies and claim that there were never any scientific 'checks' on the conclusions that people made. This was because there was no distinction between systematic sound correspondences and sporadic sound correspondences. Only in the case of systematic sound correspondences can we claim to have any scientifically valid generalisations.

However, Saussure reacted against the Neogrammarians by claiming that *their* position was in fact basically unscientific. He said this because it is impossible to describe the changes in a language over a period of time until we first of all describe the language at particular points in time. To do scientific diachronic linguistics, we must first of all have two synchronic descriptions of the language taken at different times. Saussure's *Course in General Linguistics* set out to describe the basic concepts that he felt were needed before we could actually sit down and write scientific synchronic descriptions of languages.

Saussure proposed a very rigid distinction between diachronic and synchronic descriptions, and expressed the point of view that historical information was totally irrelevant in a synchronic analysis of a language. By implication, we can assume also that Saussure would regard any guesses about the future changes a language might undergo as being quite irrelevant, and should not be included in a synchronic description of a language. In a synchronic description, all we should be interested in is describing the relations between the units in a system at a point in time. This distinction between diachrony and synchrony can perhaps be compared to a movie film. A movie film is a sequence of still photographs. A description of an individual photograph would be like a synchronic description of a language. But these individual still photographs, when they are viewed quickly one after the other, indicate movements like real life. A study of these movements would therefore be like a diachronic study of language; to do such a study, you would need to compare one of the still photographs with another further up the film strip or further down the film strip.

So, Saussure and linguists who followed him in the same tradition (like Bloomfield, as we just saw) in a sense were blinded by their own theoretical approach. They failed to see language change in process (even though everybody else could see it!). Because they did not believe it could be seen, they did not look for it.

But, in the last couple of decades, linguists have gradually come to realise that this approach was wrong. They opened their eyes, and they saw evidence of changes taking place all around them in all sorts of languages. So, where was it that linguists started finding evidence of change in progress?

There are two concepts that linguists came to look at in more detail that people like Saussure and Bloomfield (and most other linguists of their time) failed to look at. These are the concepts of INDETERMINACY in language, and VARIABILITY in language.

10.2   Indeterminacy

To understand the concept of indeterminacy (or 'fuzziness' as it is sometimes called) in language, take a look at the following English sentences. Would you judge them to be grammatical or ungrammatical?

(1)   James is chopping the firewood
(2)   Daffodil must sells something at the market before she going home
(3)   The dogs don't try to keep off the grass
(4)   Remy isn't wanting any money from me
(5)   Who isn't that?

(6)   I saw a man coming from the bank get robbed
(7)   Who did you come to the pictures without?
(8)   Jennifer said she will come yesterday
(9)   I doesn't goes to church at Christmas

Some of these sentences are clearly grammatical, and we could imagine anybody who speaks English actually saying sentences like (1), (3) and (6). Some are also clearly ungrammatical, and people who speak English know they could not say things like (2), (8) and (9). But what about sentences like (4), (5) and (7)? Are they grammatical or ungrammatical? They are clearly not as grammatical as (1), (3) and (6) but at the same time, it is hard to say they are completely ungrammatical like (2), (8) and (9). In fact, they seem to be neither one nor the other, or perhaps they are both at the same time.

There are many other examples of indeterminacy that we can talk about in language. For instance, we can relate many verbs and nouns in English by the presence or absence of the suffix which we write -*tion*, So:

VERB	NOUN
emancipate	emancipation
isolate	isolation
speculate	speculation
subject	subjection
connect	connection
delegate	delegation

We also have the nouns *aggression* and *destruction*. If somebody says things like:

Argentina aggressed against Great Britain in the Falklands.
This car self-destructs after 15,000 kilometres.

we somehow feel that while these sentences are not really all that good, we could perhaps imagine somebody saying them. These sentences are also part of this no-man's land, somewhere between grammatical and ungrammatical. The words 'to agress' and 'to destruct' do not appear in the dictionary, but they are clearly not as bad as non-existent verbs like 'to teapot' and 'to underneath'.

Because there are many examples in language that are like this, linguists in the past have tended to deal only with those constructions that are clearly grammatical, and to distinguish them from those that are clearly ungrammatical. These linguists felt that the categories we recognise in language must be in a sense completely 'watertight'. But in fact, categories in language are often very fuzzy. Grammars are *not* watertight – they leak all over the place. Categories are 'fuzzy' or 'indeterminate'. By insisting that language consists of a number of very strict and rigid 'either/or' kinds of rules, they ignored a lot of what was actually going on when people use languages.

The examples we have just looked at are actually evidence of some kinds of change in process. The indeterminate or semi-grammatical status of sentence (4) is because originally in the grammar of English, verbs that indicated any kind of mental state (such as 'know', 'understand', and also 'want') could never occur in the *-ing* form, which indicates that an action is in progress.[1] So, while it is clearly possible to say:

Remy is asking me for money.

because it refers to an action, and not a mental state, it used to be completely impossible to say:

*Remy is wanting money from me.

(with the asterisk * marking the sentence as ungrammatical). But, the rule seems to be changing, and people are now starting to allow the *-ing* progressive maker to occur on verbs such as 'want'. Also, there was originally no verb in English 'to destruct', we could only say 'to destroy', and the noun form of this, i.e. 'destruction', was irregular in its derivation. But, now people are coming to say 'destruct' in some cases instead of 'destroy'. This is an example of a change in which the relationship between nouns and verbs in English is being made more regular, when the suffix *-tion* is involved.

---

[1] But note that the *-ing* as a nominaliser is quite acceptable with these forms. E.g. Wanting money is a sign of selfishness.

This concept of linguistic indeterminacy also relates to the concept of the linguistic system, used by Saussure. He argued that in describing a language synchronically, we are listing the various units (i.e. phonemes, morphemes, words, phrase types, clause types and so on) that occur in the language, and describing the ways in which these units interrelate (i.e. the grammatical rule for putting them together to make larger units). In talking about describing *the* system of a particular language, he is implying that for every language, there is one system and one system only.

But here too, the theoretical approach does not seem to be consistent with what is going on in language. There is sometimes a need to recognise that within a single language, we might have to describe more than one system, though these different systems are themselves interrelated. Let's look at the phonology of Motu, to see how an approach where we have more than one system operating at once produces a simpler description of the language, and one that fits with the intuitions the speakers have about their language.

If you look at the basic vocabulary of Motu, you will find that the language has five vowel phonemes, i.e. /i/, /e/, /a/, /o/ and /u/, as well as the following consonant phonemes:

$$
\begin{array}{llll}
\text{p} & \text{t} & \text{k} & \text{k}^{\text{w}} \\
\text{b} & \text{d} & \text{g} & \text{g}^{\text{w}} \\
\text{m} & \text{n} & & \\
\text{v} & & \gamma & \\
& \text{l} & & \\
& \text{r} & & \\
& \text{h} & &
\end{array}
$$

Of these consonant phonemes, only /t/ has any noticeable allophonic variation. We saw earlier that we can state the distribution of its allophones as:

$$
\text{/t/} : \begin{cases} \text{[s] before front vowels} \\ \text{[t] elsewhere} \end{cases}
$$

The labio-velar phonemes /k^{w}/ and /g^{w}/ are treated as unit phonemes in Motu for reasons of simplicity. If we treated them as sequences of two phonemes, i.e. velar stops followed by the phoneme /w/, then we complicate our description of the phonology in two ways:

218

(a)   We have to introduce a separate phoneme /w/, which occurs in this environment only. This phoneme would be unlike all other phonemes in the language, which are unrestricted in their distribution.

(b)   We would have to revise our statement of the phonotactics of the language to allow consonant clusters of just this type. Otherwise, syllables in Motu are of the type CV only (i.e. a single consonant followed by a vowel).

But, if we include other, more recently introduced words in the language, we find forms like these:

tini	'tin'
maketi	'market'
su	'shoe'
traka	'truck'
hospitala	'hospital'

These words break some of the rules of phonology we have just described. The original neat complementary distribution between [t] and [s] has been destroyed for one thing. And for another thing, the language now allows words with consonant clusters, in initial position (e.g. /tr-/) and in medial position (e.g. -sp-)

Linguists of Bloomfield's point of view would simply ignore these loan words by saying that they are not really a part of the language. They would probably include those loan-words that had actually been made to fit the patterns of the language. So, they would probably be happy to include the form /makedi/ for 'market', which some people actually do use, because it avoids the disruption of the complementary distribution between [t] and [s]. They would also probably be quite happy for their dictionary to include words like /gavamani/ 'government', because the consonant clusters have been eliminated. But, to ignore these words (or to describe only those words that fit "the system") is to ignore the way people actually use the language. This kind of description, which recognises only a single phonemic system for the language, is clearly inadequate.

To describe the language adequately, we need to recognise *two* phonemic systems, one for original Motu words, where [t] and [s] are not phonemically distinct and where there are no consonant clusters, and another system for loan words, where [t] and [s] are phonemically distinct, and where there are some kinds of consonant clusters. Speakers of the language are normally aware of these separate systems, and could probably tell you which system a word belongs to if you asked them. The variation in some forms that we see is a result of competition between the two systems. Change is clearly underway in the phonology of Motu. We find that some foreign words are completely adapted to the original phonemic system; some words are sometimes adapted to this system, and sometimes they obey the rules for the second system; and finally, other words only seem to obey the rules for the second system, and are never fully adapted to the original system. More and more words are coming into the last category, so we could assume that when the number of such words becomes large enough, then this will become the *new* phonemic system of the language, and the original system will cease to operate. So, eventually, we could expect [t] and [s] to become separate phonemes, as we saw in section 4.3 earlier. Motu [t] and [s] at the moment are actually indeterminate in their phonemic status. In some ways, we can say that they are allophones of one phoneme. In other ways, they seem to be phonemically distinct. This is therefore another example of how linguists have ignored the fact that linguistic systems are 'fuzzy'.

10.3 Variability

The other important concept that earlier linguists were blind to and which stopped them from seeing changes in progress was the concept of VARIABILITY. Linguists traditionally believed that language is basically a 'yes-or-no' kind of thing, as we have just seen. While geographical varieties of language (i.e. dialects) and social class varieties of language (i.e. sociolects) can to some extent be described as single 'systems', it is rather more difficult to deal with differences of style within individual speakers within a single system. Probably all speakers of all languages alter their speech so that it matches the formality of the situation, even though they may not realise they are doing it.

Linguists found it hard to describe these different styles of speech within a single fixed set of rules. For them, a rule either applied or it did not, or perhaps it was completely up to the individual speaker whether or not it would apply (i.e. the rule would in such cases be described as 'optional').

For instance, in English, there is a passive rule, which changes sentences like:

'Wartovo chased the boys along the beach.'

into sentences like:

'The boys were chased along the beach by Wartovo.'

These two sentences refer to the same thing, and linguists argued that the choice of one form over the other was completely random (that is to say that the passive rule was applied completely optionally). But the choice of the passive form over the active form is *not* completely random if we look at actual usage. Compare the following two paragraphs, which differ only in that one contains active forms:

I

We expect children to learn to behave like adults by the time they are teenagers. We give them models of behaviour to follow, and we punish them when they do not follow them. When they do things the way we like them to, we reward them.

II

Children are expected to learn to behave like adults by the time they are teenagers. They are given models of behaviour to be followed, and they are punished when they are not followed. When things are done the way we like them to be done, they are rewarded.

I think we could probably agree that paragraph I sounds more 'conversational', while paragraph II sounds more 'literary', even though they are both basically saying the same things. If we looked at the use of the active and the passive constructions in English, we would probably find that the active form is predominant in these kinds of situations:

- letters to friends
- private conversations with close relatives
- messages scribbled on the dust of somebody's car window
- at home (if you speak English at home)
- a note pinned to a lecturer's door saying why you couldn't come for class

On the other hand, the use of the passive form will probably increase in these kinds of situations:

- letters applying for jobs
- formal speeches
- public notices
- in the classroom
- an essay for a lecturer

The difference between these two sets of situations is that the first set is considered to be more casual or informal, while the second set is considered to be more formal. When speakers feel that the situation is casual, they tend to use more active sentences, but when speakers feel that the situation is more formal, they tend to use more passive constructions.

It is difficult to write these facts into a grammatical rule, so linguists just ignored them, and described the passive rule as 'optional'. One of the most influential linguists of the present day, Noam Chomsky, has even expressed these kinds of views. He says that a grammar should describe 'an ideal speaker-hearer relationship', and it should ignore factors outside language (such as the formality of a social situation). But language is not an 'ideal' system at all. It is in fact highly variable.

The importance of the concept of variability in language as an indication that language change was in progress was first described in detail by the American linguist William Labov. He studied the way people speak in the city of New York. He found that there was in fact no such thing as a 'New York dialect'. For instance, he found that some New Yorkers would say [kʰaː] for 'car' while other New Yorkers would say [kʰar]. He did a survey to find out which people used which form, and came up with the following results, according to the social class background of the speaker:

	[r] always present	[r] some- times present	[r] never present
working class	6%	12%	82%
lower middle class	22%	37%	41%
upper middle class	24%	46%	30%

These figures indicate working class New Yorkers have no [r] in such words in 82% of cases, whereas upper middle class New Yorkers have no [r] in only 30% of cases. The lower middle class speakers lie somewhere in the middle, as they 'drop' their [r] in 41% of cases. Clearly, as we go higher in New York society, we find that people use [r] in such words more and more.

But the story did not end there. He also found that the same person might use [kʰa:] sometimes and [kʰar] at other times. The choice was not completely free however, in the same way that the choice between active and passive forms of a sentence is not completely free. What he found was that speakers from all classes preferred the form [kʰar] in situations that they felt were more formal,

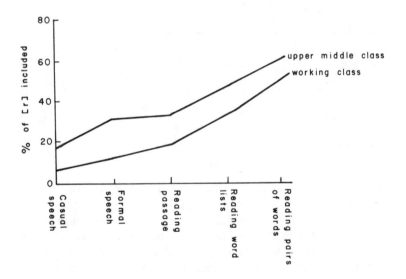

and they were less insistent on this form when they felt that the situation was more casual, and were more likely to use [kʰa:]. So look at the table below, which shows how many working class people and how many upper middle class people used the form with [r] in situations of different degrees of formality.

10.3 Variability

Something more interesting comes up when we look at the behav-
ior of the class *between* these two classes; that is, when we look at the
lower middle class New Yorkers. Their behaviour is now added to
the same table we just looked at:

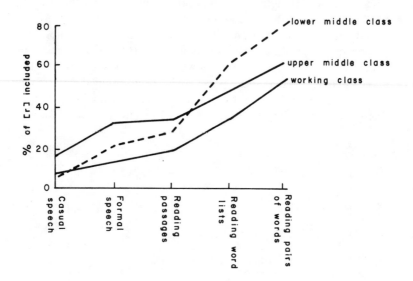

You will see that when they are using their most careful forms of
speech, they actually put in *more* [r] sounds that the people who are
socially above them. This seems to be a contradiction in a way,
because we saw earlier that the higher one's social class, the more
likely a speaker is to use the former [kʰar] rather than [kʰa:].

What this table indicates is that all speakers are aware that it is
more socially acceptable to use the forms with [r] than the forms
without [r]. The more careful someone is, the more likely they are to
include the [r]. In addition, there is a clear indication that it is the
higher social classes that are widely regarded as speaking 'correctly'
(i.e. with the [r]), even though the table indicates that they don't
always speak that way. People of the lower classes in stratified societies are forever trying to adopt the behaviour of their social superiors, and so also try to speak like them. There is not only social

prestige in the clothes people wear, the cars people drive and who people mix with, but there is also social prestige in the way people speak.

Of all the social groups in a stratified society, it is usually the lower middle class that feel socially most insecure. The working class are working class, and they cannot hope to rise any higher. They know their 'place'. The upper middle class are already marked as being socially superior in so many ways — by their cars, by their clothes, by their houses and by the people they mix with. So, they don't have to worry too much about the way they speak. But the lower middle class are somewhere in between. They are not working class, and they are high enough in the social system that people might think they *could* be upper middle class. But they do not have all of the obvious things that their social superiors *do* have, like the cars, and the houses and the clothes and so on. So, what tends to happen is that they try to improve their social position in the way that they speak. They therefore try to speak a kind of English that they consider to be more "correct". This is why we get the LOWER MIDDLE CLASS CROSSOVER on the table. This kind of crossover is very common in studies of linguistic variation: it shows that there is a prestigious form that speakers are consciously trying to adopt. It is a kind of linguistic 'keeping up with the Jones's.' It is an indication that linguistic change is in progress.

This kind of situation can actually lead the lower middle class into HYPERCORRECTION. That is to say, people sometimes actually use a particular linguistic variable in a place where the higher classes would never use it, and where we would predict it would never occur for historical reasons. For instance, in words like 'father', 'Dakota' and 'data', the lower middle class might actually pronounce these as 'farther', 'dakotar' and 'datar', especially when they are trying to impress members of the upper classes.

It is clear therefore, that English in New York is changing. Back in the 1930's, the normal pronunciation of words like 'car' was without the [r]. If you listen to old movies, you will very clearly hear that in stories set in New York, the characters hardly ever pronounced their [r] sounds in such words. In the 1950s and 1960s, there was an increase in the number of [r] sounds that people used, and this has led to the present situation. Presumably, after some time, the whole city will be pronouncing the [r] all the time, and a language change will have been completed. (But, although we can see that the change is heading in this direction, we cannot tell how long it will take for the change to be complete.)

This discussion of the role of linguistic variability and social prestige in language change very neatly explains how a language like English changes. English is the language of a large-scale society that is stratified. But not all societies are like this. What of the small-scale societies of Melanesia, where traditionally people know and are related to most of the people they have contact with? The structure of such societies is radically different: it is pointless to speak of upper middle class and working class in traditional Melanesian societies. Yet, Melanesian languages change just like the languages of stratified societies. We can find synchronic evidence of change in Melanesian languages too. For instance, in the Lenakel language of Vanuatu, there is variability word finally between the sounds [s] and [h]. Initially and medially, there are minimal pairs to show that these two sounds are phonemically distinct. Word finally however, the distinction is presently being neutralised, and we get free variation between forms like the following:

məs ~ məh	'die'	
ɔs ~ ɔh	'take'	
pugas ~ pugah	'pig'	

However, the situation is not quite as simple as this. For one thing, the free variation is more common with some speakers than with other speakers. For another thing, the variation tends to occur with some words more often than with others, while with some words, there is no free variation allowed at all, and only [s] occurs.

So, what factors are involved in the spread of changes in such societies? The answer is that western linguists do not really know. It is presumably only possible to find out from a well-trained linguist from a Melanesian society, who really understands the dynamics of such a society. Until then, our understanding of language change will be incomplete.

10.4 The Spread of Change

In the preceding section, we saw how a linguistic change can spread from one small group of society so that it eventually affects the whole society. We saw that in socially stratified societies, the force behind the spread of a change was social prestige.

As we saw earlier, the Neogrammarians, when speaking of sound change, claimed that sound changes in languages are conditioned by purely phonetic factors. They said that if a sound change applied in one word, then the same change took place in all other phonetically comparable words at the same time. So, for instance, when final voiced stops were devoiced in German (a change we have referred to a number of times already) the Neogrammarians would argue that all final voiced stops underwent this change simultaneously.

Now that we are in a position to observe language changes taking place, we can also check this assumption of the Neogrammarians. In fact, we can now show that this view of language change is quite misleading. Sound changes are not like mechanical processes, obeying set rules in all words at the same time.

For instance, we briefly mentioned the change in Lenakel, by which the phonemic distinction between /s/ and /h/ is presently being neutralised in word final position, with the archiphoneme having the form [s] or [h] in free variation. However, there are actually two categories of words that we can look at with respect to this change:

(a) The first category of words includes less common words in the language which never have this alternation. With these words, we find only final [s] and we never find an alternative form with [h].

(b) The second category of words does allow free variation. These words tend to be the more common words in the language. Also, some words in this category are more likely to enter into free variation than others.

Here, we clearly have a change in progress, and this change is in a sense gradually creeping through the vocabulary. Eventually, it will probably cover all words that now have final /s/, but it has affected only some of these words at this stage. This evidence is clearly in contradiction to the Neogrammarian position, because the change:

$$s \rightarrow h \, / \, \underline{\hspace{1cm}} \, \#$$

227

has applied arbitrarily to some words, and not others (though, when the change is complete, it will certainly look as though it had applied to all words at once). (The Paamese example dealing with labiovelar consonants mentioned in Chapter Six illustrates exactly the same process also.)

We can give another rather different kind of example of a linguistic change in progess, and we can see that this change is also gradually extending itself through the language rather than affecting all possible forms at once. This example involves a grammatical change rather than a sound change, and the language is Tok Pisin.

In Tok Pisin, the difference between singular and plural noun phrases is marked by the morpheme *ol*, which is added at the beinning of a noun phrase (or , sometimes, between a demonstrative and the rest of the noun phrase). (The plural maker *ol*, incidentally, has the same form as the third person plural pronoun 'they'; Tok Pisin shares this grammatical feature with a great many Pacific languages) E.g.:

man	'man'	ol man	'men'
liklik mangi	'small boy'	ol liklik mangi	'small boys'
traipela banana mau	'big ripe banana'	ol traipela banana mau	'big ripe bananas'
dispela haus	'this house'	ol dispela haus/ dispela ol haus	'these houses'
dispela swit-pela popo	'this sweet pawpaw'	ol dispela swit-pela popo/dispela ol switpela popo	'these sweet pawpaws'

There is a change in progress by which a plural marker derived from English is entering the language. This plural marker has the form *-s* (with the allomorph *-is* after nouns ending in *-s*). At present, this plural marker is optionally added to the head of the noun phrase (though the marker *ol* is always present, whether or not the suffix is used). This double marking of plural noun phrases is made only with some speakers. It is the English-educated speakers who are initiating this change, which seems to have reached its maximum spread in the Tok Pisin of university educated speakers of the language. What is interesting for the present discussion is to see which nouns are more likely to take the -s plural marking in Tok Pisin.

Among the group who most frequently mark plurals by both *ol* and -s, we find that some words very frequently take this double plural marking. This category includes words like:

ol risosis bilong yumi	'our resources'
ol politikel divelopmens bilong nau	'modern political developments'
ol stafs bilong yunivesiti	'university staff'

Words which behave in this way can all be described as being 'learned' words. They are the words that are borrowed straight from English to fill gaps in the vocabulary of Tok Pisin. Probably none of these kinds of words appears in any standard Tok Pisin dictionary, and would not be understood by the lesser educated masses.

In the second category of nouns, we find only occasional use of double plural marking, with -s/-is. Such words are the more everyday words of the language. They are the sorts of words that are found in the dictionary, which the ordinary grass roots[2] speaker of Tok Pisin would use and understand. But, even within this category, we find some variability. Nouns of English origin *may* take the double marking, whereas nouns of non-English origin may *not* take the double marking, e.g:

ol de(s)	'days'
ol hama(s)	'hammers'
ol plaua(s)	'flowers'
ol yia(s)	'years'
ol pekato/*ol pekatos	'sins' (from Latin)
ol diwai/*ol diwais	'trees' (From a New Britain language)
ol pikinini/*ol pikininis	'children' (from Portuguese)
ol kanaka/*ol kanakas	'grass roots people' (from Hawaiian)

---

[2] 'Grass roots' is a fairly standard English term in Papua New Guinea, which refers to the uneducated masses. It contrasts with 'elite'. People generally recognise two social classes at the national level, and give them these names. The term 'working class' is not used. There are few parallels between the Melanesian rural villagers and the Western urban working class.

Even within this category of words derived from English, there are differences as to which words are more likely to take the double plural marking than others. Words with final vowels are more free to behave in this way than words with final consonants, and words with final -s are the least likely of all to have double plural marking, e.g:

ol blanket/*?ol blankets	'blankets'
ol naip/*?ol naips	'knives'
ol tang/*?ol tangs	'tanks'
ol pes/**ol pesis³	'faces'
ol glas/**ol glasis	'glasses'
ol bisnis/**ol bisnisis	'businesses'

What we can see from this example is that even a grammatical change can come in gradually. It can first of all apply to a small part of the vocabulary that belongs to a particular word class, and it can gradually extend to other parts of the vocabulary in that word class.

   (It will be interesting to observe the future progress of this change. Perhaps the change will spread to more nouns in the language, or perhaps the marking will stay as it is. Perhaps the social prestige of the elite will be enough for the change to spread to the grass roots. Or, perhaps the grass roots will react against the tendency of the elite to exhibit their level of education in the way they speak, and a genuine situation of diglossia will result, i.e. there would be a situation where there are two quite different dialects of a language for use in different kinds of situations.)

READING GUIDE QUESTIONS
1.   Why did linguists traditionally regard language change as being unobservable?
2.   What is indeterminacy in language?
3.   What is variability in language?
4.   How did linguists in the past deal with indeterminacy and variability?

---

³ But *pes* meaning 'page' seems to be regarded as 'learned'. Speakers of Tok Pisin would probably be more likely to allow *ol pesis* meaning 'pages' than when they mean 'faces'.

5. What does the 'lower middle class crossover' refer to? What is the importance of this concept?
6. What is hypercorrection?
7. What is the basic error of the Neogrammarian view that sound changes operates with purely phonetic conditioning factors?

EXERCISES

1. In Tok Pisin, the form *save* (which, as an independent verb, means 'know') can be used as a modal to mark habitual action. Some people today reduce this free form modal to the unstressed form *sa*. So:

Em	*no save*	*waswas*
he/she	not habitual	wash

    He/she never washes

    is pronounced by some people as:

    Em no`sa-waswas

    How would you describe what is happening here in the language? Does this alternative structure relate to any other alternative structures you are aware of in the language? Can you detect any trend, or direction, in which Tok Pisin seems to be heading in its grammatical structure?

2. The vowel [ʌ] in English normally corresponds to [a] in Tok Pisin, e.g.:

ENGLISH	TOK PISIN	
nʌmbə	namba	'number'
bʌmp	bam	'collide'
tʌŋ	taŋ	'tongue'
sʌn	san	'sun'

    The vowel [æ] in English corresponds to either [a] or [e] in Tok Pisin. Some words have only [a], and some have either [a] or [e].

'Learned' words (or words indicating a high degree of education) nearly always have only [e] E.g.

ENGLISH	TOK PISIN	
mæn	man	'man'
kæbidʒ	kabis	'cabbage'
bæg	bek	'bag'
fæktəri	fektori	'factory'
blæk	blak/blek	'black'

Now, let us imagine a standard six school leaver (i.e. someone who has completed six years of education at primary level without going on to high school), who speaks Tok Pisin and some English, and that this person is speaking to a university educated person in Tok Pisin. Although the lesser educated person knows that Tok Pisin has a word *giraun malmalum* for 'mud', s/he prefers to use instead the English word. But, instead of pronouncing it *mat* as we might expect, s/he pronounces it as *met*. What do you think is going on here?

3. In Australian English, voiceless stops are generally aspirated, except after /s/, where they are unaspirated. Also, the vowel [æ] tends to be phonetically quite long when there is a following voiced consonant. So, we find the following kinds of examples:

/stɔp/	[stɔpʰ]	'stop'
/stæmp/	[stæ:mpʰ]	'stamp'
/bæd/	[bæ:d]	'bad'
/ænd/	[æ:nd]	'and'
/hæpi/	[hæpʰi]	'happy'
/prɪti/	[pʰrɪtʰi]	'pretty'

In Papua New Guinea English, all voiceless stops are generally unaspirated, and vowels are generally short (with many distinctions of phonemic length being lost: the pair 'ship' and 'sheep' are generally pronounced the same). Some Papua New Guinean speakers of English, especially highly educated women, tend to produce forms like these, which do not normally occur in either PNG English, or in Australian English:

[stʰɔ:pʰ]	'stop'
[stʰæ:mpʰ]	'stamp'
pʰri:tʰi]	'pretty'
[hæ:pʰi]	'happy'

Why?

4.   In Australian English, the suffix -ing on words like 'running', 'hoping', 'wanting' and so on, can be pronounced as either [-ɪŋ] or as [-ən]. The following graph shows the percentages of men and women in Australia who were observed using the [-ən] form rather than the [-ɪŋ] form.

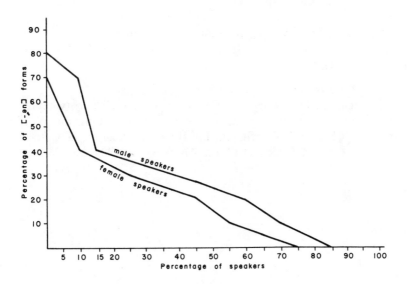

(To read this graph, the bottom line tells you what percentage of males or females we are considering. Look up from the percentage figure to the actual graph (of whichever group), and then read across to the other line, which tells you what per-

centage of times that number of men or women pronounce -*ing*
as [-ən] rather than as [-ɪŋ]. Thus, 50% of all women use [-ən]
almost 20% of the time, whereas 50% of all men use [-ɪŋ] almost
30% of thé time.) On average, men use [-ən] 24.4% of the time,
while women use [-ən] 15.6% of the time. When asked which
form they *believed* they used, the following percentages
emerged:

	women	men
1. Claimed to use [-ɪŋ] only	69%	65%
2. Claimed to use [-ən] only	3%	8%
3. Claimed to use both [-ɪŋ] and [-ən]	28%	27%

Can you offer any interpretation of these statistics?

FURTHER READING

1. Labov, William. *Sociolinguistic Patterns.*
2. Aitchison, Jean. *Language Change: Progress or Decay?* (Chapter 3
   'Charting the Changes', Chapter 4 'Spreading the Word',
   Chapter 5 'Conflicting Loyalties' and Chapter 6 'Catching
   On and Taking Off'), pp. 47-60, 63-76, 77-88.

Chapter Eleven
CAUSES OF LANGUAGE CHANGE

11.1 Theories of Language Change

Linguists have been aware for a long time that languages change over time, and that different languages change in sometimes remarkably similar ways. For as long as there has been an interest in the facts of language change, there has also been interest in trying to find out the actual *causes* of the change. Many causes have been suggested: some of these have no validity, and some are of great interest. We will now look at some of the theories that have been put forward, and assess each of them.

(a) Anatomy and 'Ethnic Character'

In the nineteenth century, some scholars attempted to find an anatomical explanation for language change, concentrating in particular on sound change. Since cultural differences were often assumed to be related to anatomical differences, sound change was sometimes also related to supposed cultural differences. For instance, there are two sets of sound changes in some of the Germanic languages of northern Europe. The so-called 'First Sound Shift' took place in the northern area in which Germanic languages were spoken (in the Gothic, Saxon and Scandinavian languages), while the more far-reaching 'Second Sound Shift' took place in the southern area (where German was spoken). A famous linguist of the nineteenth century, Jacob Grimm, tried to explain this by saying:

> It may be reckoned as evidence of the superior gentleness and moderation of the Gothic, Saxon and Scandinavian tribes that they contented themselves with the first sound shift, whilst the wilder force of the southern Germans was impelled towards the second shift.

Such statements can easily become useful supports to politically sponsored racial beliefs, and indeed have been used in this way in the past.

This was the case in Nazi Germany, and is still the case in modern South Africa. In South Africa, one of the two languages spoken by the Whites is Afrikaans (the other being English). Afrikaans shares many of the grammatical features of a creole language, i.e. grammatical simplification with regard to the original Dutch, and reduction of redundancy. Socially, there is some dispute as to the circumstances in which it evolved from Dutch, but many scholars have argued that it arose out of contact between Dutch-speakers and non-Dutch-speaking slaves and household servants. Many White South Africans reject this theory, however, and argue that their language evolved naturally and spontaneously out of Dutch. The far reaching changes that have taken place in the phonology and grammar language were put down to the revolutionary spirit of the Dutch settlers in a new land, as evidenced by the following quote:

> A conservative race living in a conservative environment does not as a rule indulge in great linguistic changes. The Dutch colonists of South Africa lived under very unconservative conditions. It was an entirely new kind of country, with new occupations and duties.

It has also been suggested in the past that there were significant differences between the languages of 'civilised' peoples and the languages of 'uncivilised' peoples. There was once a view that was commonly held among European intellectuals that modern civilisation was basically a corrupt and decadent existence, and that real human nature is to be found in the minds of what they came to call the 'noble savage'. We can obviously question the kinds of concepts that are involved here, but that is beside the point for the moment. What is to the point is the fact that scholars also attempted to find some kind of relationship between the nature of 'primitive' languages, as distinct from the nature of the languages of 'civilised' peoples. It was claimed that 'primitive' languages contained more harsh, throaty sounds than other languages. Just as civilisation was supposed to represent a degeneration of an original pure, natural state, so too was the supposed development of a preference for sounds produced further forward in the mouth. Such a change reflects the laziness that characterises modern civilisation! The 'noble savage', it was argued, has maintained language in its more pure, throaty state!

Historical linguists of this period also tended to look back with nostalgia to the grammatical structures of the proto-language from which the modern European languages are derived. They admired the highly inflectional proto-language, which was said to represent a more 'pure' grammatical state, which has declined since the development of 'civilisation' in Europe. (You will remember that ideas such as these were referred to in section 1.2.)

Such views hardly need to be discussed. All that needs to be said is that it is quite impossible to relate any features of languages (whether they are phonetic features or any other kinds of features) to *any* differences in culture between two peoples. Such views are pure racism.

These kind of beliefs are also compatible with an anatomical explanation of sound changes in African languages. It has been said that people with thicker lips, for example, are incapable of producing certain kinds of sounds. The differences between White and Black English in America have even been put down to the physical inability of Blacks to speak English 'properly'!

A final comment will be made in a more humorous vein. In the Mekeo language of Bereina, there has been a large-scale shift of alveolar sounds to velars. So, /d/ and /l/ became /ŋ/. It could perhaps be argued by holders of this theory that in making these changes, Mekeo speakers were freeing their palatal and alveolar areas for more important purposes – chewing betel nut!

There is one powerful objection to all theories of sound change based on anatomy, and that is the simple fact that any child, of whatever physical type, will learn the language of its surroundings perfectly, whatever may be the language of its physical parents. The weakness in the argument about the reason for the change of alveolars to velars in Mekeo is the simple fact that the Motuans have not experienced this change, yet they chew too!

(b) Climate and Geography!

Similarly in the nineteenth century, linguists sometimes tried to suggest that a harsh physical environment is likely to produce a set of harsh sounds in a language. What is meant by 'harshness' of sound is not usually defined, though from the examples, it appears that phonetic harshness involves the presence of many 'guttural' sounds (i.e. glottal and uvular), many consonant clusters and few vowels. The rugged terrain and harsh climate of the Caucasus Mountains in the Soviet Union was often said to have caused the languages to develop such sounds.

This can be very easily disproved however. The Eskimos live in a very harsh environment, yet their phonetic system has been described as 'agreeable'. Similarly, the Australian Aborigines of Central Australia live in a harsh environment, yet they have a sound system that has been called 'euphonic' (pleasant sounding), with a fairly small number of phonemes, few consonant clusters and no 'guttural' (or 'throaty') sounds.

The languages of mountainous areas, it was also sometimes argued, tended to change more rapidly than languages spoken closer to sea level, especially with regard to their consonants. Because of the higher altitude, there was greater effort involved in breathing, and this was supposed to make the consonants more likely to change. This argument can also be easily disproved. There are mountainous areas which have languages that have changed relatively little, and there are coastal people whose languages have undergone radical changes in their consonants.

(c) Substratum

The substratum theory of linguistic change involves the idea that if a people migrate into an area and their language is acquired by the original inhabitants of the area, then any changes in the language can be put down to the influence from the original language of the area.

Now, it is well known that someone's first language will to some extent influence the way that person speaks a second language. We can all recognise foreign accents in our own language. It is easy to tell whether it is a native speaker speaking English, or a French person, a German, a Chinese or a Papua New Guinean. Similarly, it is possible to distinguish between a European speaking Tok Pisin and a Papua New Guinean. And even among Papua New Guineans, it is possible to recognise to some extent the particular group to which a person belongs from the influence of his or her first language on the Tok Pisin spoken by that person. People from some areas, for instance, confuse /l/ and /n/, and may say *napun man* instead of *lapun man*; people from other areas may confuse /l/ and /r/ and say *rikrik kar* instead of *liklik kar*; people from other areas may confuse /s/ and /t/, and say *haut lotu* — instead of *haus lotu*. These are clear examples of substratum influence of one language on another.

Some of the features of the grammar of Black English in America, as distinct from the English varieties of the Whites, have been put down to the features of the original languages of the African slaves when they were first transported to America hundreds of years ago. There are other possible explanations for at least some of these features, but if any features were carried over in this way, we could regard this as a kind of substratum influence.

The problem with the substratum explanation of linguistic change is that it is often used to explain changes in areas where the supposed substratum language has ceased to exist. The influence of the language can therefore never be proved, nor disproved. One example that is often quoted of substratum influence is the history of French. France was occupied by Celtic-speaking people (speaking languages related to Welsh and Irish) before the time of the Roman Empire and the introduction of Latin. France is now split into two major dialect areas, between the north and the south. Some scholars have suggested that this split corresponds with an earlier split in the original Celtic language, and that these differences were carried over into these people's Latin when they switched languages. Clearly, as Celtic no longer survives in France, this theory cannot be disproved. Nor, however, can it be proved.

In Melanesia too, the substratum theory has often been used to explain some of the more unusual features of some of the Austronesian languages when compared with Austronesian languages outside Melanesia. The argument goes like this: there were originally non-Austronesian populations throughout Papua New Guinea and the Solomon Islands, and that when the Austronesian languages arrived later, the original languages influenced the newly introduced languages in different ways before being replaced by these languages. Once again, as these original languages no longer exist, it is hard to refute this theory. It is just as hard, however, to prove it correct.

(d) Local Identification

One theory, proposed by Laycock, suggests that very small languages such as those of Melanesia, may undergo changes simply so that the speakers of the languages can point to their differences from other languages. Linguistic change in this kind of situation can therefore be quite deliberate and planned. People from linguistically very diverse areas such as the Sepik, for example, have said: 'It wouldn't be any good if we all spoke the same. We like to know where people come from.' Linguistic diversity in this kind of situation is therefore a mark of identification for a community.

For example, there are four communities that speak the Austronesian language called Sissano of the West Sepik coast. One of these communities originally spoke the non-Austronesian One language, but 'settled with' Sissano speakers over a century ago and acquired the Sissano language. However, they have retained some of the original One words in their Sissano. Laycock argues that this was to assert their different history from the other three Sissano-speaking communities.

It is difficult to prove that the reasons for the development of such diversity in areas like the Sepik is the result of deliberate intervention on the part of speakers of the language. However, there is one rather interesting case from an Australian language, where people really *do* seem to have sat down and consciously done something to their language. In the Lardil society of northern Australia, there is a special speech style that is used in certain situations instead of the ordinary, everyday kind of language. This special style is used only by men who have been fully initiated into the society. It is characterised by the use of different words to refer to the same things as in the everyday style (though the grammar that is used is the same for both styles). What is interesting about this case is the fact that this special style contains sounds that no other languages in Australia contain. For instance, the word for 'vegetable food' can be represented as [m!i], which is something like the sound of a kiss, followed by [i]. A fish is called [Li], where the [L] represents an ingressive lateral fricative. (This is like the sound you make when you chew sugarcane and the juice starts running out of your mouth because your mouth is full, and you breath in so you don't lose the juice.) There is even one sound in this special style that occurs in no other language in the world (at least, as far as we know). The sound is symbolised as [p'], and it is like the sound we make with our lips when we want to imitate somebody farting! The fact that these sounds are so unusual makes it look like somebody must have deliberately invented the words so that the initiated men could very clearly mark their special social status

(e) Functional Need

It is also true that some changes take place in language because a particular language *must* change to meet new needs that its speakers face. As the functional needs of a language change (i.e. the situations in which a language is used become wider), some parts of a language may be lost, and other parts may be added. These kinds of causes do not affect the phonology, or even the grammar, to a great extent, but they do affect the vocabulary. Words referring to cultural concepts that are now irrelevant are lost and forgotten, while new words come in to a language to express important new concepts.

New words can come into a language in a number of ways.

(a)   The first source for new words is to take words that already exist in a language and apply them to a new concept. In Tok Pisin, for instance, there was originally no word for 'aeroplane'. However, there was a word *balus* that originally meant 'pigeon'. Speakers of Tok Pisin, when aeroplanes first appeared on the scene in this country, saw a similarity between these two things which flew in the sky, and applied the name *balus* to this new concept. So now we have the word *balus* in Tok Pisin, which means both 'aeroplane' and 'pigeon'.

(b)   A second source for new vocabulary to meet new needs in a language is to take words that already exist in the language and string them together according to the existing grammatical patterns of the language, and make up new compound words. This explains the origin of the Tok Pisin word *wetkot* for 'remand prisoner'. This is a compound derived from *wet* 'wait' and *kot* 'court' – somebody who is waiting for a court case to come up.

(c)   The final source of new vocabulary is foreign languages. Usually, cultural change involves contact with a foreign culture which is expressed in a different language to our own. In the case of Papua New Guinea, cultural change generally comes in by means of the English language, so we find very many English words making their way into the languages to express new concepts. For example, in modern Tok Pisin, you can hear words like the following:

intanesinol	'international'
demokrạsi	'democracy'
benediksen	'benediction'
menesmen	'management'

In fact, in some countries, there are even national committees that are set up by governments to check and control the introduction of new vocabulary into their national languages. Governments often want to 'protect' their language against the introduction of too many foreign words, as they feel that this might 'corrupt' the language in some way. We saw in Chapter One that the French Government has set up the French Academy, to keep out English words from the French language. In the case of Indonesia, there is an official Language Council which tries to find new words in Bahasa Indonesia, as far as possible using genuine Indonesian words, rather than resorting to the vocabulary of foreign languages like Dutch. (Remember that it was the Dutch who had colonial power over Indonesia until it gained its independence in 1949.)

Although a great deal of vocabulary change can be explained as being the result of new needs that the language has to meet, this cannot always explain the introduction of new words into a language, or the loss of old words. We saw in Chapter One that in the Paamese language of Vanuatu, there were originally words like *leiai* for 'bush' and *a:h* for 'garden'. The younger generation is presently replacing *leiai* with the borrowed word *bu:s*, and the word *a:h* is being replaced by the borrowing *ka:ren*. There is no *need* for these words to change at all. The Paamese are still making basically the same kinds of gardens in basically the same kinds of ways as they always have, but they appear to be getting new words for a very old cultural concept. The reason for this must remain a mystery.

(f) Simplicity

Many of the sound changes that we looked at in Chapter Two could be regarded as simplifying the production of sounds in one way or another. In dropping sounds, we are making words shorter, and therefore need to exert less physical effort to produce them. The changes known as assimilation also clearly involve a change in the effort needed to produce a sequence of sounds as the degree of difference between sounds is reduced. Fusion too, reduces the number of sounds in a word. One famous linguist, Otto Jespersen, made a great deal of the importance of simplicity as a factor in bringing about language change:

> I am not afraid of hearing the objection that I ascribe too great a power to human laxness, indolence, inertia, shirking, easy-goingness, sluggishness, or whatever other beautiful synonyms have been invented for 'economy of effort' or 'following the line of least resistance'. The fact remains that there *is* such a tendency in all human beings, and by taking it into account in explaining the changes of sound, we are doing nothing else than applying here the same principle.

There are several problems however, in using the concept of simplicity to explain the reasons for sound change. The first is that it is difficult, or perhaps impossible, to define the concept of phonetic simplicity. Simplicity is clearly a relative term. What is simple for the speakers of one language may well be difficult for speakers of another. When Kuman speakers in Simbu Province fused the two sounds /gl/ into a single velar lateral /ʎ/, the principle of simplicity can be brought up as the causal factor. However, the velar lateral is a sound that speakers of all other languages find extremely difficult to produce. Similarly, the fricatives [θ] and [ð] developed in English out of the corresponding stops, presumably for reasons of simplicity. Yet many Papua New Guineans pronouncing words containing these sounds use a [t] and a [d], finding the fricative forms too difficult. And while English speakers have no trouble with [θ] and [ð], they find it difficult to produce the velar fricative [x], a sound that Germans have no trouble with.

A second problem is that if all sound change were to be put down to simplicity, we cannot explain why many changes do *not* take place. If it is easier to say [ʌŋkaind] than to say [ʌnkaind] for 'unkind', why do not all languages change [nk] to [ŋk]? Why only some languages, and why only at some times? There clearly has to be some other factor involved.

A third problem is that some sound changes clearly do *not* involve simplicity anyway. There is no way for instance, that the change called metathesis can be called simplification, as exactly the same sounds are found before and after the change. All that has changed is the order of the sounds. And if phonetic fusion can be viewed as simplicity, then surely phonetic unpacking must be just the opposite, as this creates two sounds from an original single sound.

Finally, we can point out that simplification in one part of the language may actually create complexity in another part, so of what value is this concept as an explanation? For instance, the change known as syncope (dropping of medial vowels) can be viewed as simplification in that it reduces the number of actual sounds in a word. Yet often, syncope results in the creation of consonant clusters in languages that did not originally have them. This was certainly the case in the Lenakel (Vanuatu) example of syncope that we looked at in Chapter Two. How can we say that the change from a CV syllable structure to a CCV syllable structure involves simplification, when we give exactly the opposite interpretation to a change from CCV to CV? We say this, for instance, when we talk about cluster reduction, or about the insertion of an epenthetic vowel between consonants in a cluster to avoid such 'complexities'.

The simplification of phonology in the ways that we have described may also cause increased complexities in the grammar of the language and therefore make the language at this level 'harder' to learn. In Chapter Two, we looked at the change by which final voiced stops in German were devoiced. This was viewed as an assimilatory change, and therefore supposedly involves simplification However, this change has made the morphology of the language more complex, as we saw in Chapter Seven. Examine the following data:

SINGULAR				PLURAL			
*ta:g	→	ta:k	'day'	*ta:gə	→	ta:gə	'days'
*hund	→	hunt	'dog'	*hundə	→	hundə	'dogs'
*laut	→	laut	'sound'	*lautə	→	lautə	'sounds'
*bo:t	→	bo:t	'boat'	*bo:tə	→	bo:tə	'boats'

In the earlier stage of German, the rule for the formation of the plural of these four nouns could be stated quite simply: add the suffix /-ə/. After the rule of final consonant devoicing had applied, the statement of the plural became much more complex, because the devoicing did not take place in the plural. In the plural, the consonant was not word final, as it was followed by the plural suffix

244

/-ə/. The plural formation rule in modern German must therefore be stated as:

(a) with some words, simply add the suffix /-ə/. This class of words includes the words /laut/ 'sound' and /bo:t/ 'boat'.
(b) with some words, add the suffix /-ə/ and at the same time change the final voiceless consonant to a voiced consonant. This class of words includes the words /ta:k/ 'day' and /hunt/ 'dog'.

The form of the singular does not indicate what the form of the plural will be. Someone learning German has to *learn* that the plural of /bo:t/ is /bo:tə/ rather than /bo:də/. So, while the final de-voicing rule can be viewed as simplification in the language, it does not in itself result in an *overall* simplification of the language, as it creates complexities elsewhere.

Sound changes are very often more or less directly involved in the creation of new grammatical patterns in languages. We saw earlier that we can view grammatical change in some ways as a kind of typological 'circle', in which there is a tendency for isolating languages to move towards the agglutinating type, by phonologically reducing free forms to bound forms. Agglutinating languages then tend to move towards the inflectional type, by phonologically reducing the bound morphemes yet further. And finally, the circle is completed when inflecting languages move towards the isolating type once again, by phonologically reducing inflections to nothing at all.

Only some grammatical changes can be explained as being the result of phonological simplification however. Other grammatical changes seem to occur for quite different reasons. Grammars tend to change so that any constructions which are unnecessarily unclear and complex become clearer and less complex. Languages try to make their structures neater and simpler. For instance, there are people who complain if they hear the following nouns in English used as singular nouns:

> data
> media
> criteria

For instance, they tell us we should not say:

> The mass media in New Caledonia *expresses* only the opinions of the French colonisers.

but that we should say:

The mass media in New Caledonia *express* only the opinions of the French colonisers.

They say that *media* is a plural noun, and that the singular form is *medium*. Similarly, the singular of *data* is *datum*, and the singular of *criteria* is *criterion*.

Many people do not speak English this way however. The marking for plural on most English nouns is a morpheme which has the allomorphs /-s/, /-z/ and /-əz/, as in:

parrot	parrots
cassowary	cassowaries
cuscus	cuscuses

The existence of a separate plural marking for a few nouns such as *datum*, *medium* and *criterion* is in a sense unnecessary. Speakers of English are finding different ways of avoiding this grammatical complication.

Some of these nouns are being reanalysed grammatically as being MASS NOUNS rather than COUNT NOUNS. Count nouns are those nouns in English that have separate plural forms, like those we have been looking at. Mass nouns are nouns like:

information
mail
equipment

and they do *not* have separate plural forms. We can only say:

This information is quite insufficient to make a decision.

and (in standard English) we cannot say:

*These informations are quite insufficient to make a decision.

In the sentence above, where the noun *media* takes a singular verb and does not have a separate plural form (i.e. *medias* is not allowed), we can see that the word *media* is behaving in the same

246

way as *information* behaves. The original singular form *medium* is simply disappearing from the language when it has this meaning.

The second method that speakers of English are using to regularise the language is to keep these nouns in the category of count nouns, but to make them form their plural in the regular way. So, you will find some people who now say things like:

What is the criteria you used to come to that conclusion?
Those are not the only criterias you can use to come to a conclusion.

This has been an example of grammatical change taking place in the direction of regularisation. However, even here it is difficult to speak of simplicity as being the only factor involved, as phonological changes are at the same time working to create *other* grammatical irregularities, or perhaps other grammatical changes that are taking place at the same time are producing new irregularities somewhere else in the grammar.

(g) Structural Pressure

One explanation for sound change that has been put forward in recent years is the concept of structural pressure. You should be aware of the fact that linguists view language as collections of units at various levels, and that the units relate to each other in very specific ways at each level in a system. Languages, therefore, operate in terms of systems. If a system becomes uneven, or if it has some kind of 'gap' then, it is argued, a change is likely to take place to fill up that gap' again and produce a neat system. For instance, if a language had a five vowel system:

$$i \qquad u$$
$$e \qquad o$$
$$a$$

and the phoneme /e/ was raised to /i/, we would not be surprised to find that the phoneme /o/ would then shift to /u/ to maintain the neatness of the vowel system. There are many languages with vowel systems of this kind:

$$i \qquad u$$
$$a$$

but relatively few with vowel systems of this kind:

i   u

o

a

However, all we can say is that languages with gaps in their systems 'tend' to fill them. Any attempt at a general explanation of sound change that contains the word 'tend' is of little value. Even a superficial examination of the world's languages reveals that there are languages which have gaps in their systems. In Motu for instance, there are voiced and voiceless stops at the bilabial, alveolar and velar points of articulation:

p   t   k
b   d   g

and there are nasals at the bilabial and alveolar points of articulation:

m   n

However, there is no velar nasal /ŋ/, and there is no indication that any change is taking place in the language to fill this gap. In fact, there is clear evidence that there originally *was* a velar nasal, that was unconditionally lost, which indicates that there was actually a gap *created* in the phoneme inventory.

This brings us to the point where we should try to come to some kind of conclusion about the reasons for language change. Despite the 'tendencies' towards simplification and change under structural pressure to fill gaps in systems, there is very little we can say. Many linguists in the past gave up inquiring into the 'why' of language change. As the linguist Bloomfield expressed it in 1933:

the causes of sound change are unknown

and other linguists have claimed that the same kind of comment can be made about other kinds of language change. One linguist at a recent conference publicly stated as a joke about language change that all languages have the following inbuilt characteristics:

- a tendency towards simplification
- a tendency towards the creation of irregularities
- a tendency towards remaining unchanged

The fact that such a statement was actually taken seriously suggests that we have not come very far in 150 years of the study of reasons for linguistic change!

Actually, however, if these ideas had perhaps been expressed in a different way, they could be of value. It certainly seems that although language can be viewed as a system, there are forces in a sense lying in wait to destroy it, in addition to forces lying in wait to protect it. The fact that society needs that system to hold itself together is enough of a force to keep the system from falling apart in most instances. In the light of this comment, it is interesting to note that many linguists relate the spread of linguistic changes to periods of great social upheaval. The theory is that during periods of social upheaval, there is less likely to be direct control of children by parents, so there would be less pressure of correction, so innovations could go through 'uncorrected', and become the normal form from the following generations. The drastic phonological changes in the history of Old Irish have been put down to the introduction of Christianity in Ireland. The far-reaching changes in Mbabaram in north Queensland seen in Data Set 1 have been put down to a shift in the people's location some thousands of years ago from a lush coastal environment to a dry mountain top environment and the changes in lifestyle that this meant. The great grammatical and phonological changes between Old English and Modern English have been put down to the influence of the Bubonic Plague, which killed millions of people in England, and the Norman invasion of England in 1066. These changes were all, in a sense, waiting to 'get out', and were released by these drastic social changes.

While there may be some truth in this suggestion, we cannot take it too far. Many social upheavals, while they do greatly influence the vocabulary of a language, do not necessarily influence the phonological structure or grammatical systems at all. Christianity has been introduced into many areas of Papua New Guinea over the past century or so, yet the languages have not undergone the same degree of phonological change as Old Irish did. Other social upheavals have similarly had little effect on the phonologies of other languages in other areas. The explanation of the lack of correction of the child by its parents is actually a fairly weak one anyway. People nowadays regard correction in the home as being of little importance in the learning of a language. It seems that most of a child's learning goes on in the child's peer group (or children of the same age) rather than from the child's parents.

11.2 Pidginisation

It is only in the last couple of decades that the study of pidgin languages and the linguistic changes known as pidginisation have become academically respectable. In the initial stages of expansion in this field, the study of pidgins and creoles gained a respectable place within the semi-respectable field of 'sociolinguistics'. Since then, sociolinguistics itself seems to have blossomed into a completely respectable discipline, largely under the influence of linguists like Labov, whose work we looked at in the previous chapter. The study of pidgins and creoles increased correspondingly in status, and some linguists now see the study of such languages as involving some absolutely crucial questions in linguistic theory and the theory of language change.

Before we go on to look at what these issues are, perhaps we should offer a traditional definition of what a pidgin language is. A pidgin language is a kind of language that is characterised in the following two ways:

(a) it is a language that is nobody's first language, and is only used as a contact language between speakers of different languages
(b) it has a vocabulary and grammar that is derived from the vocabulary and grammar of some other language, and which is considerably reduced or simplified with respect to the other language.

Pidgin languages always arise quickly under situations of contact where there is no common language between speakers of two (or more) languages. Languages typically undergo the process of pidginisation in colonial types of situations, where there is a dominant language group that brings together linguistically diverse groups of people for purposes associated with commerce or government. It is this dominant language that usually provides the main part of the vocabulary of the pidgin language. There are, for instance, pidgin varieties of English, French, Spanish and Portuguese spoken in all parts of the world by people who were formerly colonised by these European powers.

Linguists have lately become so interested in questions about the origins of different pidgins in the world that there have been attempts to locate the oldest records of different pidgin languages, to try to see how they evolved. Pidgin languages have traditionally been regarded as poor imitations of 'real' languages, with no structures of their own. For instance, the early governor of the colony of Papua, Sir Hubert Murray, called early Tok Pisin a 'most atrocious form of speech'. The result of prejudices like these has been that few people even bothered to record the early development of pidgin languages. Some linguists have been so keen to see how pidgins evolve that there was recently a serious proposal to set up a project to artificially produce a pidgin and see how it started and how it evolved. The idea was that a number of people who speak quite different languages were to be brought together in one place and 'fed' a number of basic words that they could use to communicate. Then, the researchers were to simply stand in the background for a period of several months to see what kinds of grammatical patterns emerged to put these words together to express meanings. The fact that this project was even officially proposed is an indication of how seriously some linguists were searching for answers on the question of the origin of pidgins. (The proposers of this project intended to use Papua New Guineans who spoke only their vernaculars or *tok ples*, and to throw them together in a situation that they could not possibly have been expected to understand. Although the possible advances to scientific knowledge from this project were great, the project was refused permission by authorities in Papua New Guinea for its great exploitative and inhumane aspects.)

Tok Pisin in Papua New Guinea is typical of many varieties of English-based pidgins found throughout the world. It arose when speakers of a number of different New Britain and New Ireland languages were thrown together on sugar plantations in Samoa about a century ago, along with people from the Solomons and Vanuatu. As these people had no common language, they took the English that they heard from their English-speaking bosses and used it as a basis for communication among themselves on the plantations. When these people were sent back to New Britain and New Ireland at the end of their contracts, they took a knowledge of this new language with them, and it eventually spread to the rest of the New Guinea Islands area, to the New Guinea mainland, and recently to the Highlands (where it is still spreading).

The vocabulary of Tok Pisin is largely of English origin. If you look at the dictionary of the language, you will find that about 80% of the words in the language are derived from English words, e.g.:

haus	'house'
dok	'dog'
rot	'road'
ren	'rain'
trausis	'trousers'

Of the remaining 20%, most of the vocabulary comes from the languages of the New Britain and New Ireland people who were the original labourers on the Samoan plantations. So, we find Tolai words such as the following:

kakaruk	'chicken'
kiau	'egg'
buai	'betel nut'
kunai	'*kunai* grass'
kulau	'drinking coconut'

The remaining words in the language that do not come from English or from New Britain and New Ireland languages come from a variety of sources. Such words include:

rausim	'take out' (from German *heraus*)
beten	'pray' (from German *beten*)
pekato	'sin' (from Latin)
binatang	'insect' (from Malay *binatang* 'animal')

The vocabulary of Tok Pisin is also clearly 'reduced' with respect to that of English. While Tok Pisin does have some areas of special vocabulary that English does not have, there is on the whole a greater range of vocabulary in English than there is in Tok Pisin. For instance, Tok Pisin lacks vocabulary to discuss many concepts in law, in science and in many other areas of life.

Grammatically, if we compare Tok Pisin with English, we find that it is much simpler in its structure. There is much more regularity in its grammatical structures for one thing. While English has many unpredictable past tense forms of the verb, Tok Pisin verbs are the same in all their forms. So, while in English we have to learn the past tense forms of the following verbs separately:

bring	brought
ring	rang
string	strung

verbs in Tok Pisin exist in only a single, invariant form. Differences in tense (and aspect) are marked by independent grammatical words. E.g.

> *Em bin   i   kam*
> s/he past verb phrase come
> 'S/he came.'

> *Em bai   i   kam*
> s/he future verb phrase come
> 'S/he will come.'

The absence of a marker can indicate either present tense, or the fact that tense is irrelevant in the particular case, e.g.:

> *Em   φ i   kam*
> s/he   verb phrase come
> 'S/he $\left\{ \begin{array}{l} \text{came} \\ \text{is coming} \\ \text{will come} \end{array} \right\}$.'

Tok Pisin also differs from English in that it has far less redundancy built into its grammatical system. For example, in English, plural marking is expressed in a variety of different ways in a sentence, often in more than one way at once. For instance, it can be marked in the following ways:

(a) by a separate form of the noun, i.e. *dog* vs. *dogs, child* vs. *children, man* vs. *men, woman* vs. *women*

    (b) by a difference in the form of a demonstrative, i.e. *this* vs. *these, that* vs. *those*

    (c) by a separate form of the verb, i.e. *am* vs. *are, is* vs. *are, does* vs. *do*

So, in the sentence:

> Those women are singing.

the idea of plural is actually included in three separate items. Contrast this with the singular form:

> That woman is singing.

In Tok Pisin however, the idea of plural is expressed only once in the sentence, and even then it is optional. We can say:

> *Dispela meri   i   singsing i   stap*
> this   woman verb phrase sing verb phrase continue
> 'This woman/those women is/are singing.'

to refer to one or to many women. If we want to specifically mark the fact that there is more than one women involved, we can use the plural marker *ol* at the front of the noun phrase. Thus:

> *Ol   dispela meri   i   singsing i   stap*
> plural this woman verb phrase sing verb phrase continue
> 'These women are singing.'

Note that none of the other parts of the sentence change in the plural as they do in English.

    Some of the differences in grammar between Tok Pisin and English are related to differences in grammar between English and the Melanesian languages of New Britain and New Ireland. The original plantation labourers were largely speakers of Austronesian languages, and there is clear evidence of the influence of Austronesian grammatical structures in modern Tok Pisin. For instance, the verb phrase marker *i* that occurs in the Tok Pisin sentences we looked at earlier derives from the Tolai third person marker with verb phrases, e.g.:

> *To   Pipira   i   mamaɪ*
> article Pipira verb phrase chew betel nut
> 'Pipira is chewing betel nut.'

The existence of two separate forms of the pronoun 'we' is also derived from the structure of Melanesian pronoun systems rather than from the English system. Thus, in Tok Pisin we have two separate pronouns corresponding to the single form 'we' in English. Firstly, we have *yumi* which means 'we' when you are including the person you are speaking to. Secondly, we have *mipela* which means 'we' when you are excluding the person you are speaking to.

What is particularly interesting about the process of pidginisation however, is that while there is clearly evidence of the influence of the dominant language (in this case English), as well as the subordinate languages (in this case, some of the Austronesian languages of Melanesia), there is something else going on also. For instance, if we compare the grammatical structure of a simple intransitive sentence in Tok Pisin, which is an English-based pidgin, with the same kind of sentence in Haitian Creole (spoken in the West Indies), which started out as a French-based pidgin, we find that there are remarkable similarities between the two. Compare the structures of the following sentences in the two languages:

> Tok Pisin   *Em   no   bin   save*
> Haitian Creole *Li   pa   te   konē*
>   s/he   not   past   know
>   'S/he didn't know.'

The forms in one language are put together according to the same set of grammatical rules (even though the actual forms themselves are quite different).

Let us now compare the structures of the corresponding sentences in English and in French, the languages from which these two languages are said to be derived. In English, the structure of the sentence:

$$\left\{ \begin{array}{c} \text{He} \\ \text{She} \end{array} \right\} \text{didn't know}$$

involves the following facts:

(a) The first element is the subject pronoun.

(b) The second element is the verb 'do', which is put there to carry the tense marking. In this case, the tense is past, so the verb appears in the form 'did'.

(c) The third element is the negative marker 'not', which optionally appears in a special suffixed form '-n't', which is attached to the preceding element.

(d) The fourth element is the verb 'know', which occurs in a so-called infinitive form, i.e. it does not mark any differences in tense.

The corresponding French sentence has the form:

$$\left\{ \begin{array}{l} \text{Il} \\ \text{Elle} \end{array} \right\} \text{ne connaissait pas}$$

The significant facts here are that:

(a) The first element is again a subject pronoun, of the form *il* meaning 'he' or *elle* meaning 'she'.

(b) The second element is the form *ne*, which indicates negative.

(c) The third element is the verb root *connaiss-* which means 'know'.

(d) The fourth element is the tense marking suffix *-ait*, which indicates the fact that the event took place in the past.

(e) The fifth, and final element, is the form *pas*, which also indicates negative. To express the negative in French, this must be marked twice, with *ne* before the verb and *pas* after the verb.

The structures of the English and French sentences can be represented in the following ways:

English:

SUBJECT	DO + TENSE	NEGATIVE	VERB

French:

SUBJECT	NEGATIVE	VERB + TENSE	NEGATIVE

These structures are clearly quite different between the two languages. We cannot simply substitute the forms of one language with the forms of the other. To substitute the French forms with English forms but keeping the French structure for example, would produce the impossible English sentence:

$$*\begin{Bmatrix} \text{He} \\ \text{She} \end{Bmatrix} \text{not knew not}$$

The question we need to ask ourself is this: if the structures of English and French are so different, how is it that the structures of the two pidgin languages that are derived from them are so similar? Both Tok Pisin and Haitian Creole share the following basic structures:

SUBJECT	NEGATIVE	TENSE	VERB

The two pidgin languages are closer in structure to each other than either is to French or to English. Clearly, this cannot be because of the influence of the dominant languages, as they are so different. Similarly, it cannot be due to the common influence of the subordinate languages, as these are different in each case. We have already seen that in the case of Tok Pisin, tne subordinate languages are the Austronesian languages of New Britain and New Ireland. In the case of Haitian Creole, the subordinate languages were the languages of parts of West Africa, the original languages of the slaves who were taken to the West Indies centuries ago.

One explanation that has been proposed to explain these facts is to suggest that speakers of all languages are born with some kind of basic idea about how to simplify their language in situations where it is necessary. It is in situations of contact with speakers of other languages that we bring this knowledge into operation. What we are saying then is that we all have a set of ready-made instructions in our heads to tell us how to get rid of as much irregularity and as much redundancy as we can, and to speak a kind of basic, understandable language where all we have to learn is the vocabulary. The reason that Tok Pisin and Haitian Creole are so similar in their structures is that people in both places (i.e. the Melanesian sugar plantation workers and West African slaves) shared this same basic set of instructions about how to simplify language. This knowledge is competely independent of the particular language we speak — it is knowledge that we are *born* with, even before we speak any language at all.

If this theory is true — and it is just that, an unproven theory — then it would be interesting to see just what the full set of instructions that we are supposed to be born with actually looks like. One way of doing this would be to look at as many situations involving pidginisation as we can, and see if we can find any consistent differences between pidgins of the world, and the languages they are 'derived' from. In the light of this comment, let us look at the case of pidginised Motu. Pidgin Motu (or, Hiri Motu as it is officially called) is related to vernacular Motu (often called Motu Korikori or 'pure Motu') in the same way as Tok Pisin is related to English. The two share the same vocabulary (except that the Hiri Motu vocabulary is rather more restricted than that of vernacular Motu, as we would expect). There are significant grammatical differences however. These differences involve the following particular points:

(a) Objects to verbs in vernacular Motu are expressed as bound forms attached as suffixes to the verb. These suffixes have the following forms:

	singular	plural	
first	-gu	inclusive	-da
		exclusive	-mai
second	-mu	-mui	
third	-a/-ia	-dia	

In pidgin Motu, objects are expressed by full form pronouns that have the same form as the subject pronouns. The difference between subject and object is marked by the position of the form in the sentence. The full form pronouns are the same in both vernacular Motu and pidgin Motu, i.e.

	singular	plural	
first	lau	inclusive	ita
		exclusive	ai
second	oi	umui	
third	ia	idia	

(b) Subjects to verbs are marked as prefixes to the verb in vernacular Motu. The basic subject markers are:

	singular	plural	
first	na-	inclusive	ta-
		exclusive	a-
second	o-		o-
third	e-		e-

In pidgin Motu, subjects are expressed by placing the full form pronoun in the subject position in the sentence. There is no further subject marking on the verb as there is in the vernacular.

(c) To make a verb negative in vernacular Motu, there is a different set of subject markers. These have the forms below:

	singular	plural	
first	asina-	inclusive	asita-
		exclusive	asia-
second	to-		asio-
third	se-		asie-

In pidgin Motu however, negation is marked by placing the free form *lasi* after the verb phrase.

The following examples are presented to illustrate the differences between vernacular Motu and pidgin Motu. The two languages are mutually unintelligible, even though most of the actual forms are identical.

> Motu
> *Ia   e-   ita-mu*
> s/he s/he see you

> Hiri Motu *Oi ia   ese   itaia*
> you s/he subject see
> 'S/he saw you.'

> Motu
> *Asi-na-rakatani-mu*
> not I leave   you

> Hiri Motu *Oi lau rakatania lasi*
> you I leave   not
> 'I didn't leave you.'

11.2 Pidginisation

There are many other structural differences between vernacular Motu and pidgin Motu, which have not been mentioned here. The point of these examples, you should remember, was to see if we could find any common facts in the differences between the dominant languages and the pidgin languages they have produced. The following points do seem to emerge:

(a) The pidginised form of a language has much less redundancy

(b) As we saw in the case of Tok Pisin, irregularities had been eliminated. Although we did not look at any examples of this in Hiri Motu, the same differences can be seen here also. While there are some irregular verbs in vernacular Motu, these are all made fully regular in Hiri Motu.

(c) The pidgin forms of a language have very few bound form morphemes. Concepts that are expressed by means of suffixes and prefixes in the dominant language are expressed by independent morphemes in the pidginised form of the language. So, perhaps the set of instructions we are born with that tells us how to simplify our language tells us to do these things (as well as many other things that we have not found out yet).

One further interesting point to come up from this is that in some sense, these instructions seem to match very closely to the normal processes of language change that we have been looking at in this book. For instance, if you compare the English of today with the English of a thousand years ago, you will find that the grammatical differences involve a reduction in redundancy, less irregularity and the loss of many bound forms and their replacement by free forms. In the past, pidginisation has been viewed as a special kind of language change that emerges only under certain very special conditions. Now, some linguists are suggesting that *all* language change involves the same kinds of changes as are involved in pidginisation. The suggestion is that these inborn instructions on how to simplify a language are in fact operating on us the whole time. They are like a constant 'pull' on our language, dragging it in one direction. These instructions are, in a sense, the 'causes' of language change. Language change is therefore genetically programmed into us. So, we should not be looking for explanations of why languages change, but why they do not change. Pidginisation, according to such a view, is not such a special case after all. The only special thing about it is the speed and extent of normal processes of change taking place.

Modern English is really just pidgin Old English, that took a few hundred years to evolve instead of just a single generation!

READING GUIDE QUESTIONS

1. How do we know that language change is not caused by anatomical, cultural or geographical factors?
2. What is the substratum theory of language change, and what are its weaknesses?
3. Can language be deliberately changed by members of a speech community?
4. How valid is it to say that languages change because they *have* to in order to meet new social needs?
5. To what extent is 'simplification' a factor in causing language change to take place? What are some problems associated with this explanation of language change?
6. How might structural pressure cause a sound change to take place?
7. What is a pidgin language?
8. Why is it that we know very little about the initial stages of the formation of a pidgin?
9. In what ways is Tok Pisin grammatically simpler than English?
10. What influences are there in the formation of the structure of Tok Pisin lexicon and grammar?
11. Can the influence of pidgins be explained solely as the result of the influence of the grammars of the dominant languages and the subordinate languages? Why?
12. What proposal has been made to account for similarities between different pidgin languages?

DISCUSSION AND EXERCISES

1. Introductory linguistics textbooks often stress the idea that all languages are approximately equal in their level of difficulty, that is, there is no truly simple language. Do you think that this is true? Do you think that a so-called 'simple' language is more efficient than a more complex one?
2. Can you see any more general importance of the discussion of pidginisation than its relevance to the study of language change?
3. We saw in Chapter Eight that certain grammatical changes could be seen taking place in modern Tok Pisin. These involved

the phonological reduction of certain forms, and the development of grammatical structures for the marking of relative clauses. Can you think of any more changes that are taking place in the language? Can you relate these kinds of changes to the process of pidginisation in any way?

FURTHER READING

1. Aitchison, Jean. *Language Change: Progress or Decay?* (Chapter 7 'The Reason Why', Chapter 8 'Doing what Comes Naturally', Chapter 9 'Repairing the Patterns', Chapter 10 'The Mad Hatter's Tea-party', Chapter 12 'Language Birth', and Chapter 14 'Progress or Decay?'), pp. 111-128, 129-143, 144-153, 15-169, 191-207, 222-235.

2. Anttila, Raimo. *An Introduction to Historical and Comparative Linguistics* (Chapter 9 'Why Does Language Change? Social and Linguistic Factors'), pp. 179-206.

3. Bickerton, Derek. *Roots of Language.*

Chapter Twelve
CULTURAL RECONSTRUCTION

Different people who practise historical linguistics may have their own particular reasons for their interest. Some may enjoy the intellectual challenge of applying a difficult technique to 'dig' into the past and find out about things that we could not know otherwise. Some may be looking for 'universal' features of language and language change in an effort to determine what it is that makes us uniquely 'human' (if, in fact, we are uniquely human). And others may study historical linguistics in an effort to use the information it can provide to tell us something about the non-linguistic history of the people who speak a language. In this, our final chapter, we will try to find out just what sorts of information historical linguistics *can* give us about a society's non-linguistic history, and how reliable this information is.

12.1 Archaeology

Once we start considering the question of cultural reconstruction, there are various ways we can tackle this problem. Archaeologists attempt to reconstruct cultures on the basis of the material remains left by people of the past. They uncover material that has been buried by natural processes of soil movement, and can use different scientific methods to provide actual dates for the existence of particular cultural features and changes in cultures, as long as they leave some kinds of material remains.

For instance, archaeologists are able to tell us that there have been people living in what is now Papua New Guinea and Australia for at least as long as there have been people living in what is now Europe. They can tell us with a fair degree of certainty that people have been living in Australia for about fifty thousand years. There are even some fairly strong suggestions that these dates are too young, and some archaeologists are expecting to find solid evidence that people have been living in Australia for perhaps as many as eighty thousand years. And remember, these are findings on what is now the Australian continent. Eighty thousand years ago, the sea levels were much lower than they are today, and there may be evidence of even earlier populations that was destroyed when the sea levels rose and destroyed the sites they lived in.

In Papua New Guinea, archaeologists have solid evidence that people have been living in the high inland mountains for at least twenty-five thousand years. This is much less than in Australia, but we need to consider a couple of additional points. Firstly, if people were living in the mountains that long ago, there must have been people living on the coast earlier than that. It is obviously only possible to get to the mountains by first coming from the coast! Secondly, at that time, what is now Australia and Papua New Guinea was actually a single huge island. It would be difficult to imagine that just the Australian part was occupied much earlier than the Papua New Guinean part. So, archaeologists are also expecting to find evidence of people living in Papua New Guinea going at least as far back as the Australian evidence. In fact, there is a possibility that this evidence has been found on the Huon Peninsula near Finschhafen. There are stone axes that have been found there that are very similar to stone axes that have been found in Australia and other parts of southeast Asia, and these stone axes come from soil layers that are well over fifty thousand years old.

Archaeologists are able to tell us something of ancient trade routes for goods like *kina* shells, *toea* shells, clay pots and other goods. They can often suggest who were the economically dominant groups in these economic networks. They can also tell us something of population movements and the spread of cultural changes from one area to another. For instance, they can tell us that Australian Aborigines did not have dogs until about ten thousand years ago. Presumably, the dog was introduced as a result of some kind of cultural contact, either in the form of trading visits, or in the form of a migration of some group into Australia. Archaeologists can also tell us that about five thousand years ago, a new kind of pottery style appeared in parts of coastal Papua New Guinea and island Melanesia generally, which had not been known before that date. Also, around the same time, we start finding evidence of pigs in Melanesia, whereas before that time, there had not been any evidence of pigs. The assumption is again, that there had been some kind of cultural contact, and in this case the contact was with people who had pigs, and who practised a certain kind of pottery making.

But there are many things that the archaeologists cannot tell us. They cannot tell us about a people's oral literature for instance, and they cannot tell us anything about their kinship system. And even though they can tell us that there has been cultural contact in the past, they cannot always tell us where the cultural contact came from, and they cannot always tell us what was the exact nature of the contact.

12.2 Oral History

Another way we can attempt to reconstruct a culture is to look at a people's oral history. Eyewitness accounts of events are often passed on from one generation to another. In particular, oral histories are important for recording genealogies, or family histories. For instance, oral historians are sometimes able to tell us the approximate time that a particular village was established (with time being measured in generations rather than in years), where the people had originally lived, who was their leader at the time, and why the move actually took place.

Many other facts can be recorded in oral history also, but there is often a problem in interpreting oral history. Some stories that are passed on from generation to generation are just 'myths' or 'legends', that reflect the religious and social system of a community, and provide the basis for its religious and social organisation. Oral tradition of these types is of little interest to the oral historian because they are based more on faith than on fact. For instance, the oral historian would not be particularly interested in the story of the origins of the coconut in parts of Melanesia that we looked at in Chapter One. Other stories however, are based on actual historical events. The problem that we often face in dealing with stories such as these is that although they are based on actual events, the stories may have changed in some way. For instance, it is posssible that two different groups of people may pass on differing accounts of the same event that differ in details, or which perhaps conflict in some of their basic elements. Oral historians can therefore only accept evidence on which all tellers of a story agree, or evidence which appears independently in different stories. Because of these problems of accounts being influenced by a community's interpretation of an event, oral historians usually claim that their evidence is only reliable for a time period of about two hundred and fifty years into the past.

One very interesting example that we can look at is a story of a

'Time of Darkness', that is told in many societies of Madang and Morobe provinces, and all of the Highlands provinces. Although these stories differ to some extent according to where the story was told, or who the particular story-teller was, there is still a remarkable degree of agreement over this whole area. The story is, in its basic form something like this:

> The people heard a loud noise (or sometimes, felt an earthquake, or both), and felt that something awful was going to happen. Black clouds started to build up and blocked out the sun. Very quickly, the whole place was in darkness like the darkest night. People went into their homes to hide, and they heard something falling from the sky onto their rooves. When they looked out, they saw it was raining ash. The darkness stayed for three or four days. When the sun reappeared, people found that the whole countryside was covered, and many gardens had been destroyed, and many houses had collapsed.

This story sounds quite disastrous. However, while people from Enga who tell the story believe that the time of darkness was a terrible thing, they also believe it actually had beneficial long term effects. After this tragedy, the gardens grew better, which meant the population expanded and people had more wealth (in the form of pigs) for exchange. Many cultural developments were said to follow directly from the Time of Darkness.

This story sounds very much like a description of a distant volcanic eruption, even down to the details about the long-term benefits mentioned in the Enga version of the story. This is presumably compatible with the enriching of the soil from volcanic ash.

This interpretation of the story can in fact be checked scientifically. There are deposits of volcanic ash in a layer about 2.5 centimetres thick to be found in the area indicated on the map below. The areas where stories of the Time of Darkness are reported are also marked on this map.

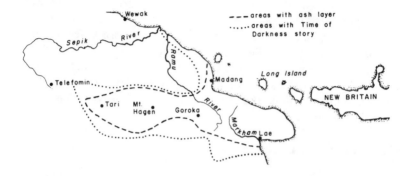

These two areas coincide very closely, so presumably the story and the layer of ash *are* connected historically. Geologists are able to locate the source of the ash as the volcano on Long Island, and they are able to suggest that there was a major eruption probably sometime between 1640 and 1820. The people who tell the story of the Time of Darkness in Enga Province claim very definitely that the story is "historical" rather than "legendary", and the most common date people give for the event is somewhere in the period 1820 to 1860. (These dates were arrived at by counting back generations from the present.) The version of the scientist and the version of the oral historian are quite clearly compatible therefore. (Even the dates given overlap to some extent. Perhaps the actual overlap indicates that the eruption took place closer to 1820, rather than any of the other possible dates.)

But many much older historical events can also be recorded in oral history. For instance, the great Polynesian sea voyages to the various Polynesian islands are often recorded in oral form. Polynesian stories often speak of migrations from some homeland in the distant past, and they name this homeland */savaiki/. They do not tell us, however, where */savaiki/ was located. The name was taken with the Polynesians wherever they went, and applied to the new places they discovered. The name Hawaii (phonemically /hawaiʔi/, for instance, is a regular reflex in Hawaiian of the name for the original Polynesian homeland, and Samoan oral history tells of a migration from a homeland which is called /savaiʔi/ in Samoan. In fact, one of the four large islands of Samoa is today called /savaiʔi/.

Some Australian Aboriginal groups from northern Queensland also have stories of people 'walking' from coastal islands to the mainland. This seems to be pure legend now, but it may be that the stories date from an earlier time when the sea levels were much lower than they are now, and the islands actually *were* connected to the mainland by land.

12.3 Comparative Culture

We have seen that by comparing a number of languages that share certain similarities, we can reconstruct a proto-language that can reasonably be set up as the ancestor language of these languages. If we regard culture as involving a 'system' of interrelated facts (in the same way that a language is a system of interrelated facts), then it should be possible to adapt the comparative method of historical linguistics, and reconstruct a proto-culture from the evidence of the various cultures that are descended from it.

However, any technique of cultural reconstruction using an adapted comparative method must presumably be applied more like grammatical reconstruction or semantic reconstruction, than the rather more neatly worked out system for phonological reconstruction. The actual units of the cultural system and the precise nature of the interrelationships between these units are perhaps even more difficult to define than the units and their interrelationships in grammar and semantics. The range of 'possible' changes in culture are even harder to define than the range of 'possible' changes in grammar and semantics also. This therefore leaves us in a position where culture reconstruction by the comparative method is theoretically possible, but that any conclusions we come to must necessarily be rather shaky.

Let us now look at an example of comparative culture, and see how we might use the evidence of a variety of cultures to reconstruct an earlier cultural system. In Samoa, we find that there is an institution called the /fono/, which is a kind of meeting house. Most /fono/ are oval in structure, with a series of posts in the ground and around the actual building. The /fono/ has 'members', who come from certain groups in society, and membership in these groups is passed on from father to son. The members of these groups select from their number the person they regard as the most capable to represent them in the /fono/. Such a person is called a /matai/, and he sits inside the /fono/ during the meetings, while the people he represents sit outside. In the meetings in the /fono/, all decisions are arrived at by consensus.

In Kiribati, the communities have a large rectangular meeting house. In each community, there are various groups who have rights to sit in the house, while others sit underneath the building during meetings. Decisions are arrived at by consensus. The similarities between the two cultural systems of Kiribati and Samoan are so obvious that we would want to say that these are two cognate systems.

If we now look at a society from the island of Malakula in Vanuatu, we find the following kind of system. There is a rectangular central meeting house (called in Vanuatu Pidgin the *nakamal*) that is partitioned off into areas that are regarded as progressively more sacred as one goes towards the back. Men can only go inside as far as the 'grade' to which they have been initiated, and initiation into the highest grade requires enormous payments of pigs and other forms of wealth. Outside, there is a series of carved blackpalm images that are in memory of dead people, and to which the spirits of these people would return for certain ceremonies.

Even this system from Vanuatu, while quite different from that of Samoa and Kiribati on the surface, has some basic similarities: the central meeting house to which there is restricted access, and the representatives outside (in one case living, in the other case dead) and the decisions being reached by consensus. We could therefore regard these as being features of the proto-culture from which all of these different cultures have evolved.

The problem now, of course, is exactly what kind of proto-culture should we reconstruct? While it seems reasonable to reconstruct the existence of some kind of central meeting house with some kind of restricted access, should we reconstruct an oval meeting house (as it is in Samoa) or a rectangular meeting house (as it is in Kiribati and Vanuatu)? Perhaps all that we can say is that it was probably longer than it was wide. And, was the access restricted by birthright (as in Samoa), or by wealth (as in Vanuatu)? It is probably not possible to make a decision on this point with the data we have looked at

However, the restriction of people to certain privileges by birthright seems to be a predominantly Polynesian cultural feature, which has spread also to Fiji and even parts of Vanuatu (but not Malakula), so this perhaps represents the cultural innovation. Another question we could ask is: who were the representatives outside the meeting house? There are various possibilities: firstly, they may have been people who were not eligible to enter the meeting house because they lacked the wealth (or, perhaps because they were not 'born into' membership, if the Polynesian system turns out be closer to the original), or secondly, they may have been people who were not eligible to enter because they were dead (and whose presence was indicated by carved posts instead). Again, on the evidence that is available, we are not really in a position to come to a conclusion on this.

Cultural reconstruction in Polynesia, and even in parts of Melanesia, is comparatively simple, because there were no 'substratum' populations to influence the cultures in different ways in different areas. Also, the populations were separated by large areas of ocean, which meant that day-to-day cultural contact between peoples was more difficult, and that cultures therefore had more chance to develop independently. Cultural reconstruction in the rest of Melanesia, and in fact in the rest of the world, is much more complex than the example we have just looked at. There is always the problem of the nature of the culture of the preceding population (and remember that we are speaking of populations going back probably more than fifty thousand years). Not only that, but there has been continual cultural contact between people in these areas on a day-to-day basis for all of these thousands of years, with the result that cultural innovations have spread in a criss-cross pattern all over the mainland.

12.4 Historical Linguistics

We have now looked at archaeology, oral history and comparative culture as methods of reconstructing the cultural history of a society. These different methods all provide information that partly overlaps, and is partly different. Archaeology and comparative culture can take us a long way into the past. Only archaeology can give us reasonably accurate dates for cultural features, and only comparative culture can tell us anything about the non-material culture of a society. Oral history can tell us something about the history of a society, again with fairly accurate dates, but it cannot take us very far back in time. Both oral history and comparative culture allow us to reconstruct the non-material culture of a society, but again, there is a difference in the possible time-depth. There is also a difference in the amount of detail that can be provided. While oral history provides a fair amount of detail this is not true of comparative culture.

The final technique of cultural reconstruction that we can employ is historical linguistics. Historical linguistics can allow us to go back quite a few thousand years in time. The questions we need to ask ourselves are firstly, what sorts of information can historical linguistics provide us about the cultural history of a society, and secondly, how does the information gained in this way compare with information that we can obtain from archaeology, oral history and comparative culture?

Let us deal with the initial question first. There are various kinds of cultural information that can be deduced from an examination of the reconstructed history of a people. Each of these kinds of information is discussed below.

(a) Relative Sequence of Population Splits

Take a situation such as the following, where there is a language family, with four members, subgrouped as shown.

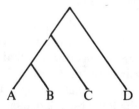

A   B   C   D

Here, we have a group of languages descended from a common ancestor. Languages A, B and C all belong to a single subgroup, while language D belongs to a different subgroup of its own within the same family. The languages A, B and C further subgroup such that A and B are more closely related to each other then either is to C. This subgrouping is of course arrived at by considering the shared linguistic innovations or changes that have taken place from the original proto-language.

A situation like this will tell us that at one stage in the history of these languages, there was a single language (Proto-ABCD) which must have been spoken in a single community. This community then split, perhaps by migration, perhaps by a simple lack of contact without any migration taking place, with a separate community developing, speaking language D. The rest of the community at this stage still spoke a common language (Proto-ABC). Next, of course, we can say that the C-speaking community split off from the AB-speaking community. Finally, the A and B languages split.

This kind of subgrouping is compatible only with non-linguistic evidence which supports the breakaway of D before the breakaway of the other languages. Similarly, non-linguistic evidence must support the breakaway of C before the split of A and B for this subgrouping hypothesis to be valid.

For instance, if we look at the language of Polynesia and island Melanesia, we can draw a very rough subgrouping map of the following kind:

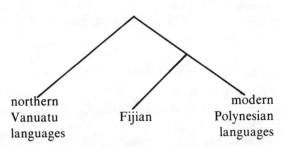

northern
Vanuatu   Fijian   modern
languages   Polynesian
                                      languages

From this we can assume that all of the modern Polynesian languages go back to a common ancestor, and that this split off from an earlier language that was ancestral to proto-Polynesian and Fijian. Furthermore, we can assume that this split took place *after* the ancestor of Fijian and the Polynesian languages Fijian split off from the language ancestral to the languages of northern Vanuatu. If we are talking about language splits, we are presumably talking about some kinds of splits in the populations of the speakers of those languages. In the case of Polynesia and island Melanesia, where the languages involved often occupy small isolated islands, we must also be speaking of the relative age of migrations of peoples.

It should be pointed out that we are speaking of the *relative* age of population splits, and not the *absolute* age. That is, we can only say that the Fijian-Polynesian split took place later than the split with northern Vanuatu. We cannot say *when* these splits actually took place. The technique of glottochronology however, was an attempt to provide actual dates for population splits, though there are few linguists who take this very seriously now. It should also be pointed out that just by looking at the family tree, we cannot tell which group moved away and which remained in the original location (or, indeed, if both groups moved away, in different directions). From the family tree we looked at earlier, we cannot tell if it was D that moved away from proto-ABC or vice versa.

(b) The Nature of Cultural Contact

Often, when we are able to isolate borrowed words from indigenous words directly inherited from a proto-languges, we can tell something about the nature of the cultural contact that took place at the time the borrowings were made. Compare the following pairs of words in English, for example:

law	justice
freedom	liberty
kingship	royalty

The words on the left are native English words, while those on the right are words borrowed from French after the invasion of England in 1066 by French-speakers. People would generally agree that the issues described by the words in the righthand column would be more worth dying for than those described by words in the lefthand column. A banner reading JUSTICE AND LIBERTY is a more effective call to revolution than one reading LAW AND FREEDOM. This is so, even though the concepts referred to are more or less the same. This fact suggest therefore, that something was regarded as 'better' simply if it had a French name at the time that the borrowings were made. That the French language actually did have social prestige over English at the time is indicated by the following statement made in English at the time:

Vor bote a man conne Frenss, me telth of him lute

which translates into modern English as:

Unless a man knows French, one thinks little of him.

273

Another example of this kind comes from the American Indian language called Ṇavajo. The Navajo word for corn is /na:da:ʔ/. Non-linguistic evidence tells us that the Navajo have only fairly recently acquired corn, and that they acquired it from their neighbours, the Pueblo Indians, who spoke a different language. Historically, we can reconstruct this Navajo word as going back to a compound meaning 'enemy-food'. This therefore suggests something about the nature of the cultural contact that took place between the Navajo and the Pueblo when they first came into contact and when the Navajo first saw corn — they were enemies.

Finally, if we examine the vocabulary of Tok Pisin and compare it with that of English, we could reconstruct the original 'master/slave' type relationship without knowing any of the historically recorded facts. The fact that Europeans were called *masta* and Melanesians were called *boi* (and these terms are of course quite frequently used still today!) indicates quite clearly who was the controller and who was the controlled. A middle-aged European in a work situation is always a *masta*. His son is a *pikinini masta,* even though he might be only six years old, and has no responsibilities as a boss. A Melanesian of the same age is often still a *boi*. A Melanesian who has "made it" to the top in many work situations is still not a *masta*. He must be satisfied to be called a *bosboi* — but he is still a *boi*.

The existence of terms in Tok Pisin like *bagarap* for 'out of order, ruined' and *as* for 'basis, reason, bottom' provides further evidence for this kind of relationship between speakers of the two languages at the time that Tok Pisin was emerging as a distinct language in its own right. Ordinarily the words 'buggered up' and 'arse' in English are felt to be appropriate only among close friends. If they are used between people who are not close friends, they are regarded as insulting terms. The fact that these words were used by Europeans to Melanesians clearly indicates that Europeans felt it was 'alright' to speak in an insulting way to Melanesians. (Melanesians then took these words and stripped them of their emotional overtones under the influence of hyperbole (as mentioned in Chapter Eight), and gave them the respectable meaning they now have.) For example, there is nothing wrong with a minister standing up before the Sunday congregation in church and saying:

*Yumi olgeta i save **bagarapim** laip bilong yumi olgeta taim*
'We are always ruining our lives.'

and going on to add:

As bilong dispela, em olsem yumi no save harim toktok bilong papa Got.
'The reason for this is that we do not obey the word of God, the Father.'

(c) Sequences of Cultural Contact with Respect to Population Splits
It is also possible to tell if certain cultural contacts took place before or after a population split took place.

Let us look at the example of the introduction of sweet potato in the Pacific. We know from the archaeological evidence that it is a fairly late introduction into the whole Oceanic area (including Papua New Guinea). It did not arrive in Papua New Guinea until around the sixteenth century. We also know that it came from South America, where it was cultivated by the indigenous Indians. It was introduced into Polynesia and parts of island Melanesia such as Vanuatu by a westerly movement from the South American Indians. Its introduction into Papua New Guinea was more indirect. The Portuguese introduced it into Europe from South America in the fifteenth and sixteenth centuries, who then introduced it into eastern Indonesia. From there, it was introduced into Papua New Guinea, after having been carried right around the world!

Some scholars have argued these facts are supported by the linguistic evidence. There is a word of the form /kumala/ which is used for sweet potato right throughout Polynesia. This word is possibly a direct borrowing from the word in Quechua, a language of Peru, which is /kumara/. This word is also found in many island Melanesian languages, such as Fijian and some of the Vanuatu and Solomons languages. (It is incidentally, also the word for *kaukau* used in Vanuatu Pidgin.) Normally, the island Melanesian languages underwent a large number of phonological changes that would make such a form rather more difficult to recognise. For instance, in the language of Paama (Vanuatu), the phoneme *\/k/ of proto-Oceanic was regularly lost, e.g.:

PROTO-OCEANIC	PAAMESE	
*a kai	a:i	'tree'
*a ika	ai	'fish'
*kapika	ahi	'Malay apple'
*masakit	mesai	'sick'
*penako	hena	'steal'
*a tansik	atas	'sea'

If the proto-Oceanic language had a word */kumala/, we would therefore expect Paamese to have something like /umal/ according to the regular changes. In fact, Paamese has /kumal/ preserving the /k/ just as in the Polynesian languages. This therefore suggests that Paamese acquired the word (along with the thing it referred to) from the Polynesian people *after* the language had undergone the loss of the phoneme */k/.

(d) The Culture of a Society

Given the fact that a language bears a very close relationship to the culture of the people who speak it, we can also tell *something* about the nature of the culture of a people simply by looking at the language they speak. This is just as much so with a reconstructed language arrived at by applying the comparative method as with any other language.

A major aspect of the relationship that holds between a language and the culture of its speakers is the fact that there is always lexical richness in areas of cultural importance. Similarly, there is little lexical development in areas of little cultural importance. So, for example, the Eskimos have numerous words for different kinds of snow, while the Bedouin Arabs, who are desert people, have many names for different kinds of camels and associated technology.

When we apply this kind of reasoning to a reconstructed proto-language, we call this the *Wörter und Sachen* (German for 'words and things') technique. A considerable amount of research has already been carried out on reconstructing the vocabulary of the proto-Austronesian language that was spoken about ten thousand years ago, and from which all of the Austronesian languages spoken in the Pacific and southeast Asia are derived. The reconstructed vocabulary includes items like the following:

taro	*tales	boat	*waŋka
yam	*qubi	sea travel	*parasu
banana	*punti	sail	*layaɣ
sugarcane	*tebus	paddle	*besai
coconut	*ɲiuɣ	steer	*quliŋ
sago	*rumbia	bail out	*limas
breadfruit	*kulur	fish hook	*kawil
muli/lemon	*limau	derris poison	*tuba
pandanus	*pandan	high tide	*ɣusah
buai/betel nut	*buqa	giant clam	*kima
yar/casuarina	*aɣuqu	octopus	*kuɣita
		seaweed	*limut
		conch	*tamburi
fallow land	*talun	fish scale	*qunapi
cultivate	*teba		
garden	*quma	clay pot	*kuden
to weed	*wawau	bow	*busuɣ
shoot, sucker	*suli	shoot	*panaq
		broom	*sapu
domestic pig	*beɣek	needle	*zaɣum
wild pig	*babui		
root up ground (of pigs)	*sua		

Applying this technique, the overall picture that emerges of proto-Austronesian society according to the Austronesian scholar Blust is that:

> They were settled people, occupied villages which contained some kind of public building and dwelling units, raised on posts (and thus entered by ladders), with thatched gabled roofs, internal fireplaces, and a number of storage shelves and wooden headrests. They possessed domesticated pigs, fowls and dogs. They hunted, wove, potted, used needle and thread, tattooed themselves, chewed betel nut and drank some kind of intoxicating drink. Iron

was known, as was writing (in whatever form). They had a well developed maritime technology, but also
cultivated root crops, as well as rice
and millet. They hunted heads, and
used the bow and bamboo stakes in
their hunting.

There is one further interesting point. For proto-Austronesian,
there are two reconstructed words for 'pigs':

babuy	wild pig
beɣek	domesticated pig

Archaeological evidence indicates that there were originally no pigs
in Melanesia and Polynesia. Also, the Oceanic languages only have
a reconstructible form for 'tame pig', but not 'wild pig'. This fits in
nicely with the archaeological evidence. We could conclude that it
was Austronesian-speakers who first introduced pigs into Melanesia
and Polynesia. It is logical that proto-Oceanic would only have a
word for 'tame pig' — we would hardly expect people to have wild
pigs with them on their ocean-going canoes when they arrived in this
part of the world!

(e) The Homeland of a People

The *Worter und Sachen* technique can also tell us something about
the original homeland of a people. (Note that the original homeland
or proto-homeland is often referred to in the literature by the German term *Urheimat,* corresponding to the term *Ursprache* meaning
'proto-language'.) We can even use this technique to tell us something about the migration routes people may have followed to get
where they are now. For example, from the proto-Austronesian
vocabulary that we have just examined, it is obvious that the people
must have lived on an island, or on the mainland very close to the
sea. They clearly lived in a tropical rather than a cold environment.
They lived in an area that had crocodiles, as there is a reconstructible word */buqaya/ meaning 'crocodile'. This fact alone rules
out anywhere in Polynesia or parts of island Melanesia as the proto-
Austronesian homeland, as these areas have no native crocodiles.
Using all the data that we have, we can reconstruct for these people
a homeland around southern China. We do know that around ten

thousand years ago, the Chinese pushed southward, presumably pushing out the ancestors of the modern Austronesian speakers, who then spread to the Philippines and Indonesia, and eventually to the Pacific area.

We can use the *Wörter und Sachen* technique to make some guesses about the actual routes followed by different people in reaching their present locations. There is, for example, a word for 'owl' everywhere in Polynesia except those areas that do not have owls, and the reconstructed word in proto-Polynesian for 'owl' is */lulu/. In Hawaii however, the word for owl is /pueo/, which is clearly not a reflex of */lulu/. From this, some scholars have argued that Hawaii might have been settled from an area such as the Marquesas to the south where there are no native owls. On arriving in their new home, Hawaii, they had to find a new name for a bird that was now new to them.

Biologists have argued that certain mosquito species were spread into Polynesia by human settlement. In fact, in eastern Polynesia (Hawaii, Tahiti, the Marquesas), the first Europeans in the area hardly noticed any mosquitoes at all. In these areas, the original Austronesian word for mosquito, */ɲamuk/, occurs with the different meaning of 'sandfly'. The mosquito is known by other names, in Hawaiian as, /makika/ (possibly from English) and in Maori as /wae-roa/ (a compound meaning 'long-legs'). This suggests that there were no mosquitoes when the Polynesians first arrived in these areas and the original word was transferred in meaning to the sandfly. When the mosquitoes did arrive, perhaps a few generations later, the people had to find a new name for them, either by borrowing or by creating a new compound from words that already existed in the language.

It is also in considering the original homeland of a people that we consider the AGE-AREA HYPOTHESIS. This is a hypothesis that says: the area with the greatest diversity in terms of the number of first-order subgroups within that area is likely to be the original homeland. In saying this, we are assuming the lowest number of population movements to account for the geographical distribution of the subgroups (and remember that in historical linguistics, we always choose the *simplest, most reasonable* solution to a problem). Let us take an example. We have a family of languages divided up into the following subgroups geographically:

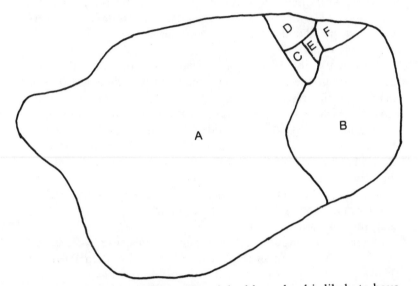

By the age-area hypothesis, the original homeland is likely to have been the area in which the subgroups BCDEF meet. This would require that we set up only a single major population shift, that of subgroup A to the west. On the other hand, if we suggest that the far west of this area were the original homeland, then we would need *separate* movements for the populations of B, C, D, E and F to their present locations in the east.

In Melanesia and the Pacific, the greatest area of subgrouping diversity in Austronesian languages is to be found in Melanesia, and in Melanesia, the greatest area of diversity is to be found in Papua New Guinea. We therefore suggest an original homeland for Oceanic languages in Papua New Guinea. If it were to be shown that all of the non-Austronesian languages of **Papua New Guinea** were to be related, the most likely areas of original settlement would be either the Sepik or the Bird's Head of Irian Jaya, as the following map suggests from the diversity of the number of distinct 'phyla' of languages in these areas.

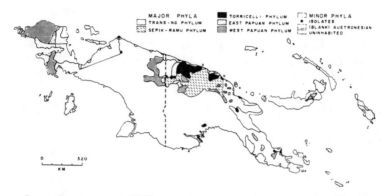

Sometimes, we find that languages or language families are 'splintered' or DISCONTIGUOUS; that is, they are spoken in areas that do not join, and are separated by other languages or other families. We could take this as evidence that some kind of migrations have taken place, as we work on the assumption that languages and language families should occupy contiguous (or adjacent) areas unless they are actually forced apart by some other factors. For example, in Europe, most of the languages belong to the so-called Indo-European language family. The Hungarian, Finnish and Turkish languages do not belong to this family, yet they are related in a separate family of their own, the Ural-Altaic family. The fact that these languages are widely separated geographically as the map below shows, suggests that these were the original languages of Eastern Europe, and that the Indo-European languages were later arrivals.

 Ural - Altaic Languages

Indo - European Languages

The case of the languages of the Tufi area in Oro Province is interesting also. In the map below, it can be seen that there are many discontiguous languages. The Maisin language is spoken in three separate areas, Notu in three areas, Korafe in two, Ubir in two and Arifama-Mainafia in four. Apart from this, there are fairly large areas of unoccupied land. The inland Orokaiva people had a reputation traditionally of being a very warlike people, and quite possibly pushed earlier neighbours out of their area to this previously uninhabited coastal area, resulting in this very mixed-looking linguistic map. The distribution of languages in this case suggest that this is in fact some kind of 'refugee' area.

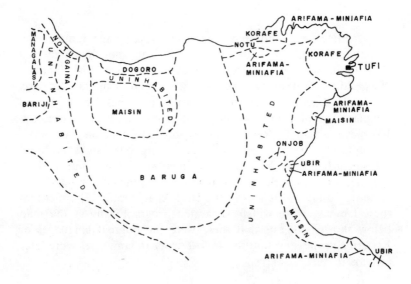

Having now looked in detail at the kinds of information that historical linguists can provide about cultural history, we should ask ourselves an additional question: how *reliable* is this information, and how well does this information tie in with information provided by archaeology, oral history and comparative culture?

In general terms, what historical linguistics can tell us about cultural history depends on how we subgroup languages in a particular family, and what we reconstruct in the vocabulary of a proto-language. Our statements about cultural history can therefore only be as accurate as our subgrouping and our lexical reconstruction.

We have already seen that subgrouping is not always certain. In some cases, there may be contradictory evidence when we are trying to set up subgroups, depending on what sorts of facts we choose to rely on more. For instance, some scholars have argued that the area of greatest subgrouping diversity within the Austronesian language family is in the Austronesian languages of Taiwan, off the coast of southern China. This fits in nicely with the theory we have presented in this chapter of an Austronesian homeland in southern China. However, linguists who claim this are relying on shared grammatical and phonological innovations, and just what is a 'retention' and what is an 'innovation' depends on how we actually reconstruct the proto-language. If our reconstruction is wrong in the first place, then our subgroupings will also be wrong. Other linguists, for instance, have claimed that it is in the Melanesian area that we have the area of greatest Austronesian diversity (though most of these arguments have rested on lexicostatistical evidence, which is not very reliable, as we have seen). If this were true, then we would be speaking of a Melanesian homeland for proto-Austronesian, rather than southern China.

Also, if our reconstruction of the vocabulary of the proto-languages is inaccurate, then any statements about the nature of the original culture and the original homeland that are based on this will also be misleading. It is in fact not difficult for our lexical reconstruction to be wrong. For instance, in the Algonquian languages, a family of American Indian languages spoken in northeastern North America (mostly in Canada), it is possible, by strictly applying the comparative method, to reconstruct in proto-Algonquian a word for 'whisky' and a word for 'train'. The word for 'whisky' can be reconstructed as a compound of the form 'fire-water', and the word for 'train' can be reconstructed as a compound of the form 'iron-horse'. Yet it is quite obvious that the Algonquians did not know about whisky and the trains until European contact, which came well after proto-Algonquian had split up into numerous daughter languages. This is clearly a case where there has been a parallel development in all of the Algonquian languages. Parallel semantic developments in related languages are especially hard to detect. So the reconstruction of writing and iron in proto-Austronesian society is particularly suspicious, especially since there is no direct evidence of the actual use of writing and iron until thousands of years later, in most cases only after outside cultural contact.

We must therefore also be suspicious of reconstructions of homelands for proto-languages on the basis of lexical evidence such as this. Another question that we must ask ourselves is this: how widespread does a form have to be in a language family for it to be reconstructed as a form in the proto-language? For instance, many of the reconstructed words we looked at earlier for proto-Austronesian are reconstructed only on the basis of evidence in the languages of Indonesia, the Philippines and Taiwan. Many of the forms that are reconstructed for proto-Austronesian refer to things that have only entered southeast Asia relatively recently. Some biologists have suggested recently that plants like sugarcane, breadfruits and many bananas are actually native to Melanesia. Earlier on, they simply did not exist in Indonesia, the Philippines and Taiwan. If this is correct, then it would appear that some species of plants have been introduced into southeast Asia from Melanesia. This would then make it extremely difficult to support the proposal put forward by most Austronesian linguists that the Austronesian languages spread in an eastward movement from southern China. The only possible homeland in this case would be a Melanesian homeland! The evidence is therefore inconclusive.

READING GUIDE QUESTIONS

1. What is archaeology and what kinds of historical information can archaeologists provide?
2. How reliable is the historical evidence provided by oral historians? What factors influence the reliability of their data?
3. What is meant by the term comparative culture? What kinds of historical information can it provide?
4. How can historical linguistics tell us something about the relative order in which population splits and movements take place?
5. What can we tell about the nature of cultural contact between two societies from linguistic evidence?
6. How can we tell something about the relative timing of a borrowed cultural feature from linguistic evidence?
7. What is the *Wörter und Sachen* technique of cultural reconstruction?
8. What problems are involved in applying the *Wörter und Sachen* technique?
9. How can we make guesses about a people's homeland and migration routes from the linguistic evidence?

EXERCISES

1. Should we make hypotheses about cultural history from linguistic evidence independently, or should we restrict our guesses
only to possibilities that are suggested by 'real sciences', such as
archaeology and biology?

2. To what extent do you think it would be possible to devise a
'comparative method' for the reconstruction of a culture? Are
there any special problems that would be faced which we do not
face in reconstructing proto-languages?

3. The following words have been reconstructed for proto-
Algonquian, the ancestor to the American Indian languages
spoken in the areas shown in the map below.

      *weʃawe:minʃya   'American beech tree'
      *name:kwa   'lake trout fish'
      *a:çkikwa   'harbour seal'
      *atehkwa   'woodland caribou'

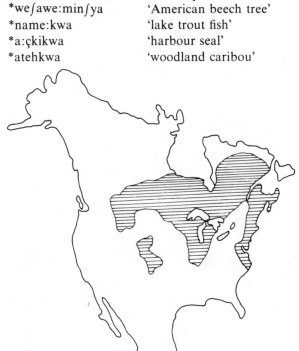

The maps below show the area where the reconstructed species are
found. What would you propose as the homeland for proto-
Algonquian ?

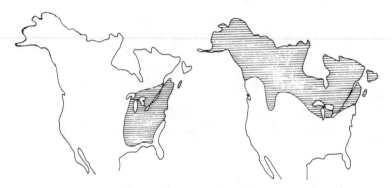

American beech tree   lake trout fish

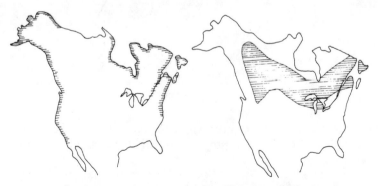

harbour seal   woodland caribou

4. Examine the following map showing the distribution of Austronesian languages on the island of New Guinea. Assume that the
Austronesian languages originated outside Papua New Guinea,
and say where you think they might have come from. Give your
reasons.

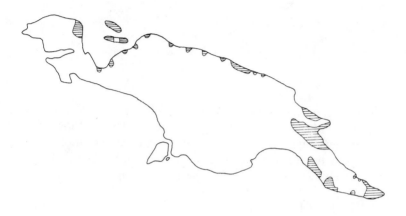

5. In southern New Ireland and northern East New Britain, we
have the following languages, as shown on the map:

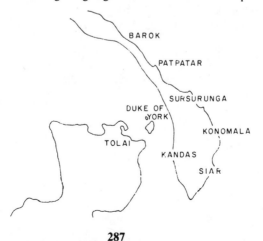

These languages are all related within a single subgroup. The internal subgrouping can be suggested as follows, according to the lexicostatistical evidence:

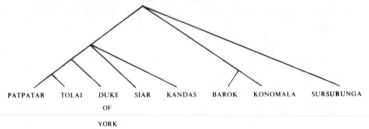

PATPATAR	TOLAI	DUKE	SIAR	KANDAS	BAROK	KONOMALA	SURSURUNGA
		OF					
		YORK					

Can you suggest a possible pattern of migration that is consistent with this subgrouping, and with the fact that the nearest related subgroup is spoken to the immediate north of Barok? (Note that the languages spoken to the south of Tolai are completely unrelated non-Austronesian languages.)

FURTHER READING

1. Bynon, Theodora. *Historical Linguistics* (Chapter 7 'Language and Prehistory'), pp. 262-280.
2. Anttila, Raimo. *An Introduction to Historical and Comparative Linguistics* (Chapter 21 'Change and Reconstruction in Culture and Linguistics'), pp. 377-388.
3. Swadesh, Morris. 'Linguistics as an Instrument of Prehistory' in Hymes (ed.) *Language in Culture and Society*, pp. 575-84.
4. Denoon, Donald and Lacey, Roderic (eds.). *Oral Tradition in Melanesia*.
5. Swadling, Pamela. *Papua New Guinea's Prehistory: An Introduction*.

DATA SETS

The following sets of data are used in the exercises at the end of several chapters as an aid in acquiring different skills. Rather than repeat each set of data in each chapter, these data sets are attached as an appendix, and students are referred to the data sets by number in each particular question.

1. Palauan (Micronesia)

1.	*hatay	→	ʔaδ	'liver'
2.	*layaγ	→	yarəs	'sail'
3.	*ɟalan	→	rayl	'road'
4.	*apuy	→	ŋaw	'fire'
5.	*mata	→	maδ	'eye'
6.	*cinaγ	→	sils	'light'
7.	*cucu	→	tut	'breast'
8.	*bulan	→	buyl	'moon'
9.	*batu	→	baδ	'stone'
10.	*ikan	→	ŋikəl	'fish'
11.	*huɟan	→	ʔull	'rain'
12.	*laŋit	→	yanəδ	'sky'
13.	*buŋa	→	buŋ	'flower'
14.	*pəɲu	→	wel	'turtle'
15.	*dəŋəγ	→	reŋəs	'hear'

2. Nganyaywana (Northern New South Wales)

1.	*ŋa:naŋ	→	anaŋa	'who'
2.	*wi:gan	→	igana	'snow'
3.	*ba:baŋa	→	abaŋa	'father'
4.	*mi:gin	→	igina	'star'
5.	*mi:l	→	ila	'eye'
6.	*ga:bulga:n	→	abulgana	'shark'
7.	*bargan	→	argana	'boomerang'
8.	*winba	→	inba	'fire'
9.	*buruluŋ	→	ruluŋa	'fly'
10.	*wambuɲa	→	mbuɲa	'kangaroo'
11.	*bagar	→	gara	'meat'
12.	*ganay	→	naya	'yamstick'
13.	*dimin	→	mina	'nits'
14.	*guruman	→	rumana	'boy'
15.	*wigay	→	gyaya	'food'

16.	*gugaŋa	→	gwaŋa	'child'
17.	*gubila	→	bwila	'possum'
18.	*giɲinma	→	ɲirma	'scratch'

3. Mbabaram (North Queensland)

1.	*wula	→	lo	'die'
2.	*ŋali	→	li	'we'
3.	*ḍawa	→	we	'month'
4.	*guyu	→	yu	'fish'
5.	*guwa	→	wo	'west'
6.	*ḍana	→	ne	'stand'
7.	*bamba	→	mba	'belly'
8.	*ŋaba	→	bo	'bathe'
9.	*wuna	→	no	'lie down'
10.	*ḍiba	→	be	'liver'
11.	*gumbi	→	mbi	'penis'
12.	*naga	→	ga	'east'
13.	*ɲulu	→	lu	'he'
14.	*gunda	→	ndo	'cut up'

4. Yimas and Karawari (East Sepik)

		Yimas	Karawari	
1.	*sɨkɨr →	tɨkɨt	sɨkɨr	'chair'
2.	*yakus →	yakut	yakus	'*bilum*/ string bag'
3.	*samban →	tamban	samban	'lover'
4.	*panmari →	panmaḷ	panmari	'male'
5.	*sɨsɨn →	tɨrɨn	sɨsɨn	'tooth'
6.	*nanɨn →	nanɨŋ	yanɨŋ	'fat'
7.	*sambaym →	tambaym	sambaym	'basket hanger'
8.	*nawkwan →	nawkwan	yawkwan	'chicken'
9.	*nam →	nam	yam	'house'
10.	*sambɨn -→	tambɨn	sambɨn	'tail'
11.	*sɨmun ﹥	tɨmun	sɨmun	'cane'
12.	*pariapa →	paḷapa	pariapa	'verandah'
13.	*manbaw →	manbaw	manbo	'death adder'
14.	*tumbaw →	tumbaw	tumbo	'crocodile'

Note: [ḷ] is a palatal lateral and [ɨ] is a high unrounded central vowel.

5. Lakalai (West New Britain)

1.	*kani	→	ali	'eat'
2.	*ikan	→	ia	'fish'
3.	*lima	→	lima	'hand'
4.	*paʔa	→	vaha	'leg'
5.	*ʔate	→	hate	'liver'
6.	*kutu	→	utu	'lice'
7.	*ʔunsan	→	hura	'rain'
8.	*ʔanso	→	haro	'sun'
9.	*lipon	→	livo	'tooth'
10.	*danu	→	lalu	'water'
11.	*taŋi	→	tali	'cry'
12.	*tapine	→	tavile	'woman'

6. Suena and Zia (Morobe). Slightly regularised

	Suena	Zia	
1.	ni	ni	'bird'
2.	ɟo	yo	'mercy'
3.	wo	wo	'meat/fish'
4.	oro	oro	'lime'
5.	pu	pu	'pig'
6.	wa	wã	'boat'
7.	su	su	'soup'
8.	wi	wi	'penis'
9.	mu	mũ	'sap'
10.	be	be	'mouth'
11.	pigi	pĩgi	*kambang*/lime'
12.	me	mẽ	'shame'
13.	ari	ari	'vagina'
14.	goroba	gorobo	'black palm'
15.	moka	moko	'inside'
16.	wena	weno	'nose'
17.	tuma	tumo	'back of neck'
18.	duba	dubo	'throat'
19.	ɟaɟo	yaɟo	'name'
20.	ema	emo	'man'
21.	me	me	'true'

7. Korafe, Notu and Binandere (Oro Province)

Korafe	Notu	Binandere	
1. ɟoka	ɟo	do	'mercy'
2. ɟoʔka	ɟo	do	'inside'
3. ɟaʔka	ɟa	da	'*buai*/betel nut'
4. ɟawo	ɟawo	dao	'name'
5. biɟo	biɟo	bido	'banana'
6. seka	seka	teka	'new'
7. susu	susu-	tutu	'meaning'
8. toʔká	to	to	'hole'
9. –	tewo	teo	'bowl'
10. dubo	dubo	dubo	'throat'
11. dika	di	–	'tooth'

8. Northern and Southern Paamese (Vanuatu)

Northern	Southern	
1. eim	aim	'house'
2. amai	amal	'reef'
3. a:i	a:l	'stinging tree (*salat*)'
4. oul	aul	'maggot'
5. out	aut	'place'
6. he	hel	'step'
7. mea	mela	'get up'
8. takul	takul	'sago'
9. hae	hale	'outside'
10. keil	kail	'they'
11. teilaŋ	teilaŋ	'sky'
12. tahe	tahel	'wave'
13. moul	maul	'alive'
14. mavul	mavul	'broken'
15. houlu	haulu	'many'
16. ateli	ateli	'basket'

9. Motu (Central Province)

1. *tama	→	tama	'father'
2. *taŋi	→	tai	'cry'
3. *tari	→	tadi	'younger brother'
4. *γita	→	ita	'see'
5. *γate	→	ase	'liver'
6. *tina	→	sina	'mother'

7.	*tiavu	→	siahu	'hot'
8.	*mate	→	mase	'die'
9.	*ɣutu	→	utu	'louse'
10.	*pune	→	pune	'bird'
11.	*ðaŋi	→	lai	'wind'
12.	*leŋi	→	rei	'kunai grass'
13.	*bara	→	bada	'big'
14.	*diba	→	diba	'right'
15.	*geru	→	gedu	'nape of neck'
16	*garo	→	gado	'language'
17.	*gʷada	→	gʷada	'spear'
18.	*lata	→	rata	'milk'
19.	*labia	→	rabia	'sago'
20.	*maða	→	mala	'tongue'
21.	*wabu	→	vabu	'widow'
22.	*walo	→	varo	'vine'
23.	*vui	→	hui	'hair'
24.	*vavine	→	hahine	'woman'
25.	*api	→	lahi	'fire'
26.	*au	→	lau	'I'

10. Sepa, Manam, Kairiru and Sera (Coastal Sepik)

	Sepa	Manam	Kairiru	Sera	
1.	tamota	tamoata	ramat	reisiouk	'man'
2.	waine	aine	mwoin	tamein	'woman'
3.	mata	mata	mata	tapung	'eye'
4.	ginga	ganga	kwokala	suvətang	'nose'
5.	talngo	kungi	təlenga	tenerping	'ear'
6.	lima	debu	kawi	ləɣang	'arm/hand'
7.	lulu	ruru	sus	tuit	'breast'
8.	dala	dara	sinai	tenei	'blood'
9.	ngamali	amari	warang	rau	'sun'
10.	kalewa	kalea	kaleo	bul	'moon'
11.	wabubu	rodo	abwung	puing	'night'
12.	ndanu	dang	rian	rain	'water'
13.	makasi	makasi	nau	na	'sea'
14.	pa:tu	patu	bung	ak	'stone'
15.	bu:ka	buku	worəng	sol	'mountain'
16.	ewa	ewa	luf	teing	'fire'
17.	kai	kai	kai	ai	'tree'

18.	undu	udi	wur	bur	'banana'
19.	keu	keu	wonau	bing	'dog'
20.	manu	mang	mian	main	'bird'
21.	mota	moata	vaniu	meni	'snake'
22.	ika	ika	siasi	mwoing	'fish'
23.	ngalambuti	lango	ləmwok	lang	'fly'
24.	namu	nang	niam	nənei	'mosquito'
25.	pela	pera	pial	nou	'house'
26.	wawaraki	wauwau	bunbun	wuipul	'white'
27.	mbotambo	zimzimi	silsir	neknek	'black'
28.	ndisuau	tumura	marir	marir	'cold'
29.	kani	kang	an	ʔain	'eat'
30.	sopu	mai	miai	ma	'come'
31.	lako	lako	liak	pi	'go'
32.	teke	teke	tai	pontenen	'one'
33.	lua	rua	wulu	elting	'two'
34.	toli	toli	tuol	elting pal	'three'
35.	wati	wati	viat	elting elting	'four'
36.	lima	lima	vələri	pinggariʔ	'five'

11. Burduna (Western Australia)

1.	*pampura	→	papura	'blind'
2.	*ṯuluŋku	→	ṯuluṯku	'crane'
3.	*ŋaṯa	→	ŋaya	'I'
4.	*kawuŋka	→	kawuka	'egg'
5.	*kaṇṯaṛa	→	kaṯaṛa	'root'
6.	*papu	→	pawu	'father'
7.	*ŋampu	→	ŋapu	'tree'
8.	*waṇkan	→	waṯkan	'chest'
9.	*kuṯaṛa	→	kuyaṛa	'two'
10.	*ṯuṇṯu	→	ṯuṯu	'narrow'
11.	*muḷaŋkara	→	muḷaṯkara	'parrot type'
12.	*ṯipa	→	ṯiwa	'drive'
13.	*kumpu	→	kupu	'urine'
14.	*puka	→	puwa	'bad'
15.	*kuṇṯal	→	kuṯal	'daughter'
16.	*ŋaṇka	→	ŋaṯka	'beard'
17.	*ṯuṯuŋkayi	→	ṯuḏukayi	'honey'
18.	*paṯapuṯu	→	payawuḏu	'dangerous'
19.	*mukul	→	mu:l	'auntie'

20. *yiminʈa	→	yimiʈa	'scratch'
21. *kanpařf	→	katpař	'spider's web'
22. *puŋkuʈi	→	pukuɖi	'kangaroo'
23. *paʈaři	→	payaři	'fight'
24. *paʈa	→	paya	'drink'
25. *ŋunʈa	→	ŋuʈa	'lie'
26. *ʈukara	→	ʈuwara	'hiding'
27. *ɳuŋkun	→	ɳukun	'rotten'
28. *ʈa:paʈa	→	ʈa:waya	'wild plum'
29. *kakul	→	kawul	'testicles'
30. *pařumpa	→	pařupa	'wattle tree'
31. *pinʈa	→	piʈa	'mud'
32. *waŋka	→	waka	'speak'
33. *mininʈa	→	miniʈa	'centipede'
34. *pinkaʈi	→	piʈkayi	'dish'
35. *ʈinʈi	→	ʈiʈi	'clitoris'
36. *yukaři	→	yuwaři	'stand'
37. *kankaʈa	→	katkaʈa	'wild potato'
38. *yakan	→	ya:n	'husband/wife'
39. *kuʈuru	→	kuyuru	'word'
40. *wampapanʈi	→	wapa:ʈi	'anthill'
41. *ʈintiʈinti	→	ʈitiyiti	'willy wagtail'
42. *manʈa	→	maʈa	'arm'
43. *mintulu	→	mitulu	'fingernail'
44. *mika	→	miwa	'back'
45. *pukuřa	→	pu:řa	'devil'
46. *wanʈa	→	waʈa	'give'
47. *wanka	→	watka	'raw'
48. *jukuʈu	→	ju:du	'smoke'
49. *majun	→	mayun	'turtle'
50. *kukulara	→	ku:lara	'dove'

Language Index
Below is a list of languages used as problems, or to illustrate major points in the text. As stated in the preface, I have avoided quoting the sources of my information in the text to avoid creating a less readable, overly academic style. The list of languages below indicates the source of the information used. Sources without dates indicate personal communication, while sources listed without names indicate my own field notes or my own general knowledge.

Abau (Bailey 1975)
Afrikaans (Burgers 1968)
Alamblak (Bruce 1979)
Algonquian (Arlotto 1972)
Angkamuthi
Arifama-Miniafia (Lynch 1977b)
Aroma (Ross 1979)
Attic Greek (Cowan 1971)
Bahasa Indonesia
Banoni (Lincoln 1976)
Binandere (Farr & Larsen 1979)
Bislama (Camden 1977)
Burduna (Austin 1981)
Dusun (Prentice)
Dutch
Dyirbal (Dixon 1972)
Enggano
Fijian (Capell 1973, Cowan 1971, Milner 1972)
German
Gothic (Bloomfield 1967)
Greek (Bloomfield 1967)
Gumbaynggir (Eades 1979)
Hawaiian (Foley)
Hula (Ross 1979)
Huli (Cheetham)
Icelandic (Cowan 1971)
Ilokano (Bloomfield 1967)
Iroquois
Italian (Arlotto 1972, Cowan 1971)
Kabana (Thurston and Goulden)
Kairiru (Laycock 1976)
Kara (Beaumont 1979)
Karawari (Foley)
Koiari (Dutton)
Koita (Dutton)

Korafe (Lynch 1977b, Farr & Larsen 1979)
Kuman
Kwaio (Keesing 1975)
Lakaiai (Johnson 1978)
Latin (Arlotto 1972, Bloomfield 1967)
Lenakel (Lynch 1977a)
Maisin (Lynch 1977b)
Malay (Dempwolff 1934-38)
Manam (Laycock 1976)
Manga (Hooley 1971)
Maori (Foley)
Mapos (Hooley 1971)
Marshallese (Lynch)
Mbabaram (Dixon 1980)
Mekeo (Ross 1979)
Motu (Ross 1979)
Mountain Koiari (Dutton)
Murut (Prentice)
Muruwari (Oates 1976)
Ndao (Walker 1980)
Nganyaywana (Crowley 1976)
Notu (Lynch 1977b, Farr and Larsen 1979)
Old English (Arlotto 1972)
Old Irish (Arlotto 1972)
Orokaiva (Lynch 1977b)
Paamese (Crowley, 1983)
Palauan (Foley)
Patep (Hooley 1971)
Rarotongan (Foley)
Rumanian (Cowan 1971)
Samoan (Marsack 1973)
Sanskrit (Bloomfield 1967)
Sawu (Walker 1980)
Sepa (Laycock 1976)
Sera (Laycock 1976)
Sinaugoro (Ross 1979)
Sissano (Laycock 1973)

Southeast Ambrym (Parker 1970)

Spanish (Bloomfield 1967)

Suena (Farr & Larsen 1979)

Tagalog (Dempwolff 1934-38, de Guzman 1974)

Tahitian (Clark 1979)

Toba Batak (Dempwolff 1934-38)

Tok Pisin (Lynch 1979)

Tolai

Tongan (Foley)

Ubir (Lynch 1977b)

Uradhi

Wagau (Hooley 1971)

Yaygir (Crowley 1979b)

Yimas (Foley)

Zia (Farr & Larsen 1979)

BIBLIOGRAPHY

Aitchison, Jean, 1981. *Language Change: Progress or Decay?* Fontana Paperbacks.

Anderson, Wallace L, and Norman C. Stageberg (eds.), 1962. *Introductory Readings in Language.* New York: Holt, Rinehart and Winston.

Anttila, Raimo, 1972. *An Introduction to Historical and Comparative Linguistics.* New York: MacMillan.

Arlotto, Anthony, 1972. *Introduction to Historical Linguistics.* Boston: Houghton Mifflin.

Austin, Peter, 1981. 'Proto-Kanyara and Proto-Mantharta Historical Phonology', *Lingua,* 54:295-333.

Bailey, D.A., 1975. 'The Phonology of the Abau Language' in Work Papers in Papua New Guinea Languages, Vol. 9. *Abau Language, Phonology and Grammar,* Ukarumpa. pp. 5-58.

Beaumont, C.H., 1979. *The Tigak Language of New Ireland.* Pacific Linguistics B58, Canberra.

Bickerton, Derek, 1981. *The Roots of Language.* Ann Arbor: Karoma Publishers.

Biggs, Bruce G., 1972. 'Implications of Linguistic Subgrouping with Special Reference to Polynesia', in R.C. Green and M. Kelly (eds.), pp. 143-160.

Bloomfield, Leonard, 1967. *Language.* London: George, Allen and Unwin.

Bruce, L., 1979. *A Grammar of Alamblak (Papua New Guinea),* unpublished Ph.D dissertation, Australian National University, Canberra.

Bolinger, Dwight, 1968. *Aspects of Language.* New York: Harcourt, Brace and World.

Burgers, M.P.O., 1968. *Teach Yourself Afrikaans.* New York: David McKay.

Bynon, Theodora, 1979. *Historical Linguistics.* Cambridge: Cambridge University Press.

Camden, Pastor Bill, 1977. *A Descriptive Dictionary: Bislama to English.* Vila: Maropa Bookshop.

Capell, A., 1973. *A New Fijian Dictionary.* Suva: Government Printer.

Clark, Ross, 1979. 'Language,' in Jesse D. Jennings. *The Prehistory of Polynesia.* Cambridge: Harvard University Press, pp. 249-270.

Cowan, William, 1971. *Workbook in Comparative Reconstruction.* New York: Holt, Rinehart and Winston.

Crowley, Terry, 1976. 'Phonological Change in New England', in R.M.W. Dixon (ed.), pp. 19-50. *Grammatical Categories in Australian Languages.* Canberra: Australian Institute of Aboriginal Studies.

———— 1979. 'Yaygir', in R.M.W. Dixon and Barry J. Blake (eds.) pp. 363-384. *Handbook of Australian Languages,* Vol.1. Canberra: Australian National University Press.

———— 1982. *The Paamese Language of Vanuatu.* Pacific Linguistics.

Dempwolff, Otto, 1934-38. *Vergleichende Lauthlehre des Austronesischen Wortschatzes* (Zeitschrift für Eigeborenen-Sprachen, Beiheft No. 15, 17, 19). Berlin: Reimer.

Dixon, R.M.W., 1972. *The Dyirbal Language of North Queensland.* Cambridge: Cambridge University Press.

———— 1980. *The Languages of Australia.* Cambridge: Cambridge University Press.

Dixon, R.M.W., and Barry J. Blake (eds.). 1979. *Handbook of Australian Languages,* Vol. 1. Canberra:-The Australian National University Press.

Denoon, Donald and Roderic Lacey (eds.), 1981. *Oral Tradition in Melanesia.* Port Moresby: The University of Papua New Guinea and the Institute of Papua New Guinea Studies.

Eades, Diana, 1979. 'Gumbaynggir', in R.M.W. Dixon and Barry J. Blake, (eds.), *Handbook of Australian Languages,* Vol. 1. Canberra: Australian National University Press, pp. 244-361.

Farr, James and Robert Larsen, 1979, 'A Selective Word List in Ten Different Binandere Languages', mimeo, Summer Institute of Linguistics, Ukarumpa.

Foley, William Auguste, 1976, 'Comparative Syntax in Austronesian,' unpublished Ph.D dissertation, University of California, Berkeley.

Grace, George W., 1969. 'A Proto-Oceanic Finder List,' in *Working Papers in Linguistics* 2:39-84 (March), University of Hawaii, Honolulu.

Green, R.C. and M. Kelly, (eds.), 1972. *Studies in Oceanic Culture History, Vol 3.* Pacific Anthropological Records No. 13. Honolulu: Bernice Pauahi Bishop Museum.

de Guzman, Maria Ondulio, 1974. *English-Tagalog and Tagalog-English Dictionary.* Manila: G.O.T. Publishers.

Hooley, Bruce A., 1971. 'Austronesian Languages of the Morobe District, Papua New Guinea', in *Oceanic Linguistics,* 10(2): 79-151.

Hymes, Dell, 1964. *Language in Culture and Society.* New York: Harper and Row.

Jennings, Jesse D., (ed.), 1979. *The Prehistory of Polynesia.* Cambridge: Harvard University Press.

Jespersen, Otto, 1922. *Language: Its Nature, Development and Origin.* London: Allen and Unwin.

Johnston, Ray, 1978. 'Steps Towards the Phonology and Grammar of proto-Kimbe,' mimeo, Summer Institute of Lingusitics, Ukarumpa.

Keesing, R.M., 1975. *Kwaio Dictionary.* Pacific Linguistics C35, Canberra.

Labov, William, 1972. *Sociolinguistic Patterns.* Philadelphia: University of Pennsylvania Press.

Langacker, Ronald W., 1968. (2nd edn.) *Language and its Structure.* New York: Harcourt, Brace and World.

Laycock, D.C., 1973. 'Sissano, Warapu and Melanesian Pidginisation', in *Oceanic Linguistics,* 12:245-278.

_____ 1976 'Austronesian Languages: Sepik Provinces', in S.A. Wurm. (ed.), *New Guinea Area Languages and Language Studies Vol. 2: Austronesian Languages.* Pacific Linguistics C39, Canberra, pp. 399-418.

Lehmann,Winifred P., 1962. *Historical Linguistics: An Introduction.* New York:Holt, Rinehart and Winston.

Lincoln, Peter Craig, 1976. 'Describing Banoni, an Austronesian Language of Southwest Bougainville', unpublished Ph.D dissertation, University of Hawaii, Honolulu.

Lynch, John, 1977a. *Lenakel Dictionary,* Pacific Linguistics C55. Canberra.

_____ 1977b. 'Notes on Maisin — an Austronesian Language of the Northern Province of Papua New Guinea?', mimeo, University of Papua New Guinea.

_____ 1979a. 'Changes in Tok Pisin Morphology', mimeo, University of Papua New Guinea.

_____ 1979b. *Introduction to Phonetics and Phonology.* Port Moresby: University of Papua New Guinea.

_____ 1980. 'Proto-Central Papuan Phonology,' mimeo, University of Papua New Guinea.

MacDonald, R. Ross and Soenjono Darjowidjojo, 1967. *A Student's Reference Grammar of Modern Formal Indonesian.* Washington: Georgetown University Press.

Marsack, C.C., 1973. *Teach Yourself Samoan.* London: The English University Press.

Meillet, Antoine, 1967. *The Comparative Method in Historical linguistics.* Paris: Librairie Honoré Champion.

Milner, G.B., 1972. *Fijian Grammar.* Suva: Government Printer.

Oates, Lynette, 1976. 'Muruwari', in R.M.W. Dixon, (ed.), *Grammatical Categories in Australian Languages,* Canberra: Australian Institute of Aboriginal Studies, pp. 342-347.

Parker, G.J., 1970. *Southeast Ambrym Dictionary,* Pacific Linguistics C17. Canberra.

Pawley, Andrew, 1972. 'On the Internal Relationships of Eastern Oceanic Languages', in R.C. Green and M. Kelly, (eds.), *Studies in Oceanic Culture, History, Vol 3, Pacific Anthropological Records* No. 13. Honolulu: Bernice P. Bishop Museum, pp. 1-142.

Pei, Mario, 1966. *The Story of Language.* London: Allen and Unwin.

Pulgram, Ernst, 1961. 'The Nature and Use of Proto-Languages', in *Lingua,* 10:18-37

Ross, Malcolm, 1979. 'Reconstructing Proto-Central Papuan,' mimeo, University of Papua New Guinea.

Sapir, Edward, 1949. *Language: an Introduction to the Study of Speech.* Harcourt, Brace and World.

Shopen, Tim, 1978. 'Research on the Variable (ing) in Canberra, Australia', in *Journal of the Linguistic Society of Australia,* 5:42-52.

Swadling, Pamela, 1981. *Papua New Guinea's Prehistory: An Introduction.* Port Moresby: Gordon & Gotch (in association with the National Museum and Art Gallery).

Walker, Alan Trevor, 1980. 'Sawu: a Language of Eastern Indonesia', unpublished Ph.D dissertation, Australian National University, Canberra.

Wurm, S.A. (ed.), 1976. *New Guinea Area Languages and Language Studies, Vol, 2: Austronesian Languages,* Pacific Linguistics C39. Canberra.

INDEX

abbreviations 32
absolutive 172
Academy, French 242
accusative 170-3
addition, phonemic 74-5
Afrikaans 47, 236
age-area hypothesis 279-282
agglutinating 164, 165, 168, 245
Alamblak 174-5
allomorph 152
allophonic change 71-3, 76, 81
alternation, morphological 126, 152-3, 154-5
analogy 129-133, 135, 175, 177-8
anaptyxis 33
anatomical influence on language change 235
Angkamuthi 29, 74
apocope 29-30, 39, 81
archaeology 263-5
area, linguistic 178
areal features 178
assimilation 39-47, 81, 242, 244; distant, 45; immediate, 45; regressive, 41
autonomous phonemics 144

back formation 176-8
Bahasa Indonesia 13, 152, 242
Bandjalang 163-4, 170-1, 172
Banoni 44, 62, 66-7, 75-6
bifurcation 179-180
Bislama 19, 37-8, 46
Bloomfield, Leonard 214, 219, 248
Blust, Robert 277-8
borrowing 134-5, 242-3
broadening, semantic 179, 180, 241
Brugmann 127, 135

change, sporadic 189
Chomsky, Noam 222
cluster reduction 29, 244

cognate 90, 91, 92, 93, 102, 103, 106, 109, 118, 128, 134, 192, 195, 196-7, 203
combinatory sound change 58-60
common descent 188-190
comparative method 89-103, 103-110, 116, 121, 124, 128, 135, 142
complementary distribution 80, 84, 104-5, 106, 108-9, 110, 124-6, 128-9, 219
compression 31
conditioned sound change 58-60, 72, 73-4, 78, 79, 103-5, 107, 124-7
conditioning environment, loss of 80-2
conditioning, grammatical 144-6
consonant harmony, 46
contrastive distribution 80, 84, 108-9, 110, 125
correspondences 83-103, 104-6, 107, 108, 109-110, 117, 123, 125, 128, 134, 142-3; sporadic 124, 126, 128-135, 195, 214; systematic 122-3, 127, 128, 195, 214
count nouns 246-7

Danish 134
diachronic linguistics 11, 71
dialect 136-146, 192-3, 202; geography 144
diffusion 175, 178
diglossia 230
discontiguous languages 281, 282
dissimilation 47, 126
drift 189
Dutch 187

Enggano 46, 189
epenthesis 33-4, 244
ergative 170-3, 175
etymology 121-2, 127; folk 132-3; popular 132-3
euphemism 181
euphony 238
excrescence 33

303

family 15-8, 192-3, 202; tree 136, 143, 187, 197-200, 206
feature, phonetic 35-6
Fijian 13, 28, 74, 78, 84-5
folk etymology 132-3
fono, Samoan 268
French 36, 117-9, 132-3, 164-5, 187
fusion, phonological 35-6, 133, 242-3; morphological 166-7

geographical influence on language change 237-8
German 45, 118-9, 154, 187, 244-5
Germanic Sound Shift, First 235; Second 235
Gillieron 142-3
glottochronology 201-2
Gothic 123-6
Grassmann, Hermann 47, 125-6, 127
Greek 123-6; Attic 36-7
Grimm, Jakob 123-4, 127, 235

Haitian Creole 255, 257
haplology 30
Hawaiian 57, 64-5, 90-103, 104, 107-9, 128-9
Hiri Motu 17, 151, 152, 163, 258-9
homeland 278-284; Austronesian 278-9; Polynesian 267-8
homonyms 76, 182
homophones 76
homorganic sound 33
hypercorrection 223
hyperbole 181-2, 274

Icelandic 122
iconic symbols 12
Ilokano 34-5
indeterminacy 215-220
inflectional 164-5, 168, 237, 245
innovation, shared 188-190, 271
inspection method 195

interference, semantic 182
isogloss 138-140
isolate 149
isolating 163, 165, 168-9, 245
Italian 117-8, 169, 187

Jespersen, Otto 243
Johnson, Samuel 21
Jones, Sir William 14, 121, 122
Junggrammatiker 127

Kabana 203-4
Kairiru 39
Kara 27
Koiari 195-7, 201-2
Koita 174, 195-7, 201-2
Kuman 243

Labov, William 222, 250
Lardil 240
Latin 17-8, 27-8, 116-9, 123-6, 131, 168-9
Lenakel 30, 226, 227, 244
lengthening, compensatory 37
lenition 27-32
Leskien 127, 135
lexicostatistics 190-3, 196-200, 202-6
loanwords 82-4, 118, 134-5, 203, 219-220, 273-5
loss, phonemic 73-4
loss, complete phonemic 74
loss, partial phonemic 74

macrophylum 192-3, 202
Mbabaram 249
Maori 103-5
mass nouns 246-7
Mekeo 237
merger, complete phonemic 78
merger, phonemic 76-8
mesophylum 192-3, 202

metaphor 181
metathesis 34-5, 189, 244
microphylum 192-3, 202
Motu 32, 34, 43, 57, 72-3, 74, 76, 79, 82, 83-4, 105-7, 134-5, 162, 173, 218-220, 237, 248
Mountain Koiari 195-7, 201-2
Mpakwithi 74
Muller, Max 21

nakamal 269-270
narrowing, semantic 179
Navajo 274
neogrammarians 121, 127, 129, 135-6, 141-7, 161, 206, 214, 227
New York English 222-4
nominative 172
noun, count 246-7; mass 246-7

object 170-1, 174
off-glide 38
Old Irish 37, 249
One 240
on-glide 38
onomatopoea 12
oral tradition 265-8
ordered sound change 64-7

Paamese 13, 137-143, 144-5, 167, 176, 242, 275-6
palatalisation 18-22, 43, 72, 105
Palauan 25
parallel development 189-190
phonemic addition 74-5; space 37; loss 73-4; loss, complete 74; loss, partial 74; merger 76-8; merger, complete 78; merger, partial 78; shift 75-6; split 79
phylum 280
pidgin 250-1
pidginisation 250-9
popular etymology 132-3
portmanteau morpheme 168

pre-language 149
prothesis 34, 74, 76
proto-Austronesian 189
proto-culture 269-270
proto-culture, Austronesian 276-8
proto-Indo-European 123-4
proto-language 13-8, 89, 109-110, 116-120, 188-190
proto-Oceanic 189-190
proto-Polynesian 91, 98, 100-1, 104

Rarotongan 90-103, 104, 107-9, 128-9
Rask, Rasmus 122-3
reanalysis, grammatical 175-8, 246-7; morphological 93, 152
reconstruction 89-103, 106, 116; internal 149-159
reduction, phonological 165-6; morphological 168
redundancy 253-4
reduplication 126
reflexes 89, 91, 95, 97, 98, 101, 268
regularisation 245-7
rephonemicisation 75-9
research, exploitative 251
retention, shared 188
rhotacism 27-8
Rumanian 117-8
Russian 187

Samoan 90-103, 104, 107-9, 128-9, 150, 151-3
Sanskrit 14, 123-6
de Saussure, Ferdinand 11-2, 214-5, 218
separation of levels 144
serial verbs 174
shift, phonemic 75-6; semantic 180
simplification 242-7
Sinaugoro 105-7, 134-5
Sissano 240
Southeast Ambrym 30
SOV-language 173-4, 175, 178
space, phonemic 37
Spanish 117-8

spelling pronunciation 133-4, 135
split, phonemic 79; semantic 179-180
Sprachbund 178
stereotypes, racial 235-7
stock 192-3, 202
structural pressure 84, 247-8
Suau 19
subject 161-172, 174, 175
subgroup 136, 187-8, 271-3
subphonemic change 71-3
substratum 238-9, 254-5, 270
SVO-language 173-4
Swadesh-list 193-4
synchronic linguistics 11, 71
syncope 30, 244

taboo, linguistic 203-4
Tagalog 35
Tahitian 204
Tasmanian 17
Time of Darkness 266-7
Tok Pisin 17, 27, 28, 29, 33-4, 76-7, 151,
    165, 179, 180, 181, 191, 213, 228-230,
    238-9, 241, 251, 252, 253, 254-5, 257,
    274-5
Tolai 13, 162, 163, 176
Tongan 90-103, 104, 107-9, 128-9
typology 162, 245

umlaut 46-7, 81

unconditioned sound change 57-8, 64,
    72, 74, 78, 103
unpacking 37-8, 244
upheaval, social 249-250
Uradhi 25, 77-8
Ural-Altaic 281
Urheimat 278
Ursprache 278

Van der Tuuk 150
variability 220-6
verb chain 174
Verner, Carl 126, 127
vocabulary, core 191, 193-5; peripheral
    191
vowel breaking 38-9; harmony 46, 67
VSO-language 173

wave model 143, 206
weakening 26-32, 96, 99
work mixes 31-2
Worter und Sachen 276-8

Yaygir 27
Yimas 174